GROWING YOUR OWN
FRUIT & VEGETABLES

To Adam, Grace, Eleanor and James
To John, Will, Joe and Margot

GROWING YOUR OWN
FRUIT & VEGETABLES

A STARTING OUT GUIDE

Alison Chivers & Mary Canning

CONTENTS

'I used to visit and revisit it a dozen times a day, and stand in deep contemplation over my vegetable progeny with a love that nobody could share or conceive of who had never taken part in the process of creation. It was one of the most bewitching sights in the world to observe a hill of beans thrusting aside the soil, or a rose of early peas just peeping forth sufficiently to trace a line of delicate green'. ~Nathaniel Hawthorne, *Mosses from an Old Manse*

Growing herbs   158

Growing fruit   178

Pest and diseases   280

What to sow when gardening calendar   232

Common gardening terms   258

Index   260

Bibliography   266

Acknowledgments   267

About the Authors   267

INTRODUCTION

Friends often tell me they would love to start a vegetable patch and grow some of their own food, but have no idea how to start. This book will give you a simple, step-by-step guide to creating a fruit and vegetable garden from scratch so that you can grow your own food. I hope to impart some of the knowledge and 'tricks' learnt from growing up in a family of three generations of Australian gardeners. With a little preparation, some basic knowledge and enthusiasm anyone can have a vegetable garden in any sort of backyard or climate.

My father grew up in country New South Wales and, together with his four brothers, he tended the family vegetable patches. They watched their father enrich the earth, taking note of which vegetables he sowed together, which he sowed apart, how he made compost and what he did to avoid pests.

It wasn't long before the boys had sole responsibility for the garden and with it (supplemented by rabbit catching), the family's food.

Later, he had a family of his own and we moved around New South Wales, from the rich soil of temperate New England to the mid-west, the arid sandy soil of Broken Hill and then to Sydney's temperate climate and my father built one vegetable garden after another. Before removalist vans had even left the driveway he'd be digging up lawn and creating the new family vegetable patch.

My father possessed two generations of gardening knowledge and passed it on to my siblings and me—the third generation. My brother, sister and I were soon out mixing carrot seed with sand to ease sowing, mulching rows of leeks and pinching out tomato laterals.

What my father gave us was not only a love of the natural world but a generational history of how things grow in Australia.

It is that knowledge that, over the years, I have written down in journals and have put into this book. I hope it will give you the skills to grow some of your own food.

Above all, I hope it instils in you a love of fruit and vegetable gardening to pass onto your own children, as I have to mine.

> The first gatherings of the garden in May of salads, radishes and herbs made me feel like a mother about her baby—how could anything so beautiful be mine. And this emotion of wonder filled me for each vegetable as it was gathered every year. There is nothing that is comparable to it, as satisfactory or as thrilling, as gathering the vegetables one has grown.
> ~Alice B. Toklas

Right: Alison's father, Les.

Opposite page: James, Alison's son picking fennel.

PLANNING YOUR VEGETABLE PATCH

ASSESSING YOUR SPACE

Before you build a vegetable patch in your garden you first need to work out the best location for it—this is critical. Most vegetables need 'full sun'; this means at least six hours of sunlight a day. So you need a position where shadows from the house or the neighbour's house, fences or trees won't cover the plot for much of the day. If you put your plot in the shade you won't get any fruit or vegetables. Fruit and vegetables also need to be sheltered from strong winds and frost.

How big your vegetable garden will be depends on the space available and how much you want to grow. Relatively small gardens can still produce significant crops. There are a number of space-saving techniques you can try, including planting vegetables in pots and containers that can be fitted in anywhere around the yard or balcony, using vertical spaces like walls, fences and trellises to grow climbing crops, or planting vegetables amongst the ornamental garden. Many vegetables also come in dwarf cultivars and occupy less space.

Consider drawing a plan of your property, including any buildings, trees, fences and fixtures. Watch your garden as the sun goes over the sky during the course of a day and block out areas of shade on your plan. This can be a valuable exercise in determining the best place to put your vegetable patch.

THINGS TO CONSIDER

Time
How much time you can spend in the garden will, in some ways, determine how big you make your vegetable patch. Some seasons, particularly spring, require more time than others. Generally, you need to spend at least a couple of hours per week in the garden.

Aspect
A northerly aspect is ideal, as you will get more sun. So try to ensure that your patch will run from north to south. Sunny walls are a good option for growing fruit, either vines, like grapes or passionfruit, or fruit trees, which can be espaliered over the walls. At night, walls that receive daytime sun will re-radiate the warmth and improve the growth of the tree. All gardens contain microclimates—areas where the temperature, wind, drainage and sunlight differ from the rest of the landscape. These areas can be used to good effect when building a vegetable garden. Further considerations when deciding where to build the patch are access to

a water supply and your own access to the new garden as it is important not to stand on the soil too often, as doing so will compact it.

Competition

A vegetable patch should be clear of any overhanging or large trees and any garden plants, as they will compete with the vegetables for water and nutrients.

Climate

Australian climatic zones are broadly divided into six main regions. For the purposes of this book, we have divided the zones into four main gardening zones: tropical, subtropical, temperate and cool (a subzone of temperate—those areas with hard winter frosts and temperatures that can fall below zero). Since vegetable gardening is affected by temperature, rainfall, humidity, weather and the season, what can be grown and when is different depending on the zone you live in. Some crops are suited to cool areas and need a frost so will obviously be unsuitable for growing in the tropics. Others need long, hot growing periods that do not exist in the cooler climates. Growing vegetables in the tropics is also affected by the amount of rainfall and humidity, which, in turn, affects the timing of when the crops can be grown.

Spring and autumn are the two seasons when most planting is carried out. In frost-prone areas the timing of the first and last frost will further determine when you can and can't plant your vegetables. Fruit and vegetables grown out of season will invariably fail.

With climate change scientists predicting a hotter climate for Australia, with an average rise in temperatures of around 0.4 to 2°C by 2030, with more hot days over 35°C and a reduction in the number of frost days (CSIRO, Intergovernmental Panel on Climate Change), gardeners need to plan for more severe conditions than those experienced in the past. Ways to modify the climate around you and to protect and prolong harvests need new consideration and other ways to grow plants will need to be found. In hotter summers, vegetables may need to be protected by shade cloths or polytunnels. Unpredictable rain patterns will also mean more thought will need to be put into drainage. Plants, like gardeners, will find ways to adapt.

Drainage

Prepare your new garden properly and it will reward you from the start, saving time later on as you won't need to go back and re-build or move it. After ensuring that the designated space is in the sun you have to make sure that it is well-draining. Vegetables don't like 'getting their feet wet', they like soil that drains away water and doesn't stay wet. Good drainage is essential.

If your land is flat, inspect it after a heavy rain to see if the water has pooled, or drained away. If it has pooled the soil will be poorly draining and drainage will need to be improved before constructing the garden bed.

If your land is steep, water will drain away rapidly leaving the soil dry. Building a terrace, which slows the flow of water and allows it to percolate downwards, is a possible solution.

On a sloping site, you may first need to dig a trench, so that the water will drain away before you build your garden. In high rainfall areas a drain may need to be put in front of, or behind, a retaining wall to divert excess water. Make sure to build the patch across the slope and not up and down it.

You can also check drainage by digging a hole about a shovel-length deep and filling it with water. If it takes more than half an hour to drain then the drainage will need to be improved. One way to do this is by digging the soil over and then adding gypsum (calcium sulphate, also known as Plaster of Paris, bought from nurseries or hardware stores) to break up the clay. Adding a layer of coarse river sand, gravel or ash to the soil just above the sub-soil will further help drainage. Patience is required to really improve the soil and drainage. By incorporating loads of well-rotted compost, manure and a thick layer of hay or straw and leaving it to earthworms to pull the organic matter down over six months, you will achieve an excellent humus rich soil.

Where drainage is poor, building raised beds with a load of good-quality topsoil (from a landscape supplier) or building a no-dig garden are both faster options.

Ground preparation

Once you have decided where to put the garden, clear the area of weeds and rake it flat. If you are making a bed where there is lawn, you will need to strip it away using a knife with a sharp blade to undercut it and then turn over the soil underneath with a fork or shovel.

CLIMATE CLASSIFICATION OF AUSTRALIA

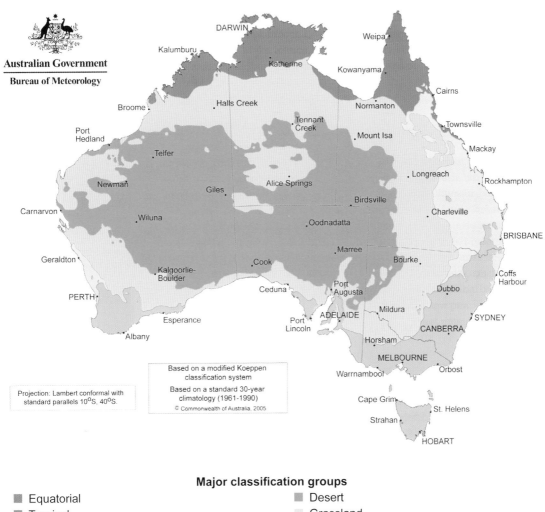

Australian Government

Bureau of Meteorology

Based on a modified Koeppen
classification system

Based on a standard 30-year
climatology (1961-1990)

© Commonwealth of Australia, 2005

Projection: Lambert conformal with
standard parallels 10°S, 40°S.

Major classification groups

■ Equatorial	■ Desert
■ Tropical	■ Grassland
Subtropical	■ Temperate

Map copyright of the Bureau of Meteorology (www.bom.gov.au).

BUILDING A GARDEN

TYPES OF GARDENS

Garden bed system

Vegetables were traditionally grown in rows with spaces between the rows. Depending on the size of the garden you are going to create you can divide the space into a series of beds, divided by pathways wide enough to walk or push a wheelbarrow down, so at least 45 cm wide. Make sure each bed is narrow enough to be able to reach across from one side; about 1.2 m wide is usually wide enough. The beds themselves can be level with the surrounding ground or edged with wood, old sleepers (make sure they are untreated, or creosote-free, sleepers), bricks, bush rocks or whatever you have at your disposal.

Pathways bordering garden beds allow useful access.

Here garden beds are level with the ground and narrow enough to work easily in.

Young seedlings in a raised garden bed.

Raised garden beds

Raised beds are in fashion now but have, in fact, been in use for centuries. Plans drawn in 920AD for a Benedictine monastery in Switzerland show a central walk bordered with nine raised beds on either side, each with an allocated crop. Early English settlers at Jamestown in Virginia built raised rectangular beds, close to their houses and protected by fences.

Raised beds may be any height or made out of any material. They are an excellent choice if space is limited, soil drainage is poor, the area is waterlogged or the soil is clay. Pre-fabricated raised beds can be bought in hardware stores and nurseries—these are often made of colourbond or corrugated iron, are very easy to put up and come in a range of sizes. Raised beds are also an excellent choice for people who cannot fully bend.

To make your own raised bed, use any wooden planks, untreated railway sleepers, bricks, blocks or stones to make the walls. Mark out where you want to build the garden. Remove any weeds. The beds can be any length or height but width is important as it must be possible to reach the centre from each side.

If building with blocks or bricks, set them into a shallow trench for stability. For wood, sink planks 5 cm into the ground and support them with square pegs or posts. Allow for drainage by leaving some weep holes at the base of the walls. Lay out the first layer of timber to create a low wooden wall. Repeat the process by stacking timber sections to raise the height of the wall. Drive nails into the corner joints on each layer of timber to keep it stable. When at the height you want, fix the top row by driving nails in at an angle through the vertical joints. A simpler method is to drive some short picket stakes into the ground to hold the sleepers in place.

Once the framework is constructed, dig over the soil inside the box. Stretching weedmatting across the bottom and up the sides will help prevent weeds and tree roots from growing. If the raised bed is deep, the bottom part can be filled with sticks and branches, broken bricks and any rubble you have lying around. This will aid drainage and reduce the amount of soil you will need. Cover the branches, etc, with old hessian bags, industrial felt, landscaping geotextile or shade cloth to prevent the soil from falling through. Fill the bed with soil and well-rotted compost and/ or manure. Or use the layering method described below and create a no-dig garden inside the frame by adding straw, hay and compost.

Raised beds have a number of advantages. The soil warms up more quickly in spring and so planting can start earlier than in garden beds. The soil inside is generally looser than soil in the garden, thereby encouraging deeper roots. In humid areas, they allow for better air circulation. An irrigation system can easily be installed by running a pipe beneath the bed or attaching a drip system to the walls.

In hot weather, however, soil in a raised bed will heat up faster than in the garden. Make sure to keep the bed moist and well mulched.

No-dig garden beds

In spots where drainage is poor you can make a no-dig garden. Pioneered by the Australian gardener Esther Dean, in the late 70s, a no-dig garden is easy to make, grows excellent vegetable crops and allows you to make a garden in the most unlikely of spaces, including over concrete. It is essentially a garden made up of layers of organic matter, built up to at least 30 cm, but higher if you desire. It relies on worms and other organisms to 'dig' the soil.

Once you've settled on a site, make the edging, as you would for a raised garden, or simply mark out the space on the ground. Wet the soil or lawn underneath. Then you can start building the layers.

For the first layer, overlap 1 cm thick layers of newspaper or cardboard, making sure that no space peeps through. Wet it thoroughly. If you are building over concrete, place a pile of sticks and rough materials, like garden prunings and branches on the concrete first then place the newspaper over these, which will aid drainage.

Next add a layer of hay, straw or pea straw, palm fronds and/or grass clippings. Hay and straw are available from produce shops, nurseries and some landscaping suppliers. Over this layer, spread some organic fertiliser like pelletised chicken manure, blood and bone or worm castings and a layer of well-rotted cow, sheep, horse or chicken manure or compost. Next add another thick layer of straw. Water each layer as you go. You can stop at this layer or keep building until you reach the height you want.

If you have chickens, use the spent straw and shavings from the chicken shed. Once the bed is as high as you want, make depressions in the surface of the straw layer and fill them with compost. Seedlings can be planted straight into these. Large seeds and potato tubers and

Another idea for a raised garden bed—this one at the rear of a suburban apartment block.

rhubarb crowns can also be sown straight into a no-dig garden.

No-dig gardens are topped up each year with a further layer of mulch, compost or manure.

Pots and containers

Many vegetables and herbs do very well in containers and pots. They are an efficient use of space and can be placed anywhere—on a deck, balcony, courtyard or on a verandah in hanging baskets. Pots enable anyone to grow some of their own food. They can be highly decorative or as simple as a polystyrene box with holes punched in the bottom.

There are a few simple rules for successful vegetable gardening with pots. The pot or container must be big enough to allow space for the plant's root zone. If you want to grow root crops you will need a deep container. If you are growing a top-heavy crop, like tomatoes, you need to ensure that the container won't blow over and that there is adequate space for staking.

The pot and growing medium must have good drainage. If the drainage is too slow the roots will rot; too fast and the plant will dry out. A balance must be found between the competing needs of drainage and water retention. This is where a good-quality potting mix is vital.

The choice of a premium potting mix, with an Australian standards mark, is critical to the success of vegetable gardening in pots. The potting mix needs to contain organic matter and nutrients. Some mixes will contain a slow-release fertiliser, a wetting agent—to help the soil absorb water and prevent the mix drying out—and vermiculite or washed river sand to lighten the mix and help with drainage. Wetting agents are, for the most part, not allowed in strict organic gardening.

Garden soil is no good in pots as it compacts when confined. Making your own potting mix is easy and allows you to get a medium that is alive and thriving with micro-organisms and nutrients. Experiment to see what you find is the best mix, but basically you need a coarse material to allow air around the roots, a water-retaining material and a material that adds nutrients.

Depressions in a no-dig garden filled with compost and awaiting planting.

Lettuce growing in a pot.

Right: Chives growing in a retaining wall.

BASIC VEGETABLE POTTING MIX RECIPE

One part coarse builder's sand or perlite (a volcanic rock extract)

Two parts compost

Two parts rehydrated coconut coir, vermiculite or sphagnum moss.

Additional nutrients can be added by incorporating some fine garden loam, small amounts of blood and bone (for phosphorous) or well-rotted manure, dolomite (to raise the pH and add calcium and magnesium) or seaweed meal (for nitrogen).

The other vital requirement for the potted vegetable garden is sunlight. Most vegetables need at least six hours of full sun a day; pots need to be put in a place where they will receive this. In hot climates, however, you will find that there are times when vegetables will need some shade. Plants in pots also need to have good air circulation around them and protection from strong winds.

Vegetables in pots will need an all-purpose or balanced fertiliser throughout their growing season; soluble fertilisers and liquid seaweed are particularly good ways to feed plants in pots.

The final thing to look out for with a potted garden is watering. Pots can dry out quicker than the garden bed so you need to be vigilant. Keep vegetables moist—check this by sticking your finger into the pot. To water them, water until the water runs out of the drainage holes. If you have the pot in a saucer it is a good idea to have it standing on stones so the roots aren't perpetually in water.

When re-using pots it is a good practice to scrub the pot with hot soapy water or a weak bleach solution between uses to help prevent the risk of transferring soil diseases.

Climbing gardens

To make good use of space, consider growing vegetables up walls and trellises, over sheds, up old ladders and pot stands. Vegetables such as peas, climbing beans, choko, soybeans, Malabar spinach, climbing summer squash and sweet potato will climb up frames. Climbing fruits

A garden bed along a driveway has been transformed into an edible border.

include passionfruit, kiwi fruit and grapes.

A simple frame can be made by attaching wire to wooden stakes or star pickets or making tripods out of bamboo stakes by tying them at the top with twine and weaving it down and around the stakes.

Strawberries are often grown in growbags attached to walls. Ensure the wall attracts enough sunlight.

Edible landscaping

Vegetables, herbs and some fruit, especially the permanent or perennial ones, like rhubarb, strawberries and artichokes, can be planted anywhere in the garden and make attractive plants interplanted among flowering plants. Lettuce, thyme, parsley, endive and beetroot, for example, can be planted along low borders in ornamental gardens. Celery, silverbeet, sage, rosemary, cabbages and kale can be planted to create a higher border. If your garden is a native one you need to be mindful of native plants disliking phosphate, so be careful with fertilising.

Right: Lettuces in growbags attached to a shed wall.
Below: Oregano, thyme and chives planted around a fruit tree.

BEFORE YOU START

In Australia, convicts were set to work three days after the First Fleet landed in 1788. Captain Phillip landed with a supply of pea, cabbage, onion, spinach, beet, lettuce, wheat, barley, buckwheat and oat seeds as well as a number of fruit trees. Most of the young plants withered and died. The hot Sydney summer together with the reasonably infertile soil was the first lesson of Australian gardening: the need to improve and nurture the soil.

SOIL

Good soil is fundamental to successful fruit and vegetable gardening. If your soil is good it will provide plants with all of the nutrients, water and air they need to thrive. Poor soils are low in nutrients and tend to result in weaker, stunted plants. Think of soil as a living thing. It requires care and feeding to thrive.

Australia, with its ancient soils, has some of the most nutrient deficient soils in the world. The top layer of soil is often thin and contains very little organic matter and humus. Humus is basically the dark carbon-rich material in soil produced by fully broken down vegetative or animal matter.

There are simple ways to improve soil and prepare it for successful fruit and vegetable growing. All soil is improved by adding well-rotted organic matter. This is an on-going process. 'Organic matter' means anything that has a living origin. It can be dug into the soil, broken down into compost or spread over the top as a mulch. It includes compost, decaying plants, fallen leaves, green manure plants, seaweed, grass clippings, pond sludge, animal manure, bark, wood chips, sawdust, wood ash, straw and hay and so forth.

Before you start any vegetable planting you need to ensure that your soil is fertile and healthy. What you need to do to improve your soil will depend on what type of soil you have, although basically all soils will be improved by the addition of copious amounts of organic material. By pressing a clod of soil in your hand you should be able to tell what sort you have.

Soil type

Soil is essentially a mixture of broken-down rock, water and organic matter.

Sandy soil is made up of relatively large bits of rock and too much air. It is light soil, low in nutrients and moisture, as it cannot hold them. It is easy to dig but porous. It will feel gritty and will not form a ball when pressed together.

Clay soil is made from small particles of rock. It is heavy soil and drains poorly, tending to become waterlogged. It remains in large clumps when dug and sets a hard crust when dry. Clay soils do not have enough air in them and plant roots keep bumping into walls of clay. When balled in the hand clay soils will hold the ball shape.

Silty soil feels like sandy soil only silkier.

Peat soil is dark and spongy and dries out easily. It cannot be rolled into a ball. It has a high acid content and so will need an addition of lime to grow plants other than acid-loving ones.

Loam is the ideal soil; it is the right mix of clay, sand and air, organic matter or humus and is crumbly with a rich brown colour and earthy smell. Loam soils have already been enriched with organic material. To achieve a loam soil you need to add organic matter at every possible opportunity by heavy mulching.

If your soil is sandy or silty the best way to improve it is to add lots of organic matter—compost and manures. If your soil is clay you can reduce compaction by adding gypsum. An application of lime is also beneficial. Salt-affected soils are improved with gypsum as well.

Soil pH

All soil is either alkaline (sweet) or acid (sour). This is measured as the pH (potential of hydrogen) of the soil, which means the concentration of hydrogen ions in the soil—the more of them the more acidic the soil. It is worth measuring when you start your garden or if your plants are showing signs of nutrient deficiency. If the pH is outside the normal range, some nutrients are not available to plants. You can test the pH of your soil by purchasing an inexpensive pH soil-testing kit, available from nurseries. Soil pH is measured on a scale of 0 to 14. Seven is neutral, soils above 7 are alkaline and soils below 7 are acidic. You will need to do a number of tests as the basic pH can vary between the levels of the soil, so dig the garden over and take several samples from different spots around it.

Most Australian soils are slightly acidic. Most vegetables do best in slightly acidic soil with a pH range from 6 to 6.5, including tomatoes, capsicums and eggplant. Fruit such as strawberries and blueberries also like an acidic soil. Other vegetables, such as spinach, cabbage and broadbeans and also certain fruit trees, prefer a sweet or alkaline soil and will often need to be limed.

Adjusting the pH level

If soil is too acidic, raise the pH with an application of agricultural lime or dolomite. Lime and dolomite contain calcium, an essential nutrient easily lost from the soil and in need of regular replacement. An annual application of about one handful per square metre is sufficient to remedy this and sweeten the soil. To apply lime, wet the soil and scatter the lime over it, then dig or rake the lime in. It is best added at least six weeks before planting to give it time to start adjusting the soil. Dolomite has the added advantage over lime of containing magnesium, another essential nutrient. Wood ash is another good source of calcium and potash, to raise the pH.

Lime shouldn't be added to the soil at the same time as blood and bone or manure, as the effectiveness of one is counteracted by the other and nitrogen is lost from the soil. Make sure not to add lime around young seedlings.

If your soil is too alkaline (as it is in large parts of South Australia, Western Australia and arid regions of central NSW) the pH can be lowered by adding agricultural sulphur or iron chelates as well as copious amounts of compost, which is usually acidic. Other organic materials to help acidify soil include pine needles, sawdust (best added once you have let it rot into a mulch) and peat moss. Lowering the pH of an alkaline soil is often a thankless task, particularly over large areas. With alkaline soil, avoid using lime, dolomite and wood ash, as these increase the alkalinity. Chicken manure is also best avoided. Plants, however, that do thrive in alkaline soil include celery, globe artichoke, lettuce, beans, brassicas, asparagus and onion.

SUMMARY

If your soil is acidic, with a pH of 6.5 or below, you will need to add lime or dolomite to sweeten it and make it less acidic. Increase the pH, if the vegetable requires a pH of 6.5 to 7. If your soil is alkaline, with a pH of 7.5 or higher, and the vegetable requires a more neutral pH of 7 or a more acidic soil (of say 6 to 6.5) you will need to add acidic materials like compost to lower the alkalinity.

HOW TO IMPROVE YOUR SOIL

All plants need nutrients to grow but these are often deficient in Australia's poor soils. If you improve the soil, more nutrients become available for your plants. Adding copious amounts of well-rotted compost and manures are the best way to achieve long-term improvement to all soils. Fertilisers are a fast way to provide these nutrients, but won't help to improve the structure of soil. Add these to the soil or potting mix, before planting and again while the plant is growing, as they are absorbed through the plant's roots. They can also be sprayed onto the leaves as a foliar spray. Organically, gardening is all about the health of the soil and so the focus is not on fertilising plants but on improving and maintaining the structure, fertility and micro-organisms of the soil. Composting, adding manures, growing green manures and mulching will all help to ensure this.

FERTILISERS AND LIQUID FEEDS

Essentially the primary elements that plants need and that fertilisers provide are nitrogen (N), phosphorous (P) and potassium (K). Nitrogen is essential for good leafy growth, phosphorous helps develop strong roots and aids flower and fruit production. Potassium is critical for strong stem cell thickness and promoting flowers, colour and quality of fruit. The NPK ratio on bought fertilisers is on the packaging and different fertilisers will have different ratios depending on what the fertiliser is for. Secondary elements include calcium (Ca) for healthy cell walls and root growth, magnesium (Mg) vital to photosynthesis, and sulphur (S) for flavour and odour.

Fertilisers often also contain vital trace elements, needed only in 'trace' or minute quantities, including iron (Fe), manganese (Mn), boron (B), copper (Cu), zinc (Zn) and molybdenum (Mo). Trace elements can also be bought separately.

Fertilisers are either synthetic or natural. They can be in a granular form and release nutrients slowly (known as slow-release fertilisers) or a liquid form for a quicker application.

Synthetic fertilisers are made from chemicals and are not organic. They are used because they are fast-acting, have a balanced ratio of elements, are cheap, easy to access and use, and are soluble (broken down with watering). You can rake them into the soil before sowing, or use as a 'top dressing' while the plant is growing to give it a growth spurt. The fertiliser is sprinkled onto damp soil around the plants and watered in. If you use them, care needs to be taken that they are not being washed into waterways and bushland.

Natural fertilisers are organic and include blood and bone, manures, compost, rock minerals, seaweed and fish emulsions. These are broken down by micro-organisms to add nutrients to the soil in a form that plants can take up. They also add bulk and structure to the soil, greatly improving its quality and encouraging soil micro-organisms. Vegetables grown organically do tend to taste better.

Seaweed solutions

Seaweed solutions condition the soil, not fertilise it, by stimulating microbial activity and improving the plants' ability to absorb nutrients. They also contain some trace elements. Most Australian soil is low in boron, magnesium, potassium, zinc and selenium. The easiest way to supplement these is to use seaweed fertiliser regularly, either by adding it to a filled watering can or by using it as a foliar spray.

Mineral Fertilisers

Rock dusts are an organic way to add nutrients often lacking in compost. They include phosphate rock, dolomite or ground limestone, which adds lime and calcium, sulphur from volcanic deposits and potassium from wood ash.

Potash or sulphate of potash is named after the traditional practice of leeching wood ash in large metal pots. Potash is a mineral form of potassium and is essential for plant growth, disease resistance, fruit flavour and development. Potassium can be found in wood ash, which can be sprinkled on the garden. It is also present in the herb comfrey, which can be used as mulch or fermented into a tea to water onto plants. It is a good idea to add potash to soils when starting out and again when planting tomatoes, potatoes, broad beans and peas. Citrus will also benefit from an annual application. Potassium has been found to help minimise diseases such as black spot, powdery mildew and rust.

Liquid Fertilisers

Liquid fertilisers and liquid feeds are used for fertilising plants once they are growing. They boost growth and can help stressed plants fight disease. You can buy them or very easily make your own.

Known as 'teas', homemade liquid fertilisers simply involve collecting a handful of the raw material, placing it in a bucket of water and leaving it to ferment for a few days. Strain the 'tea' with a gardening sieve or a piece of old muslin and dilute it with water in a watering can to the colour of weak tea and then water the vegetables.

Right: A liquid tea being prepared. Once fermented and strained it can be diluted and used to water your vegetables.

TIPS

The golden rule for applying any fertiliser is to always water the soil before you apply it and again afterwards to water it in.

Don't apply lime and blood and bone or rock dusts at the same time as the lime acts to lock up the phosphates.

Different fruits and vegetables have different needs when it comes to feeding or fertilising them. Some leafy greens, cabbage and corn for instance, like a fertiliser high in nitrogen, which stimulates leaf growth. High-nitrogen fertilisers include shop-bought soluble fertilisers (these are not organic, and often contain synthesised chemicals like ammonium and nitrate), chicken manure, coffee grounds, blood and bone, composted grass clippings, comfrey and comfrey tea, nettles and fish emulsions. These are best applied when preparing the soil for planting and during the main growing season. Planting vegetables that need a lot of nitrogen after a 'nitrogen fixing' crop such as a legume (see sections on Crop Rotation and Beans) is the best organic practice to ensure they receive the nitrogen they need.

Other vegetables, like carrots and beetroot, may require a boost from a fertiliser that is low in nitrogen, as nitrogen will produce leafy growth at the expense of root growth. These fertilisers include compost, some liquid fertilisers (check the package) and leaf mould.

TEAS INCLUDE:

Compost tea—made with half a bucket of homemade compost and water.

Worm tea—using a handful of castings from a worm farm and a bucket of water.

'Liquid manure'—the manure itself can be put in a sack or old stocking and popped into the water like a teabag.

Weed tea—any weeds in the garden, chopped up, will release nutrients for a rich tea.

Nettle, comfrey or borage tea—chopping up the plants as they go in will help the tea to brew.

Comfrey makes a wonderful tea as does borage (below).

Above: Manure added to the soil increases soil fertility.

MANURE

Adding animal manures to soil is a traditional method for increasing soil fertility. They are essential to organic gardening as they also enhance the structure of the soil and encourage micro-organisms. Manures include poultry (which can be bought in pelletised form), cow and sheep, horse and goat. The first two are the easiest to come by and can be bought in 20 kg bags from nurseries and hardware stores, or delivered by the cubic metre from landscape suppliers. Bought manures are not necessarily 'organic' unless they come from organic or free-range farms. Composting manure in the compost heap before using it will help rid it of residues. Rabbit, guinea pig and bird droppings can also be added to the compost heap.

The most important rule when using manure is to ensure that it is well rotted. Never use fresh manure as this will burn tender plant roots. Also make sure to wear gardening gloves and cover any scratches and sores on your skin when working with manures.

Poultry manure is a good source of nitrogen and phosphorous. Add two buckets every square metre to the soil when growing leafy greens.

Cow manure is low in nitrogen and so makes a good mulch and all-round fertiliser.

LEAF MOULD

Leaf mould is the broken-down product of autumn leaves and grass clippings. It makes a wonderful soil conditioner. Simply collect deciduous leaves, heap them up in an open enclosure and leave them to break down. Chopping them with a mower and adding a bag of manure will help decomposition.

GREEN MANURE CROPS

An excellent way to re-invigorate and fertilise soil, boost carbon and improve its structure is to plant a green manure crop at a time when the bed would otherwise be fallow. Green manure crops are often nitrogen-fixing plants that not only draw nitrogen to the soil but will help prevent soil erosion in a vacant bed, will smother weeds and aid the drawing up of nutrients to the soil surface.

There are many green manure plants to choose from and what you choose will depend on the season in which you are planting, what you plan to plant in the patch next and the type of soil you have in the garden bed.

Leaf mould collected in an open wire enclosure.

A thriving green manure crop.

A wooden compost bay being used to store leaf mould.

Green manures include lucerne or alfalfa for neutral to alkaline soils. Sow these from spring to summer. Buckwheat is another—it takes two to four months to grow and is good for poor soils. Plant it in spring to midsummer; bees and hoverflies are attracted to it. Lupin is good for acid and sandy soils and if planted from spring to midsummer will take about three to four months. Green manures you can grow over winter include broad beans and peas, which are sown in autumn or winter and are excellent for heavy soils. Cut them off at soil level, leaving the roots in the ground and plant a nitrogen-loving vegetable next, like leafy greens, over the roots. Rye is good for all soils, particularly heavy clay, and is grown over winter. It is good for attracting beneficial insects. Other green manures include clovers, fenugreek for growing over summer, mustard grown to seedling stage and the flowering plant phacelia.

To grow a green manure crop, broadcast sow the seed thickly around the bed and then gently rake over it, pushing the rake backwards and forwards. Allow the plant you have chosen to grow to between 30 and 60 cm. Like all plants, green manure ones benefit from being grown quickly by being fed with compost, blood and bone or manure and regular watering. Care does need to be taken to ensure that the green manure plant does not flower and seed.

Once grown, dig the plants into the soil, chopping them up as you go with the edge of your shovel. Leave the plants to decompose in the soil for a few weeks before sowing your next crop of vegetables. Covering the patch with black plastic, mulch or an old carpet will aid decomposition.

Green manure plants are also an excellent addition to the compost heap.

MULCHING

Mulching around your fruit and vegetables is an invaluable practice. It is simply adding a thick blanket-like layer of organic (or inorganic) material over the top of the soil. Mulching helps retain moisture in the soil, reducing the need to water. It regulates fluctuations in soil temperature by providing a form of insulation and helps to suppress weeds. By using a variety of mulches, different micro-organisms, like earthworms, will be encouraged as the mulch breaks down and nutrients will be added to the soil.

Mulches that are good around vegetables include lucerne or hay, straw, especially spent straw from the chicken coop, wilted grass clippings, sugar cane, compost, washed seaweed, well-rotted manure, leaf mould, mushroom compost and leaves. Comfrey leaves make excellent mulch and pine needles are traditionally used around acid-loving strawberries.

Other mulches that are readily available around the yard include weeds, which you can shred or leave to wilt before applying, shredded newspaper or cardboard, vacuum fluff and other spent plants from the garden.

Above and below: A well-mulched vegetable patch means moisture is retained in the soil and weeds are suppressed.

Grass clippings are best mixed with other leaves or used in a fine layer only, to avoid them compacting around the plant and preventing air and moisture penetrating the roots.

The layer of mulch can be between 2 and 10 cm deep. There are only two rules to applying it—always wet the soil before applying mulch and leave a clear space around the plant's stem or it will rot.

Black plastic is often used as a mulch around strawberries and other permanent crops and is a good way to prevent weeds and provide warmth around plants. Ensure you weigh it down with rocks.

COMPOST

Compost is essential to the health of soil and plants. Good compost acts as a soil conditioner adding critical bacteria, moulds, yeasts, fungi and nutrients and also improves soil structure. It is an integral part of organic gardening and very satisfying and cheap to make. Without compost to enrich the soil you cannot successfully grow vegetables in Australia.

Mushroom compost is the spent medium that mushroom growers use. It can be bought from gardening centres in bags or delivered by the cubic metre from landscape suppliers and is ideal for adding bulk and nutrients. It tends, however, to be quite alkaline.

A successful compost heap needs air, moisture and warmth. With these three things everything that has ever lived can be composted to produce food for the next stage of the life cycle. Air needs to be able to circulate around

TIPS

The main rule of composting is to balance the materials you use so that you have a rough ratio of 30:1 between carbon-rich dry materials (essential for fungi) and nitrogen-rich wet materials (for bacteria). Dry, brown woody materials like straw, dried leaves, woody prunings and sawdust are high in carbon. Nitrogen-rich materials are all of the green wastes like grass clippings, hay, fruit and vegetable scraps, and garden prunings. As a rule of thumb, you need loads of brown material and less green. The end product you are trying to achieve looks like crumbly dark humus with a sweet earthy smell.

the materials in the compost heap. An easy way to ensure this is to build a heap over a bundle of sticks or coarse prunings on the ground and to throw in some sticks every now and then as you build the heap. A large stick standing in the middle of the heap acting as a chimney will help air circulation. Turning the heap every few weeks with a garden fork will also aid aeration. The compost heap needs to be kept moist but not wet. In wet weather, cover the heap with thick cardboard, an old carpet, or hessian bags to prevent it getting sodden and also retain the heat. Warmth is needed to aid decomposition.

As you add layers of green waste, a good practice is to sprinkle them with lime or dolomite, wood ash, blood and bone or chicken manure. Urine, which is high in phosphorous, potassium and nitrogen, is another excellent addition. Then add dry brown materials and another layer of green waste and so forth until the pile is a metre or more high. As you layer, add the occasional shovel-load of soil. Water the pile till moist. If turned over every week, compost can be produced in six to seven weeks.

Composting methods

There are different systems and methods of making compost. In a small backyard, a ready-made container or homemade bay are perhaps the most convenient, in larger yards a series of compost bays or heaps can be made. The finer the material is shredded the faster it will break down.

'Hot' composting heaps make compost very quickly. Also known as true composting, it involves creating the conditions for bacteria and fungi to thrive. This heats up the composting material, which significantly increases the rate of decomposition. You need at least one cubic metre of material and instead of adding to the heap over time it is constructed in one go. As with all composting methods you need a lot more dry brown materials than wet or green ones. Add the material in layers, including garden soil and old compost and a thick layer of manure. As the heap is constructed wet the layers to ensure the pile is damp and then leave it to compost. Covering it will help prevent it drying out. 'Hot' composting can be done in compost bays.

'Cold' composting uses a compost bin. Make sure that the bin, which has no bottom, is placed on bare soil so worms can get into it and it can drain. Place it in a sunny position. Add layers of green organic matter and dry materials as they come to hand. A couple of handfuls of blood and bone aids decomposition. If it develops a

sour smell, add a few handfuls of dolomite or garden lime. If you turn the material over with a fork once a week compost should be ready to use in about three months, otherwise once the bin is full, leave it and it should compost in six months. The bottom layers are ready first and can be raked out and used before the top layers are fully composted.

Compost tumblers are barrels mounted on frames, which are turned frequently. They can be bought from hardware and garden shops and are a good use of paved areas in the garden. They are also vermin-proof. Compost can be made in as little as three weeks if the organic material is well shredded. Manure or blood and bone needs to be added to the mix.

Trench composting is a good way to prepare a garden bed for a vegetable patch. Simply dig a trench, about 30 cm deep, sprinkle

in some lime or dolomite and bury all kitchen and garden waste in it. Vegetables can then be planted into the soil on top of the trench.

Bays are easily built out of old wooden pallets, timber planks, chicken wire, corrugated iron, bricks or whatever is at hand. They are effectively three-sided enclosures (with an optional removable fourth side) and no top. If you build several bays, as the compost needs turning it can be moved along to the next bay. As with all methods of composting fill the bay with a variety of materials, wetting the layers as you go. Adding sticks to the mix will help aid air flow. Cover it with carpet, old sacks or canvas when it is full. If it is turned every two weeks, compost should be ready to use in a couple of months.

Bottom left: Compost tumbler.
Bottom right: Covered compost.
Below: Three-bayed compost bay.

When starting a new bay make sure to add a bucket full of old compost to help establish the vital bacteria needed for decomposition.

Indoor composting

'Bokashi' bins are a Japanese invention using micro-organisms sprayed onto wheat bran or rice husks, which ferment all kitchen waste—including cooked and dairy foods. They come with an airtight bucket that sits under the sink and the contents can be buried directly into the garden. Care needs to be taken to cover the bokashi waste in the garden or vermin will dig it up. Covering it for a couple of weeks with chicken wire will do the trick.

A **kitchen compost** can be made simply with a sealed bucket. Toss kitchen scraps and a layer of sawdust or garden soil in, press down when full and moisten. Leave the contents to rot down into compost.

Material to compost
- All fruit and vegetable scraps from the kitchen
- Grass clippings, fallen leaves and prunings
- Manures, including bird, rabbit and guinea pig
- Used straw and hay from the chicken shed
- Wood shavings

- Tea and coffee grounds
- Garden waste infected by fungi, mould, mildew (which will be destroyed by the heat)
- Washed seaweed
- Dry materials including shredded paper, newspaper and cardboard, dry leaves, sawdust, wood ash
- Fibres from the vacuum, clothes drier, hair and nail clippings
- Eggshells (an excellent source of lime)
- Weeds
- Urine

Adding lime, dolomite and wood ash as you build the heap is a good idea, as compost otherwise tends to be slightly acidic. Adding rock phosphate and trace elements to the compost heap will also help produce the best possible compost.

Compost activators

There are some materials that can be used as activators, giving the composting process a kick-start. These include soil, which naturally contains micro-organisms and the herbs yarrow, comfrey and borage, which all contain high levels of nutrients. Chamomile flowers are also useful. Old compost, blood and bone, chicken manure, rock phosphate and urine are excellent sources of nitrogen. Store-bought compost activators are not worth buying.

What not to compost

- Large bones, bread, rice, meat and cooked food scraps
- Human, cat and dog faeces
- Coal ash
- Rotten fruit with fruit fly
- Plastic
- Salt
- Disposable nappies
- Onion weed, couch grass
- Plants affected by viruses
- Large quantities of coloured paper or ash from burnt coloured paper, which may contain acids harmful to plants
- Soapy water

Caring for your compost heap

If the compost becomes sour and smelly, add a few handfuls of dolomite lime to sweeten it.

If it becomes smelly and gooey there may be too many kitchen scraps—add a layer of dry material and give it a good stir each time a layer of kitchen scraps are added. Having a bundle of straw or sugarcane mulch nearby will make this easier. It may also be caused by lack of air. Aerate the compost and add some coarse materials, like garden prunings.

If the materials get sloppy they are too wet; dry material like straw or sugarcane mulch or shredded newspaper needs to be added.

White compost indicates that it is too dry and needs to be moistened. Dry, powdery compost indicates a lack of oxygen so turn it over.

If the compost heap appears to have stopped decomposing it may require more nitrogen. Add poultry manure, blood and bone or grass clippings.

WORM FARMS

Worm castings are a great source of fertiliser. They make an excellent tonic for ailing plants when diluted with water (one handful of castings to one watering can filled with water). Worms will eat virtually any organic waste and are very easy to keep. Worm farms can be bought from nurseries and hardware stores or can be homemade. They are essentially a stack of three to four trays with holes in the bottom. The lowest tray collects the liquid waste, which makes an excellent liquid fertiliser, the next tray contains the worm's bedding material like coconut fibre, coir fibre, straw, shredded newspaper or leaves. The top tray contains the food scraps. Cover the top with a thick layer of damp newspaper or carpet to keep the farm cool and moist. The worms move up to the food layer. Worm castings can also be dug directly into the garden.

IRRIGATION AND WATERING

Fruit and vegetables are large consumers of water. They need frequent and regular watering to thrive and seeds will not germinate unless they are kept moist. A transplanted seedling will need immediate and profuse watering so that the soil will settle evenly around its roots. It will then need regular watering until it has been established, but care needs to be taken not to overwater it. Watering will depend on the time of year, the weather, the type of plant and the condition of the soil. In summer, it is best to water in the mornings and evenings to help prevent moisture loss through evaporation. In winter, the mornings are the best time to water so foliage is not wet during the night.

Soil with a large amount of organic matter in it will hold moisture better. Sandy soils dry out quicker than clay soils. Some soils will not absorb water. These are known as hydrophobic. Wetting agents and copious amounts of organic matter will be needed to rectify them.

Heavily mulched plants are better able to retain soil moisture around them. When watering vegetables by hand it is important to water them from underneath and around the roots and not to spray the water over the top of them. Overhead watering dramatically increases the risk of fungal disease. Generally, apart from periods of hot summer weather, vegetables will need to be watered every three or four days. As a rule of thumb, plants with large leaves need more water than others.

Given the amount of water that growing fruit and vegetables will require, it is well worth considering installing a rainwater tank and a grey water system. Drip irrigation and timer-operated irrigation systems are also a good investment.

Above and right: Raised garden beds with an irrigation system installed, ensures efficient watering of growing plants.

SUPPORT AND PROTECTION

Some plants, with climbing habits, will need individual supports to bolster their limbs or stems as they grow. Others, like grapes and raspberries, will require trellised support. Garden stakes, bamboo canes, star pickets and wire are all items that from time to time will need to be purchased or improvised upon.

Polytunnels or netting over crops will help to protect them from pests and the cold. Covers will need to be removed, however, from insect-pollinated plants once they flower so they can be pollinated. Shade cloths may be required over tender vegetables in summer to protect them from the worst of the heat.

Fruit and vegetables, particularly when young, will also require protection from birds, possums, fruit bats, wallabies, bower birds, rats, mice, cats and dogs. Fences around gardens may sometimes be a necessity. One simple method of protecting seedlings is to surround them with wooden skewers; another is to cover them with cloches or small polytunnels.

Frost-sensitive vegetables will need protection in winter. Cover them with sacks, fleece or large

Above: An old beer can has been recycled to deter birds from the crops.

Right: A berry crop protected by netting.

leaves at sunset on those nights you might expect frost or plant or build a wind-break around the patch. A weekly foliar seaweed spray is also good to toughen up the plants to survive frost. If frost-sensitive vegetables are hit with frost, give them a long watering to help revive them.

The flipside of this is humidity. Where it is a problem, try to ensure that there is adequate air flow around your crops and the garden is in a spot where air flow is not blocked by hedges or walls. In humid climates, it is also important to ensure good drainage.

Left: Seedlings covered by wire cloches.

Above: It would be virtually impossible for predators of any kind to enter this well-protected vegetable garden.

SETTING UP

COSTS

Initially setting up a vegetable garden will involve some financial outlay. Depending on the type of garden you build, costs will include any building materials and gardening tools that you need as well as organic matter, such as manure and mushroom compost, to improve the soil. Once the garden is established the costs will diminish. Seeds are cheaper to buy than punnets of seedlings and if you buy non-hybrid heirlooms you can save the seed to replant the next year and significantly reduce costs. Manure can be bought in bags from nurseries as can compost mixes and seed raising mix. It can also be delivered more cheaply in loads by the cubic metre from landscape suppliers.

Liquid fertilisers and other fertilisers, dolomite or lime, and mulches like pea straw or sugar cane will also need to be bought from time to time. To cut some costs you can make liquid fertilisers of your own and, of course, your own compost and leaf mould.

Potting and seed raising mix, seed trays and labels will also need to be bought or made from things already around the house.

TOOLS AND EQUIPMENT

You don't need a whole arsenal of tools to start a garden, just a standard four-pronged fork, a spade or shovel, a hoe, a rake, a hand fork and trowel and a watering can. Gardening gloves are a good idea for protecting hands, especially when using potting mix.

BUYING PLANTS

Seeds and seedlings are sold at nurseries, markets and some hardware stores in punnets and pots. A wider variety of heirloom plants and seeds is available online or through seed catalogues. When buying seedlings don't buy the largest ones or any that are in flower. The smaller ones will actually do better in the garden and are less likely to be pot-bound. Turn the punnet over when you are buying a plant and check that roots are not growing out of it, or that they are not wound tightly around the pot. If they are, it is pot-bound and not worth buying.

It is a good idea to harden off seedlings when you get them home by putting them in the sun for a few hours each day over a couple

of days before planting them. This will increase their resilience and strength.

PREPARING THE GARDEN BED FOR PLANTING

Before you start to build the garden, remove any weeds and dig over the soil, dispelling any big clods and loosening it up. You will almost always need to add compost or manure to improve the soil and help it retain moisture. Lime might need to be sprinkled over the soil if it is acidic and you are planting fruit or vegetables that like a sweeter or more alkaline soil. Check the pH and add lime or dolomite if necessary at one handful per square metre. If possible it is best to leave the garden for as long as six weeks before planting.

Just before planting, surround the garden with slug and snail deterrents like ground-up eggshells, used coffee grounds, coarse sand or sawdust. The slugs don't like to crawl over these rough textures.

A slow release fertiliser or blood and bone is often a good idea to dig in as well. Dampen the soil down and start gardening.

If buying seedlings, it is a good idea to check the bottom of the punnet to see whether the plant is root-bound.

DIGGING

Some gardeners do not believe that you should dig the soil of a garden—they believe this encourages weeds and degrades the soil. Instead, organic matter should be merely layered on top of the garden leaving earthworms to drag it down. One of the principle aims of organic gardening is to preserve the natural fertility of the soil by reducing the amount of cultivation. Soil is improved simply by mulching and cultivating the soil surface by layering it with organic materials. Other gardeners like to dig. However, other than the initial digging when starting the vegetable patch, very little further digging should be required.

Preparing a garden bed will depend on the type of soil you have. You may initially need to deeply cultivate it, which can be done in a number of ways.

DEEP CULTIVATION

If your soil is compacted or very heavy, digging it to a depth of about 25 cm and adding a thick layer of manure or compost, then replacing the topsoil, can improve it. It is the topsoil, the first 15 cm, which is home to the beneficial organisms that make soil fertile.

Make sure to enrich this top layer with copious amounts of manure and/or compost as you replace it. Try to leave the bed for at least four weeks before planting and then add some blood and bone, dolomite and more compost. You might like to sieve the soil for an especially fine tilth.

DEEP BED SYSTEM

When first building your garden you can improve the soil structure with one massive dose of organic matter to the soil. The soil should not need to be deeply cultivated again. Do this by marking out a trench with some bamboo canes or the like, about 60 cm wide, and dig the soil to about 25 cm or the depth of the spade. Break up the subsoil and cover it with at least 5 cm of manure. Dig another trench and as you dig put the soil into the first trench, loosening it as you go. Add more manure to the soil on top. Repeat the process until the plot has been covered.

Once the bed is established there is no need to deeply cultivate it again—shallow holes for seedlings should be the only digging required.

ORGANIC PRINCIPLES

Organic gardening is all about nurturing the earth by looking after the soil. It enables you to garden without using chemical insecticides, so you produce crops that are not only better for you but for the environment.

CROP ROTATION

One of the rules of organic gardening, indeed of any sensible gardening, is to rotate your crops. This essentially means not repeatedly planting the same type of vegetable or member of the same vegetable family in the same spot season after season. Soil becomes exhausted and is depleted of nutrients if the same crop is continually planted and a build-up of that crop's particular pests and diseases becomes inevitable, making them difficult to eradicate. Crop rotation aims to build up healthy soil and reduce the need to use chemicals.

If you have more than one vegetable bed then you can devise a plan where vegetables belonging to the same family are grown in one bed and then rotated or moved on to the next bed, so that no plot sees the same crop in successive seasons. If you have just one vegetable plot you can still practice crop rotation either by sectioning off the plot with a barrier material like a weed guard or just making sure to grow specific groups of vegetables in a different part of the vegetable plot each year.

Vegetables are grouped into the following family groups and they, generally, share the same needs.

The cabbage family, Brassicaceae—cabbage, cauliflower, amaranth, broccoli, Brussels sprouts, kohlrabi, radish, turnip, mustard greens, kale, Chinese cabbage, pak choy and rocket.

The potato family, Solanaceae—tomato, capsicum, chilli, eggplant and potato.

The pea family, Fabaceae (legumes)—peas, broad beans, dwarf beans and climbing beans.

Cucurbits, Cucurbitaceae—pumpkin, squash, melon, cucumber, zucchini, marrow.

Beet family, Chenopodiaceae—silverbeet, beetroot, spinach.

Lettuce family, Asteraceae—lettuce, globe and Jerusalem artichokes.

Onion family, Liliaceae (alliums)—onion, garlic, shallot, leek and chives.

Root family, Apiaceae—carrot, parsnip, celery, parsley, celeriac and Florence fennel.

On this same trellis, tomatoes were planted the previous summer (see page opposite for photo).

Both the onion and the root family can be grown together as root vegetables. Sweet corn, pumpkin, cucumber and zucchini will all grow happily in the one bed together.

A more complex crop rotation system takes into account the different nutritional needs of vegetables and how one type of vegetable can prepare the soil for the next crop from a different family. Legumes (peas and beans) 'fix' nitrogen into the soil as they grow so it makes good sense to grow a crop after them that needs a lot of nitrogen, such as leafy green brassicas. After the brassicas have cropped grow alliums or other root crops, which are not hungry crops. Follow them with cucurbits and then with plants from the Solanaceae or potato family and then start over again.

As long as you grow vegetables from the same family in a different spot each year you will be reducing the possibility of a build-up of crop-specific pests.

COMPANION PLANTING

For centuries, gardeners have observed a symbiotic relationship to exist between particular plants when they are grown near each other. This beneficial relationship can offer protection from pests and diseases by one plant acting as a 'trap' to lure pests away, or as a 'barrier' by exuding a scent, chemical or oil that deters pests. Other companions may attract beneficial insects, or pollinators, to the companion plant. Some plants may 'nurse' another by giving it shelter. For example, planting silverbeet, rhubarb or corn (all taller plants), will provide protection, especially on hot summer afternoons. Plant these on the southern edge of the patch, next to those vegetables such as lettuce, carrots and bush beans, which require protection from the sun. This is especially true in the tropics. Companion planting is a critical organic gardening practice and will reduce the need for chemicals or insecticides in your garden.

One good practice is to plant herbs around the borders of your vegetable patch. Useful perennial herbs include rosemary, thyme, rue, sage, lavender, hyssop and chives. Annual herbs like dill, chervil, basil, fennel and summer savoury are a strong attraction for bees when they are in flower. Gardeners have had some success by using tansy and sage to help ward off aphids, fruit fly and cabbage white butterfly, while nasturtiums act as a trap crop for cabbage white butterflies and aphids.

Perhaps the most useful companion is the French marigold—it exudes a chemical from its roots that prevents nematodes (eelworms) in the soil. It is a good practice to plant these around the border of every vegetable plot, especially in places where you will brush against them and help to release their scent.

The ornamental annual *Alyssum* is an excellent plant for attracting beneficial insects, while feverfew (*Pyrethrum parthenium*) acts as a pest repellent. Some old gardeners swear that planting chamomile with vegetables will improve their smell and taste.

Above: Tomatoes and basil are traditional plant companions.

Right: Lavender is a useful perennial herb to plant around the border of the vegetable patch.

There are some plants that do not do well together, for instance apples and potatoes, beans and garlic, and cabbages and strawberries. See the individual plant entries for lists of companions and non-companions.

EDIBLE FLOWERS

Flowers in the garden are not only invaluable for attracting pollinating insects, or repelling predatory ones, but are often edible as well. Consider incorporating pansies, violets, petunias, carnations (*Dianthus*), snow peas, lavender, nasturtiums, day lilies, marigolds (*Calendula*), cornflowers and borage into your vegetable patch. Not all flowers, or all parts of flowers, are edible, however, and caution needs to be taken before eating something you're not sure of.

HEIRLOOMS

Heirloom or traditional cultivars of vegetables, many of which have been consumed for centuries, are readily available, particularly over the internet. Growing heirlooms is a way to ensure biodiversity and to eat produce that cannot be bought at the grocer's. The flavours are often richer and the plants hardier. The range of heirlooms available is enormous. You can try striped zebra tomatoes, purple Afghani carrots, purple broccoli or white eggplants

to name a few. See the resources guide at the back of the book to find out where to buy seeds. Heirlooms are **non-hybrids** which are 'open-pollinated', that is naturally pollinated by bees, other insects or the wind. Their seed can be saved and can be sown again to produce a plant like the parent plant. Local seed-saving groups have been established nationwide as a response to the modern homogenisation of our foodstuff and to help protect biodiversity and ensure the continuance of traditional vegetables.

Hybrid seeds—when you see on a seed packet that it is a hybrid this means that it has been commercially bred by crossing two different varieties to bring together two different traits in the one plant. Typically they do not produce seeds that can be saved and used to grow the same plant again, or they don't grow again at all.

BEES, OTHER BENEFICIAL INSECTS AND POLLINATION

Albert Einstein estimated that humans would have four years to live if bees left the planet. This is because many of our foodstuffs, including vegetables, need bees and other beneficial insects for pollination. Most fruit trees need bees for cross-pollination. The bee transfers the pollen from one plant to another. Other bees act as buzz pollinators. These bees, which include native blue-banded bees, teddy bear and carpenter bees, release pollen by the vibration of their wings.

The failure of fruit and vegetables to bear fruit can often be put down to a lack of bees. The death of whole honey bee colonies in America and Europe over the past few years due to what scientists think is either a disease or a 'colony collapse disorder' makes it more important than ever to try and nurture bees.

As a gardener you want to attract bees and other beneficial insects and predators like lady beetles, butterflies and hoverflies, into the garden. The more you attract the more your garden will grow. Bees come into the garden looking for nectar, their main source of energy, and for pollen, which provides them with protein and fats. To attract bees plant a wide diversity of flowers and shrubs that flower over all seasons. Bees are particularly attracted to blue flowers including borage, *Campanula*, rosemary and *Echium*, lavender, fennel and thyme. Other bee-attracting flowers include Salvias and daisies, sweet peas, Chrysanthemum, *Aster*, black-eyed Susan, Penstemon, purple coneflowers, globe thistle, zinnias, wallflower, hyssop, marjoram,

The blue flowers of rosemary are attractive to bees.

A beneficial lady beetle.

The owner of this garden reminds us of the plants that attract 'good bugs'.

basil, coriander and lemon balm, coleus (*Solenostemon*), sunflowers and comfrey.

Bees are particularly attracted to Australian natives including *Abelia grandiflora*, *Angophora*, *Callistemon*, *Eucalyptus*, *Grevillea*, *Leptospermum*, *Westringia*, *Melaleuca*, *Brachyscome* ground-covers, *Hibbertia*, lemon-scented tea tree and fan-flower.

Gardening organically, and not using pesticides and insecticides, will encourage bees and other beneficial insects.

SEED SAVING

The seed of some vegetables is easy to save and use again. Others require a fair amount of preparation and care. Saving seeds is economical and a way to ensure the protection of our biodiversity and food heritage. How seed is collected depends on how the particular plant flowers and seeds. The other main consideration is whether the plant is self-pollinating or easily cross-pollinates with other varieties.

For capsicum, chilli and tomatoes the process is relatively simple. Leave the best fruit to fully ripen. Scoop out the seed, put it in a sieve and run it under water. Leave it to fully dry out on some paper towel before storing it in an air-tight container in a dry place. Seeds can be left on the paper towel, which can be cut into small pieces and planted.

Peas and beans, which are self-pollinating, are also easy to collect seed from. Leave some pods on the plant until they dry out. Thrash the bushes on a sheet, or rub the pods with your fingers to release the seeds. Store.

For celery, celeriac, parsnips, onions and leeks let the chosen plants flower and the seed mature on the plant. When the seeds turn brown pick the entire flower head and put it in a brown paper bag, tied with string and hang it upside down. The seed will fall into the bag. Once it has done this put it in an airtight container and store for the next season.

Leave brassicas, like broccoli and cauliflower, in the garden to flower and when they have, put a paper bag over them to capture the seeds.

Above and below: Vegetables left to go to seed for seed saving.

Interplanting: Leeks and brassicas flank celery growing in the middle row.

Care needs to be taken with vegetables that may cross-pollinate, like brassicas, corn, beetroot and eggplant. If you are going to collect their seed then they need to be grown in isolation, isolated in nets, or cultivars will need to be planted several weeks apart so they flower at different times.

SUCCESSIVE SOWING

To prolong your harvest and make sure that you are not inundated with a supply of one particular vegetable at the one time a good practice to get into is that of successive sowing. Simply plan to plant or sow a small batch of the same vegetable successively every couple of weeks.

INTERPLANTING

To maximise growing space, plant fast-growing crops like salad greens, Asian greens, radish and baby carrots among slow-growing crops, like pumpkin and brassicas.

It is also a good method of reducing pest attacks on an entire crop.

SEEDS AND HOW TO SOW

Growing vegetables from seed is substantially cheaper than buying seedlings at a nursery. Growing from seed also vastly increases the choices of vegetables available to you. Many heirloom varieties are available in seed only. It is easy to propagate from seed and extremely satisfying.

A seed is essentially the embryo of the plant and a built-in food source inside a protective coating. For a seed to germinate it needs three things: moisture, air and the right temperature. The other important thing to remember is the viability of the particular seed. Seeds vary from those with short viability to those which can remain alive for many years. Always check the use-by date on the packet and use seeds within six months of opening. Store seeds in a cool, dry, dark place in sealable plastic bags.

WHEN TO SOW

When you sow seed will depend on your climate and the season in which the particular vegetable grows. The back of the seed packet will give instructions as to sowing times for the particular cultivar. Seeds sown out of season rarely germinate as both the temperature of the soil and day length are critical. A soil thermometer will tell you the temperature of the soil; otherwise the old-fashioned method of sitting on the soil with a bare bottom to check whether it is warm is a method worth considering! Covering soil with a sheet of black plastic or cloches for a few weeks before sowing or planting will help warm it up faster in early spring.

Many seeds can be sown indoors or undercover six to eight weeks before the season is right for the seedlings to be planted out in the garden. This practice leaves space in the garden for other vegetables to continue growing until the seedlings are ready. It also means that you will get the most out of the growing seasons by being ready beforehand—particularly important in cool climates with shorter growing seasons. If you stagger sowing seeds, doing a punnet or so every few weeks, you will be able to prolong your harvest. Planting varieties of differing maturity and growing periods will also do this.

The two main sowing seasons are autumn and spring. In autumn you prepare for winter-harvested crops, while spring is the time to sow for summer vegetables. The sowing seasons are predicated by the last frost of spring, ushering in the spring planting time and a warming of the soil temperature, and the first frost of winter, putting a sharp end to the last of the warm season vegetables and bringing on the conditions for those vegetables that require a period of cold weather. In the tropics, many fruits and vegetables can be grown year round, for others the rain is the key indicator that the season has finished.

Cool season vegetables are brassicas, onions and leeks. Vegetables that can be sown in cold winter soil include broad beans and peas. In spring once the last frost is over and soil is 15°C, beans, cabbages, carrots and beetroot will germinate. When soil has reached 20°C all of the summer vegetables can be planted, that is tomatoes, cucumber, capsicum, eggplant, chilli and corn.

SEED RAISING MIX

Garden soil is unsuitable for raising seeds as it compacts when placed in containers and is usually not light enough to provide the air pockets and support that the tiny roots of seedlings need. Potting mix especially developed for seed raising can be purchased or you can make your own.

POTTING MIX RECIPE

One part propagating sand or coarse river sand

- -

One part either peatmoss/perlite/ coconut fibre/ vermiculite or leaf mould

- -

Add a handful of compost

- -

All of these are available from nurseries or landscaping suppliers.

Below: Reading the seed packet will ensure you correctly space your seeds when sowing.

DEPTH AND SPACING

As a rule of thumb, seeds are planted at a depth of roughly twice the diameter of the seed. So, fine seeds are generally planted only about 5 mm deep, while larger seeds are planted deeper. Alternatively, there are some very fine seeds that need only light to germinate and so do not need to be covered at all. The seed packet will give instructions as to spacing for individual cultivars. If seeds are planted too deeply they often will not germinate or will rot.

HOW TO SOW SEEDS

If you are sowing fine or small seeds, like carrot or rocket, mixing them with some dry sand will make them easier to handle. After spreading the seeds merely press, or tamp, down into the soil with your hand lightly rather than covering them with soil. For larger seeds, like pumpkin and beans, make a drill (an indented straight line) in the soil, with a stick or the tip of a hoe and sow the seeds directly into the drill. Push soil over the seeds, backfilling the drill.

Soaking seeds in warm water overnight will help some seeds, like basil and parsley, germinate. Another trick is to add a pinch of Epsom salts to a jar of water and soak the seeds for an hour before sowing; this is good for larger seeds like beans.

SOWING SEEDS UNDERCOVER OR INDOORS

If you sow seeds undercover—in a green house, a cold frame or in the shelter of a verandah—six weeks or so before the start of the planting season, you will have seedlings ready to go.

Cold frames are glass or plastic boxes with a slightly sloping clear cover that is hinged open to allow ventilation and are ideal for raising seeds. They can be bought at nurseries or hardware stores. Place them where they will receive good light. They can be placed on the ground and either filled with seed raising mix and the seeds sown directly into them or used to house seed trays and pots. If doing the latter, a layer of gravel across the ground inside will aid drainage. The frame creates a humid microclimate that aids germination and protects young seedlings.

A seedbed is a similar form of protection; it is essentially a small raised brick or timber frame with a removable cover of shade cloth or fly screen wire.

Sow seeds into plastic trays or cells bought from nurseries or into individual pots, or any container at hand like takeaway coffee cups or old butter and yoghurt containers with holes punched into the bottom. Toilet rolls make excellent small pots for seedlings. You can use plastic trays from nurseries lined with a piece of

newspaper to prevent the potting mix seeping out and egg cartons for larger containers. Peat pots bought from nurseries or online garden sites are excellent when growing seedlings that resent root disturbance. The pot is planted into the ground with the seedling and breaks down as it grows.

It is a good idea to always label your seed containers as it is very easy to forget what you have sown.

If you are re-using seed trays or pots wash them first in a weak solution of bleach to kill off any soil-borne diseases.

To sow seeds fill the receptacle with seed-raising mix, firm it down with your hands or a small piece of wood and dampen it with a spray of water. Spread the seeds over the tray and cover with a fine layer of seed raising mix or sieved compost, depending on the size of the seeds. Keep the tray moist as the seeds germinate. Once seeds germinate they require light so trays may need to be moved during the day. Do not allow the seedling trays to dry out. Place the trays in a warm, dry location with natural, indirect light.

Covering the pots and seed trays with plastic cling wrap or a sheet of glass is a good habit to get into, as it will help maintain moisture. Ensure that the cling wrap is taken off straight after germination.

Above: Peat pots and toilet rolls are excellent for growing seedlings.
Below: Seedlings housed in a cold frame.

Keep the seedlings moist, but not water-logged. A spray bottle is the best way to do this.

Seeds need some warmth to germinate and will perform better if they are provided with some heat underneath them. Thermostatically controlled heat propagators or heating mats can be purchased. The top of the fridge or above a hot water heater will also provide enough warmth. Once seedlings grown indoors have germinated it is important to move them to a sunny window ledge or warm, protected site outside so that they don't become spindly.

A good way to help prevent seedlings grown undercover from becoming spindly is to stroke or brush them with a piece of cardboard or your fingers. Gently stroke the cardboard back and forth over the tray of seedlings daily to make them stronger and shorter.

When seedlings emerge they can be given a boost by fertilising with a half-strength solution of an all-purpose soluble fertiliser, a weak seaweed solution or a homemade compost or weed tea.

When the true leaves appear, that is, the leaves that develop after the first, or seed leaves, the tray may need to be thinned of seedlings or 'pricked out'.

PRICKING OUT

When the seedlings are 15 to 20 mm high they need more space to grow and so often need to be 'thinned' or 'pricked out'. Do this by removing the weakest seedlings leaving the strongest to grow on with more space around them. This can be done by cutting off the weaker ones at root level with a pair of scissors or by repotting the best seedlings.

To re-pot, take the seedling bundles out of the pot or tray and, after placing them on a sheet of plastic or newspaper, with a flat blade, or your fingers, gently separate the seedlings. Fill new pots with potting mix or a combination of compost, peat and sand. Make small holes with a pencil or stick in the mix. Gently lower the separated seedling into the hole and push potting mix up around the roots. Use a fine spray and water the seedling. A very weak seaweed solution is a good way to reduce transplant shock. Put the container in a sheltered spot, with some morning sun if possible. Seedlings that are not being overcrowded can be left in the original pot to continue to grow.

With seedlings in pots and containers it is important to water every couple of days and not to let them dry out—regular watering will encourage them to develop their roots.

HARDENING OFF

Before transplanting seedlings to the garden bed, when they are 7 or 8 cm high, they need to be 'hardened off' in the sun. This means putting the containers outside in a spot protected from full sun and wind for an hour or so at first and gradually increasing the amount of time over a week until they are ready to be transplanted. This is done to help minimise transplant shock.

PLANTING OUT OR TRANSPLANTING

If you have not already done so, ready the ground by adding compost and/or manure and mark out drills with the edge of a hoe or rake. With fingers, a dibbler or a stick make holes along the drill bigger than the root ball of the seedling.

The main thing to keep in mind when planting out is to disturb the roots of the seedling as little as possible. For seedlings that resent root disturbance, like brassicas, pot them in biodegradable peat pots as the whole pot is planted into the ground. For other seedlings, lift the seedling out of the pot with a trowel or flat blade of a knife, or gently upend the pot and ease out the seedling. Put the plant into the hole making sure it is not buried and that it is at the same level as it was in the pot. Don't cover the crown or the middle bit of the plant with soil. Push soil around the roots and gently firm down with your fingers around the seedling. Making a small depression, like a moat, in the soil around the seedlings will help with watering. Water the seedling in. It is important to water seedlings as soon as they are planted, even if the soil is already damp, as this helps to settle the soil around their roots and reduce any air pockets. Make sure the water pressure is low, so the seedling is gently watered and not pelted. Keep watering daily until they are well established. After watering, it is a good idea to, again, gently press the soil around the seedling to help right its position. Mulch around the seedlings ensuring that the mulch does not touch the stems.

Soaking the pot of seedlings in a bucket of water or very weak seaweed solution before planting will help give them a head start and ease transplant shock.

Above top: A seedling being 'hardened off'.

Above: Gently ease apart seedlings before transplanting.

A common mistake when transplanting seedlings is to plant them too close together. You need to be mindful of how big the vegetable will grow and space the seedling accordingly. Plants that crowd each other out are more prone to fungal diseases and will not receive the amount of sun and nutrients they require. If you want to grow more, buy dwarf cultivars.

In hot weather, it is a good idea to plant out seedlings in the cool of the evening and provide some cover for the seedlings during the day with a shade cloth, horticultural fleece, branches from a tree, or taller companion plant.

Slugs and snails are immensely attracted to young seedlings. Sharp shell grit, coarse sand, coffee grounds or commercial snail bait (if you are not growing organically) arranged in a barrier around each seedling will help deter them. This needs to be a thick, wide barrier. Your local café is a good source of used coffee grounds (which are also an excellent addition to the compost heap). Beer traps are another deterrent. Beer traps are simply old jars, or even hollow oranges, buried at a sloping angle into the soil at intervals around the plants and filled with beer. The snail is attracted to the beer, falls in and dies.

Cloches are often used to protect plants. They can be anything from traditional glass domes, woven baskets, old vases or plastic bottles with the bottom cut off. They create mini-greenhouses over the plants, warming the atmosphere and protecting them from pests, frost and wind. Tunnel cloches can protect rows of seedlings. These can be bought or made by arching wire or plastic hoops over the row and covering them with thick plastic, netting or mesh anchored to the ground with tent pegs.

Horticultural fleeces are another way to protect young plants. They are a translucent polypropylene fabric that admits light, air and rain and can be laid across a seed bed or can be draped over hoops or cages to create cloches or tunnels. Fleeces will protect seedlings from cold snaps, frost and pests by creating a microclimate and giving extra warmth.

SOWING SEEDS OUTDOORS

Some seeds need to be sown in situ. Generally all root vegetables cannot be successfully

transplanted and plants that tend to bolt, like dill, coriander, Asian greens and fennel, are best sown where they will grow. Large seeds, like pumpkin and watermelon, are also easy to sow straight into the garden.

Before sowing seeds, prepare the soil. If you haven't already done so for a previous crop, add in compost (and/or well-rotted manure if you are not sowing root vegetables). Dig it in thoroughly. As soil temperature is critical to germination make sure that it has warmed up sufficiently.

Remove any stones and sticks from the garden bed and rake it until the soil is fine, crumbly and level. The edge of a piece of timber can be used to level it perfectly. Using a rake, either press the handle into the ground to make indentations for the 'drills' or use the end of the handle or a thick stick and draw out the drills. If the soil is dry, water it until moist (but not wet) before you sow the seeds. Place the seeds along the drill at the recommended spacing and cover with soil, by pushing it into the drill over the seeds. Firm down with your hands and water in with a fine spray.

Broadcast sowing—For salad vegetables, radishes, spring onions, mesclun mixes and green manure the easiest method of sowing is to 'broadcast' the seed. Simply scatter the seed evenly over the plot and then rake over the bed in a few directions to mix in the seeds. Water gently.

A good practice to get into is to label the rows where you have sown seed and mark them out with some sticks or bamboo stakes, as it is easy to forget where seeds have been sown. You can buy plant labels or use old ice block sticks or the empty seed packets.

Top right: Watering in newly planted seedlings.

Below right: Raking soil before planting.

Below left: Old vases used as cloches to protect seedlings.

GROWING VEGETABLES

ASIAN GREENS

Quick and easy to grow, Asian greens are members of the Brassicaceae or cabbage family and include bok choy (also called pak choy or 'white vegetable' by the Chinese), tatsoi, mizuna and mibuna. Brought to Australia by Chinese market gardeners in the 19th century, there are now dozens of varieties available. They are an excellent vegetable for children to grow.

WHERE TO GROW

Grow all Asian greens in moist, rich soil, in a reasonably sunny place, anywhere in the country. They are excellent for container gardening. Make sure to use a good quality potting mix and add some manure and a dose of a complete plant food fertiliser or blood and bone. Asian greens are an excellent vegetable to interplant amongst other slower growing vegetables.

WHEN TO PLANT

Best as a cold weather vegetable, grow Asian greens from autumn to early spring in all climate zones. Avoid planting during the hottest months of the year in warm climates, as the greens tend to bolt into flower and seed. Plant seeds from late summer to spring for winter harvests. In cool climates you can, however, plant year round although you may need to provide protection from winter frosts.

SOIL PREPARATION

Dig over the area and break up any large clumps of heavy soil. Throw in a handful of pelletised chicken manure to every square metre and a bucket full of well-rotted manure or compost.

HOW TO PLANT

You can buy seedlings but the seeds are so quick and easy to germinate they are a far more economical option; furthermore, seedlings are very likely to bolt when they are transplanted. Water the area prior to sowing. Sow seeds in drills directly into the ground. Cover them with 3–4 cm of soil and water them in gently. Keep the soil weed-free and moist so the seedlings grow rapidly. After germination thin them out to about 15 cm apart.

VARIETIES

Bok choy, known to the Chinese as 'soup spoon', has thick, white stalks with dark green leaves and bright yellow flowers. Tatsoi is a smaller version with darker green leaves, formed into a tight rosette.

Mizuna and mibuna are Japanese in origin with slightly mustard-flavoured leaves and are used in salad. They are 'cut and come again' greens and can be harvested in as little as 20 days after sowing.

Chinese broccoli, also known as gai lan, is eaten just before it flowers. The entire plant can be eaten. For a repeat harvest cut through the stem leaving four young leaves, then fertilise.

Chinese cabbage or wombok is a hearted cabbage with finely textured, crinkly leaves; there are tall-hearted and loose-leaf types.

CARE AND MAINTENANCE

Asian greens need to grow quickly, so need plenty of moisture. If the soil dries out, they are likely to bolt into flower. You may need to water daily, or every second day, depending on the temperature. Give them a boost with a liquid fertiliser every couple of weeks to ensure they grow quickly. It is a good idea to mulch with straw or sugarcane to keep the soil around the plants cool.

Sow the seeds at three week intervals so you can have a continuous supply.

HARVESTING AND STORAGE

Harvest can be as fast as six to seven weeks after sowing. Harvest outside leaves first, always leaving a few leaves so the plant keeps growing.

PESTS, DISEASES AND PROBLEMS

Look out for caterpillars, aphids and slugs.

COMPANIONS AND SUCCESSIONAL SOWING

As for other brassicas, see broccoli.

ASPARAGUS

Indigenous to North Africa, most of Europe and central Asia, wild asparagus (*Asparagus officinalis*) was eaten by the ancient Egyptians, who offered bundles of it to their gods, and by the Greeks and Romans, who used it as a diuretic. The oldest surviving recipe book, the third century AD *De re Coquinaria* includes a recipe for asparagus. It is said asparagus gained enormous popularity in 16th century Europe, being a favourite of Louis XIV of France, who had greenhouses erected solely for its cultivation.

WHERE TO GROW

Asparagus is a perennial vegetable, which should grow for twenty years or more once established. It takes up to three years before asparagus plants become productive so they need to be seen as a long-term investment. It is an easy plant to grow although it requires quite a bit of space in the garden. Asparagus is a member of the lily family and the plant itself produces very attractive foliage so it is worth considering planting it as part of the ornamental garden, or under fruit trees.

Asparagus grows best in cool, temperate and subtropical climates. It will grow in the tropics but plants don't last as long and their yield is smaller. Asparagus needs a sheltered, sunny site with good drainage. This is vital.

WHEN TO PLANT

- Asparagus crowns are best planted in early spring in cool regions and from late autumn to mid-spring in temperate or subtropical regions. In the tropics, plant crowns in autumn and early winter.
- Asparagus seed can be sown from September to November in cool climates, March to September in temperate and subtropical regions and from May to July in the tropics.

SOIL PREPARATION

The key to success with asparagus is soil preparation. Asparagus doesn't like competition so clear any weeds. Sandy soil is ideal. On heavy clay or poorly draining soil grow asparagus in raised beds or mounds to improve drainage. Mixing sand in with the soil is another way to help improve drainage. Asparagus likes a pH of 6.5–7.5.

HOW TO PLANT

Asparagus can be grown from seed but is more easily grown from one-year-old, ready-to-plant crowns. These are available from nurseries and online.

To plant crowns, dig a trench 25 cm deep and about the width of a spade, loosen the soil at the bottom of the trench and dig in a 10 cm deep layer of compost and/or manure. Create a ridge in the trench and then drape the roots of the crowns over it, about 30 cm apart. Cover the crowns with 5 cm of soil and compost and water well. Mulch lightly with sugarcane or pea straw. As the spears grow cover them with soil until the trench is full, then mulch again with manure and straw.

Seeds take two to four weeks to germinate. Soak seed overnight in water and pot in small pots filled with seed raising mix. Water the pot well before and after planting the seed.

VARIETIES

Asparagus can be white, purple or green. Varieties include Mary Washington, which is best for cold climates, the purple-speared Purple Pacific and Connover's Colossal, which can be grown from seed reasonably easily.

CARE AND MAINTENANCE

In spring, feed the bed with a complete flower and fruit fertiliser, blood and bone or pelletised chicken manure. As the spears appear, mulch around them with hay, leaf mould, compost or straw and make sure that the bed is kept free of weeds.

Asparagus needs to be kept well-watered while it is being harvested. By late December stop harvesting the spears and allow the plants to continue to grow. They will start to produce tall, fern-like foliage with small white to pale yellow flowers, then small poisonous berries. Allowing it to grow enables the plant to direct its energy into developing and strengthening the crown. Give the bed a dressing of manure and blood and bone. In autumn, cut down the ferns to about 2.5 cm above the ground but only after they have started to turn yellow and dry up. Then mulch the bed with compost or manure.

A traditional way to nurture the plant is known as the mother stalk method. Allow one of the first spears from each crown to continue to grow and produce its ferny foliage. The frond will feed the crown throughout the harvest period and ultimately lengthen the harvest.

For white asparagus, cut the spear before it emerges from the ground or blanch the spears by continuing to cover them with soil and harvest when they are about 20 cm long.

Old crowns can be divided in early spring and replanted. To divide crowns carefully dig them up and with a sharp knife or secateurs cut them into large pieces and replant them in a compost enriched new trench.

HARVESTING AND STORAGE

Newly planted asparagus must not be harvested in the first year. Instead, allow the ferns to grow. This returns nutrients and strength to the roots allowing the plants to establish. In the second year harvest only a few spears. After the third year, harvest spears until they start to wane then leave any remaining small spears to grow into ferns.

Cut spears when they are about 10–15 cm long with a sharp knife just below ground level. Harvest before the bracts on the spear tip start to open. The harvest should last for up to 10 weeks.

BEANS

Beans originated in South America and have been under cultivation for thousands of years. From the Fabaceae family, the bean (*Phaseolus vulgaris*) is a legume. Vulgaris means common and is said to suggest what happens to you when you eat them! They are an easy, undemanding vegetable to grow and are ready to eat within weeks of sowing.

WHERE TO GROW

Most beans need maximum sunlight and perfect drainage. They won't grow in wet, poor-draining soil or heavy clay. Some varieties can be grown in light shade.

Asparagus is best eaten the day of harvest, although it can be refrigerated for up to five days. It can be blanched and frozen.

PESTS, DISEASES AND PROBLEMS

Asparagus have few problems although slugs and snails can be pests.

COMPANIONS
AND SUCCESSIONAL SOWING

Asparagus is a companion plant for tomatoes and parsley. Avoid onions and garlic.

One for the mouse,
One for the crow,
One to rot,
And one to grow.
~Anon

WHEN TO PLANT

Almost all beans (except cold-loving broad beans) are grown through spring, summer and autumn. Sow beans in spring but only after the soil has warmed up as they will not germinate in cold soil.

- In cold areas, sow seeds from mid spring to summer. To get a head start you can raise the ground temperature by putting covers of black plastic, old carpet or horticultural matting over the soil three to four weeks before sowing but you will usually find that once the temperature warms up beans will grow quickly anyway.
- In temperate districts, seeds can go in any time from mid-spring until the end of January.
- In warmer climates, you can plant all year round although during the hottest months you may find they need some shade. Make sure to plant a number of crops at intervals of several weeks to ensure a continuous harvest.
- In the tropics, you can grow snake beans and winged beans all year round.

Below: Butter beans (a variety of bush bean).

SOIL PREPARATION

Remove any weeds. Beans prefer sweet soil, so if your soil is acidic add a handful of either lime or dolomite. Beans also like a rich soil and will benefit from the addition of two buckets of compost and/or cow or sheep manure to each square metre of soil, dug in deeply.

HOW TO PLANT

The only way to grow beans is from seed sown directly into the spot where they are going to grow. Germination is improved by soaking bean seeds overnight in a jar of water with a pinch of Epsom salts. There are two types of beans to grow—bush beans and climbing or runner beans. They each grow a little differently.

BUSH BEANS (FRENCH BEANS)

Level the soil with a rake and break up any clods. If it is dry, give it a good soaking and leave overnight. Create seed drills by pressing a rake into the soil to mark out lines about 50 cm apart and 5 cm in depth. Space the seeds on their sides so water won't pool on them, 10 cm apart. Backfill so all seeds are completely covered with soil. Only water the seeds if the soil is dry, otherwise do not water now. Don't water again until the seedlings appear in about two weeks and the first two seed leaves have fully opened. Beans don't need much water in the early stages of growth—waterlogging causes seeds and roots to rot. Thin out any beans that are overcrowded.

CLIMBING BEANS

Climbing beans don't take up much space and so are good for small gardens. They are more vigorous and heavier croppers than bush beans. Sow seed in the same way as for bush beans.

Climbing beans need a support to grow up. This can be a trellis of chicken wire, a net or a pyramid made of three or four bamboo stakes with strings wound around them at 10 cm intervals. Sow seeds in groups of three around the base. Once the seedlings have emerged snip off the weakest two plants in each group. Gently twist the plants anti-clockwise around their supports to encourage them to climb.

Above and below: A purple climbing bean—both in flower and ready to pick.

VARIETIES

There are many varieties of beans, varying in colour from brown, red, yellow and purple and in shape from round, flat or oval. Bush beans include butter beans and green beans; varieties worth checking include Gourmet Delight, the heritage Strike, Cherokee Wax with black seeds inside yellow pods and Golden Wax with yellow pods.

There are two types of climbing beans, both insect-pollinated: perennial (or seven-year) runner beans and annuals. Perennial varieties include Scarlet Runner. You can leave perennial roots in the ground at the end of autumn and the plant will regrow in summer. Annual climbing beans, which can grow up to 2 m high, include Blue Lake and Purple King.

CARE AND MAINTENANCE

It is vital to keep beans well mulched. Make sure that the mulch doesn't touch the plant's stem. Once the flowers appear and when the pods start to form, beans need to be kept well watered.

Birds and animals are attracted to the emerging seedlings. Protect them by erecting a tunnel over the top of the rows with wire or polytube and cover it with chicken wire or mesh or surround the seedlings with a corral of wooden skewers.

When climbing beans reach the top of the support pinch out the growing point. When the harvest is finished cut the plant off at soil level and leave the roots in the ground. Legumes extract nitrogen from the air and store it in nodules in their roots thereby 'fixing' nitrogen in the soil. The soil is left more fertile and can now be used to grow nitrogen-loving plants like lettuce, spinach, silverbeet, cabbage, cauliflower or broccoli.

HARVESTING AND STORAGE

Pick beans while they are tender and make sure to harvest them regularly as this encourages more to grow. They should be ready to harvest about eight weeks after sowing. Snap the pod off the plant making sure not to damage the plant. Beans can be frozen and the seeds can be dried.

Leave the pods to fully mature on the plants if you want to dry beans. When the pod is brittle break it open or smash it and the seeds can be stored as dried beans to eat (particularly Borlotti, Black Turtle, Red Kidney and Cannellini), or can be saved to re-sow in the next season.

Another variety of climbing bean.

PESTS, DISEASES AND PROBLEMS

The most common cause of beans failing to germinate is over-watering during and straight after germination.

If plants develop yellow leaves drainage may be poor.

Beans are prone to powdery mildew. See the section on Pests and Diseases for remedies.

Late frosts when the flowers are setting can contribute to a poor harvest.

COMPANIONS AND SUCCESSIONAL SOWING

Climbing beans grow well with corn. Avoid beetroot, kale or kohlrabi.

Beans are good to grow both before and after hungry leaf vegetables as they enrich the soil with nitrogen as they grow.

BEETROOT

Thought to be cultivated from wild seabeet since ancient times, beetroot is native to the coastlines of southern Europe and western Asia and related to silverbeet, sugarbeet and mangelwurzel. Beetroot (*Beta vulgaris*) is believed by some experts to stimulate sexual imagination because of its unusually high levels of boron. During World War II, women used beetroot as a lipstick to redden their lips. People with unusually acidic stomachs may have bright pink urine after eating beetroot thanks to its high boron content.

WHERE TO GROW

Beetroot is easy to grow. It needs a well-drained position in full sun or semi-shade. It will grow in all climates but plants may bolt if sown out of season. Round ball cultivars are suitable for pots.

WHEN TO PLANT

Beetroot is a warm season crop.

- In cool and temperate climates beetroot seeds may be sown from early spring until mid March.

- In the subtropics it can be sown all year round.
- In the tropics, beetroot can be grown all year as well, although it does better if not sown in the wet season. For a continuous supply sow successive rows every four to six weeks.

SOIL PREPARATION

If you have previously added lots of organic matter to the soil, don't add any more before sowing beetroot as over-rich soil can lead to coarse roots. If you haven't previously added organic matter add a small amount of poultry manure.

Beetroot will tolerate salt and frost but it does prefer neutral to slightly alkaline soils (6.5–7.5). If your soil is acidic, add lime before planting.

HOW TO PLANT

Beetroot does much better in the garden if you sow seeds directly. The seeds are unusual. They are 'multi-germ'—a little cluster with two or three seeds inside. Two or more seedlings emerge where one 'seed' has been sown. When the seedlings emerge you have to thin them to one per clump to allow them room to develop. Otherwise soak the seeds in water for a few hours and gently separate them before sowing. You can buy seed tapes which are easier to use—these enclose the seeds already spaced out—stretch tape along a 2 to 3 cm deep drill and bury it. The tape decomposes in the soil.

After the soil has been cultivated and raked over, make shallow drills or rows about 2 cm deep and 30 cm apart with the edge of a hoe or stick. Sow the seeds with 10 to 15 cm between them, cover with soil and water well. To prevent boron deficiency, mix two teaspoons of boron into a watering can and water the seeds. Boron is a microelement in the soil. After watering, apply a thin layer of organic mulch over the top.

VARIETIES

There are numerous cultivars, which differ in colour, size and shape of the root, as well as cultivars that have been developed to prevent bolting. These include Detroit Dark Red, which is a deep red, Golden Beet with yellow roots, Egypt's Best, a traditional Italian variety, Crimson Globe and Moulin Rouge. Boltardy can be planted early, Chioggia is an Italian variety with white and pink rings and Cylindra has carrot-shaped roots.

CARE AND MAINTENANCE

Keep the soil moist until seedlings appear 10–14 days after sowing. Thin them out when they are large enough to about 8 cm apart. Keep the soil moist or the roots become tough. Beetroot will benefit from liquid feeds once a fortnight.

In districts with alkaline soil boron deficiency is common. Seedlings look like they are thirsty, as the leaves remain small and slightly shrivelled. Use two level teaspoons of boron dissolved in five litres of water and water over the plants.

HARVESTING AND STORAGE

Beetroot takes two to three months to crop. The size of beets affects the flavour, with smaller beets tending to be sweeter.

When harvesting, pull alternate roots out, giving others more room to grow. Use a fork to gently lift beets. Twist off the leaves 2 cm above the root instead of cutting them. This avoids the beetroot 'bleeding' and losing flavour. Young leaves can be picked and eaten in salads or cooked like spinach.

Beetroot will keep for several weeks in the fridge, or in the shed in cool climates. Otherwise leave them in the ground and harvest as required.

PESTS, DISEASES AND PROBLEMS

Beetroot is usually problem free. See the Pests and Diseases section for dealing with aphids and caterpillars if they become a problem.

COMPANIONS AND SUCCESSIONAL SOWING

Beetroot grows well as a companion to silverbeet and kale, brassicas, onions, garlic, kohlrabi, parsnips and swede. It doesn't like growing with runner beans. It grows well after a leaf crop in a crop rotation cycle.

BROAD BEANS

Also known as the fava bean, broad beans (*Vicia faba*) are a legume that have been cultivated since the Bronze Age. Extremely easy to grow, as a type of 'vetch' they fix nitrogen in the soil. The Portuguese include a broad bean in the Christmas cake for luck and in Sicily, some believe that a bean kept in the pantry will ensure the pantry will always be full, after broad beans saved Sicilians from starvation during a historic famine.

WHERE TO GROW

Broad beans grow best in cool areas and can withstand hard frost. They may fail to flower and bear well in tropical areas (Madagascar beans, snake beans or winged beans may be grown as alternatives). Grow broad beans in full sun in a well-drained bed.

WHEN TO PLANT

Plant from April to September in cool regions and March to July in all other regions. In the tropics, snake beans can be grown all year.

SOIL PREPARATION

Add lots of compost or manure and a handful of potash and then rake the soil to level your soil out.

If your soil is acidic, add a handful of lime to sweeten it before sowing.

HOW TO PLANT

Broad beans must be sown by seed directly into the garden bed. They are best planted in double rows about 20 cm apart.

Mark out drills 3 cm deep and space the seeds along the drills 10 cm apart. Cover the seeds with soil and water once only.

Don't water the seeds again until after they have germinated. This is usually 10 or so days later.

VARIETIES

Dwarf cultivars, which are still 1 m tall, can be grown in large containers; varieties include Aquadulce and Coles Dwarf.

Two metre tall varieties include Early Long Pod, Big Ben and Egyptian, which has been grown in Egypt for centuries.

CARE AND MAINTENANCE

Broad beans require support as the top of the plant gets heavy with pods. Do this by staking each plant individually or by putting four long wooden stakes at each corner of the bed and tether strong twine or string between the stakes around the bed to hold up the beans.

In spring, pinch out the growing tip to encourage the pods to set. Leave broad beans in the ground for as long as possible, even after harvesting the crop. Like other legumes, broad beans have nitrogen-fixing bacteria in the nodules of their root systems. This helps to enrich the soil. When you are ready to take out the spent plants, cut them off at ground level, leaving the roots in the soil and dig the plant (the haulm) into the ground so it can act as a green manure, or compost it. The flowers of broad beans attract beneficial insects and bees.

HARVESTING AND STORAGE

The peak of the broad bean crop is in mid-spring. Harvest young beans to eat in their pods or leave them to fully mature. Shell the mature pods and remove the grey skins on each bean before cooking. Harvest beans constantly to ensure a continuous crop. You can leave the beans to reach full maturity, letting them dry on the plant and then use them for soup, or save the seeds in an airtight container to replant in the following season.

Broad beans can be refrigerated for five days, or blanched and frozen.

PESTS, DISEASES AND PROBLEMS

Failure to germinate can be caused by over-watering.

Broad bean wilt is a common virus, spread by aphids. The growing point of the plant blackens and the plant may wilt and die or recover to produce mottled leaves. Avoid aphids by pinching out the shoot tip once the flowers appear. Remove and destroy diseased plants.

Rust is a fungal disease common in late-sown crops. It looks like small, brown powdery spots on the undersides of leaves and will reduce yield and growth. Good air circulation between the plants will help to prevent fungal diseases. Bad infestations may need to be controlled with a bicarbonate of soda or sulphur spray. See the Pests and Diseases section for recipes.

Also, unsupported plants can suffer from wind damage.

COMPANIONS AND SUCCESSIONAL SOWING

Broad beans are a good companion plant to brassicas and spinach. They don't like to grow with fennel, garlic or onions.

Sow broad beans in a plot that has just had a root crop grown in it. After you have harvested the beans plant seedlings of cabbage, cauliflower, broccoli, lettuce, silverbeet or Asian greens into the nitrogen rich soil created by the legume's roots.

Broad beans make an excellent winter green manure. Grow them until they start flowering and then dig them into the soil, smashing them with a shovel as you go.

BROCCOLI

A member of the extensive Brassicaceae mustard family, broccoli (*Brassica oleracea* var. *italica*) evolved from the wild cabbage and was cultivated by the Romans 2000 years ago who served it in creamy sauces flavoured with wine or herbs.

Two types of broccoli are commonly grown. The dense, green-headed broccoli we mostly buy in supermarkets is called Calabrese. The other type is 'sprouting' broccoli. It is easier to grow and throws many heads instead of one big one.

WHERE TO GROW

Broccoli likes a rich, heavy well-drained soil in a site sheltered from strong winds. It will still do well in poor soil provided it is boosted with a heavy application of manure and/or compost or fertiliser.

WHEN TO PLANT

- Broccoli likes a cold winter. In cool districts, sow seed from November to February under cover and plant out the seedlings from January to May; and again, for a summer crop, sow seed undercover in winter to plant out in August.
- In temperate climates, sow seeds in late summer in the garden, or undercover, to plant out as seedlings in March, April and May. For a later crop, sow seeds in September to plant out seedlings from October to December.

- In the subtropics, sow seed in February to transplant seedlings in April or May.
- In the tropics, you can start seeds in April for transplanting in May, June or July.

SOIL PREPARATION

Soil needs to be well composted or manured or have just hosted a nitrogen-fixing green manure crop. If soil is acidic, add a handful of lime, as broccoli prefers a pH of 6–7.5.

HOW TO PLANT

You can sow seed in punnets and when they are large enough to handle prick them out (transplant them) into 10 cm biodegradable peat pots. Use peat pots as Calabrese broccoli, in particular, resents root disturbance. Harden off the seedlings before planting them out when they are about 10 cm high. Plant the seedlings deeply with the lowest leaf resting on the surface of the soil to encourage a good root system, and firm around the plants after planting, spaced 60 cm apart.

Alternatively, sow two to three seeds 2 cm deep into the garden in clumps 45–60 cm apart. When the seedlings are big enough thin each clump to one.

Plant sprouting broccoli 90 cm apart, with 75 cm between rows. With Calabrese, close spacing produces smaller heads, while wider spacing will allow more side-shoots and a larger central head to grow over a longer period.

VARIETIES

Calabrese is fast-maturing with large, dense green heads, cropping from early summer to autumn. It is not very hardy. Winter Harvest is a good choice for colder months, while Summer Green is more heat-tolerant.

Sprouting broccoli is in the ground for a long time, from midsummer through until spring and a single plant can take up to 1 m² of ground, but it crops when few other vegetables do. Varieties include Green Duke, Green Sprouting and purple sprouting.

CARE AND MAINTENANCE

Young plants may need protection from pests and birds with crop covers or cloches. As the plant grows, earth up the stem to prevent it being blown over and mulch around it during summer. Like all leafy crops, broccoli needs to be grown quickly and so will benefit from dressings of liquid fertilisers fortnightly. Water regularly. Sprouting broccoli may need staking.

HARVESTING AND STORAGE

Cut the central head of Calabrese while it is still tightly packed before the individual flower heads open. Take about 10 cm of the main stem with a slanting cut. This will prevent water lodging in the stem causing rot. New side shoots with smaller heads will now grow in the leaf axils, so a single plant will bear for many weeks. Cut side shoots as they develop, again taking 10 cm of the stem.

Sprouting broccoli should be picked when the first flower buds show a yellow tinge, just before the flowers open. Cut or snap off the heads. It can be harvested over several months. Regular picking encourages more shoots.

Store broccoli in the crisper of the fridge for several days or blanch and freeze.

PESTS, DISEASES AND PROBLEMS

Broccoli is from the Brassicaceae family, like

cauliflower, cabbage, Brussels sprouts and kale. When growing any brassicas organically, you must be vigilant in checking for pests so they don't get out of control before you can deal with them. Many bugs can be blasted off with a hose or the plant can be sprayed with soapy water to suffocate the bugs. If bugs are particularly bad they can be thwarted by the use of exclusion netting, draped over polypipe frames.

Look out for caterpillars, laid by cabbage white butterfly, which are a huge problem from February to mid-May. See the section on Pests and Diseases.

Clubroot is an almost incurable fungal disease suffered by brassicas. Plants affected by clubroot grow very slowly and wilt on hot days. The roots of the plant become thick and congested. It can remain in the soil for years. Clubroot is worse in acidic soils and when it is very moist. Make sure to lime an acidic soil before planting and growing seedlings or buy seedlings in a sterile compost or growing medium so as not to import clubroot.

Other problems include aphids, downy mildew and magnesium deficiency, symptomatic of which is a yellowing of the leaves between the veins. Spray the foliage of the crop with 200 g of epsom salts diluted in 9 L of water.

Birds can damage brassicas. A simple solution is to protect young seedlings by stringing black cotton around twigs or corralling the seedlings with bamboo skewers, or by using cloches.

COMPANIONS AND SUCCESSIONAL SOWING

Broccoli can be grown as a companion to French beans, beetroot, chards, celery, dill, onions, garlic, peas and potatoes. Peppermint, nasturtiums, rosemary or sage nearby will help confuse pests. Avoid lettuce, runner beans and strawberries.

Crop rotation is crucial when growing any brassica to try to avoid clubroot. In a crop rotation grow brassicas after a green manure or legume and before a root crop.

SEED SAVING

It is difficult to save true seed from brassicas. As members of the brassica family tend to cross pollinate, to save seed you need to isolate the broccoli crop from all other brassicas by growing just one variety apart. Allow at least two plants to go to flower (or their sideshoots) and then form pods. When the pods are brown and dried, cut down the plant and hang it up in the shed for at least two weeks, with newspaper under it to catch the seeds. The exception is the Asian cabbages, which do not cross with other members of the brassica family.

BRUSSELS SPROUTS

Another brassica (*Brassica oleracea* var. *gemmifera*), Brussels sprouts were probably first grown by the ancient Romans before being popularly cultivated in Belgium in the 16th century from where their cultivation spread throughout Europe. In the UK, they are a popular vegetable for eating with Christmas dinner.

WHERE TO GROW

Brussels sprouts are cold or mild climate, hardy vegetables that need a winter chill. They are not suited to warm climates. Choose an open, sunny site in ground that has rich, firm soil and is free-draining.

WHEN TO PLANT

Sow seeds undercover from early spring in cold and temperate districts and plant the seedlings out six weeks later from late spring to early summer.

SOIL PREPARATION

Brussels sprouts need firm soil to keep them upright. If your soil is loose they may need to be tied to a bamboo tripod or stake. Brussels sprouts are a heavy-feeding crop so add compost and/or manure and general organic fertiliser in early spring before planting, or plant them after a green manure crop. The soil pH in which Brussels sprouts grow most successfully is 6.5–8. Therefore, if you have acidic soil add lime or dolomite.

HOW TO PLANT

Brussels sprouts have a long growing period (nine months for some sprouts, four to five for others). It is best to sow in small pots and transplant these once the seedling is well developed, so as not to take up space for so long in the garden. Sow seed into punnets or small biodegradable pots, 8 mm deep. Prick out the seedlings when they are about 10 cm tall and transplant into the vegetable plot.

For short cultivars space the seedlings 45 cm apart, and space tall cultivars 60 cm to 1 m apart, allowing 75 cm between rows. When you are transplanting the seedlings make sure to leave enough soil around the root balls to minimise transplant shock. Dampen the soil before transplanting. The trick to planting is that you need to plant the seedling deeply into the ground, first removing the lowest seed leaves and planting the seedling so the soil comes up to its first true leaves. Firm down the soil around each seedling when you have planted them.

VARIETIES

Brussels sprouts are classified according to whether they are harvested early, mid or late season and are dwarf or tall cultivars. They can be green or red. Long Island Improved is a dark green heirloom, Drumtight is suitable to a wide range of climates and its sprouts can be harvested at the one time. Fillbasket, Red Ribs and Topscore are other varieties.

CARE AND MAINTENANCE

If plants are in an exposed, windy position lessen the chance of wind damage by hilling up soil around the base of the stem for support, or stake them.

Brussels sprouts benefit from a top dressing of compost or blood and bone, manure or a complete plant food when the first buds appear and again a month later. They also like a monthly liquid feed. Mulch well around the plants to suppress weeds. Nipping out the terminal bud will encourage the sprouts to swell more quickly.

HARVESTING AND STORAGE

Brussels sprouts taste better after a frost. Harvest sprouts when they are about the size of a 20 cent piece and before they begin to open. With modern varieties of Brussels sprouts, the sprouts tend to mature at the same time. Heirlooms mature along the main stem progressively from the bottom up. Harvest the lowest ones first. To encourage the first sprouts to ripen strip off the lower leaves. To harvest the sprouts, pick them with a downward and sideways twist or cut away from the stem with a knife. With modern cultivars, where the sprouts grow at the same time, cut the main stem at ground level and pick all of them at once.

Overcooking sprouts releases sulphur, which makes them smell and taste unpleasant. Steam them lightly only and this will not be a problem. Store them for up to one week in the fridge. They can be blanched and frozen.

PESTS, DISEASES AND PROBLEMS

Pick off any pest or disease ridden leaves. Like all brassicas Brussels sprouts suffer from a number of pests and diseases. See the entry on broccoli for methods to deal with them.

If your sprouts have hollow stems they may be growing in soil that is too alkaline and have a boron deficiency. Add two teaspoon of borax to a watering can and water well or try increasing feeds of seaweed solution.

COMPANIONS AND SUCCESSIONAL SOWING

See Broccoli.

CABBAGE

Another member of the Brassica family (*Brassica oleracea* var. *capitata*), the ancestors of cabbage were natives of the Mediterranean. By the time of the Greek and Roman civilisations cabbage was a well established garden vegetable. It had extensive uses in folk medicines especially as a treatment for acute inflammation. Breast-feeding mothers still use cabbage leaves today to alleviate engorgement.

WHERE TO GROW

Cabbage will grow in any soil that is not too acidic, across the range of Australian climates. Like all of its family it likes full sun and a well-drained soil.

WHEN TO PLANT

● In both cool and temperate climates, both summer and winter varieties of cabbages can be grown. In cool climates for cabbages harvested in winter sow seeds in trays in early spring and plant out seedlings into the garden throughout spring and summer.

● In warm climates, plant seedlings in late autumn for summer cabbages and in early spring for winter cabbages.

SOIL PREPARATION

Cabbages like a well-fertilised soil. Optimally, several weeks before transplanting seedlings, prepare the garden bed by adding a handful of lime or dolomite, a load of manure or compost and a complete fertiliser. Cabbages like a pH from 6–8.

HOW TO PLANT

Sow seed thinly in rows in a seedbed or in seedtrays and transplant the best seedlings when they are about 10 cm high. Most varieties of seedlings need to be 60 cm apart, although large varieties such as Drumhead and Succession need 90 cm around them. Smaller varieties such as Jersey Wakefield can be 30–40 cm apart. Water the seedlings in well and mulch. When planting the seedlings plant them deeply, up to the first set of true leaves. This stabilises the plant.

VARIETIES

There are a number of types of cabbage. Savoy is a ball or barrel headed type with puckered foliage. Its head takes 10–12 weeks to mature, although its outer leaves can be picked from the loose heads at any time. Varieties include Savoy Express, Mantovano and Gros des Vertus.

Traditional drum and ball-head cabbages (which form a tight central head of leaves) can grow to 4 kg and take four to five months to grow. They are cold and frost tolerant.

Oxheart or Sugarloaf cabbage are the fastest maturing and most heat-tolerant of the headed cabbages, taking eight to 10 weeks to harvest. Early Jersey Wakefield is an heirloom variety.

Grow radicchio (known also as leaf chicory or endive) as you would cabbage (though as a member of the Asteraceae family it is really more closely related to lettuce). Palla Rossa, Red Verona and Red Treviso have striking deep red foliage and grow well during cooler weather.

CARE AND MAINTENANCE

Cabbage needs to be watered regularly and grown rapidly, so when it is half grown mulch it with some compost and poultry manure or start fortnightly applications of a liquid fertiliser high in nitrogen.

As cabbages grow, hill up soil around the stems to prevent them from falling over and to encourage the formation of additional stem roots that will help to support the weight of the leaves.

Mulch the soil to retain moisture as water deficiency seriously sets back growth.

HARVESTING AND STORAGE

Pick leaves from the outside, starting with the largest oldest ones, as soon as the plant is large enough. Never completely denude the plant if you want it to continue to grow. For the cabbage to form a head stop harvesting the leaves once they begin to cup inwards towards the centre of the plant. When the head has grown and is ready to pick pull the entire cabbage up, cut off the roots and compost, don't leave the roots in the soil for fear of clubfoot disease.

PESTS, DISEASES AND PROBLEMS

See the entry for Broccoli.

COMPANIONS AND SUCCESSIONAL SOWING

See the entry for Broccoli.

CAPSICUM AND CHILLIES

Capsicum and chilli (*Capsicum annuum*) are members of the nightshade Solanaceae family as are tomatoes and potatoes. Botanically fruits, they grow in much the same way.

Capsicum and chilli are native to Central and South America and have been part of the South American diet for at least 6000 years. Christopher Columbus encountered them and called them peppers. Introduced into Europe, they were grown in the gardens of monasteries in Spain and Portugal where monks are said to have experimented with them and found them to be a substitute for black peppercorns, which were so expensive that they were used as a legal currency. In ancient Japan, part of a warrior's preparation for battle was to force himself to eat chilli to help strengthen his mental state and aid in blocking fear.

WHERE TO GROW

Chillies and capsicums are tropical and subtropical plants. They are excellent in containers and will produce large crops in pots on the verandah. All chilli varieties require good drainage, full sunshine and an enriched, fertile soil. Most importantly, they require long periods of warmth, so in cooler climates consider cloches, cold frames or an horticultural fleece. They are a good crop for an ornamental garden or a hot, sunny border.

WHEN TO PLANT

In cool and temperate zones, sow seeds in pots in spring. Plant the seedlings out in early summer. In cool climates and when the soil temperature remains low make sure not to plant chillies in the garden too early as cold-checked plants will have a retarded growth from which they are unlikely to recover. Pop a cloche or upturned bottle over the seedling in the garden until the days reach 21°C. Once the days are hot seeds can be sown in the garden.

In the tropics, chillies and capsicum can be grown year round.

SOIL PREPARATION

Ideally improve the soil with well-rotted manure or compost during winter. The ideal pH range for chilli and capsicum is 6–6.5. Before planting add a handful of complete plant fertiliser or an organic plant food.

HOW TO PLANT

Sow seed thinly about 1 cm deep in seedtrays or pots containing equal parts sand and well-rotted compost or commercial seed-raising mix. Place them in a warm, sheltered position and allow them to grow for eight to 10 weeks before transplanting. For seeds to germinate they need the soil to be at least 21°C. You can create a warmer environment by covering the pot with cling wrap, a sheet of glass or a clear plastic bottle with the top cut off, or by growing the seedlings in cold frames. When the seedlings are large enough to handle prick them out into individual peat pots filled with potting mix. Alternatively, of course, you can purchase seedlings.

In summer when the weather has warmed up plant seedlings in the garden, 30 cm to 60 cm apart, depending on the cultivar, or sow seeds directly into prepared beds.

VARIETIES

Chilli and capsicum differ from each other by a single gene that produces the fiery flavoured compound capsaicin. There are hundreds of varieties of chilli, which differ in climate tolerance, colour, shape, size and degree of heat. Chilli varieties include Anaheim with long tapering mildly pungent fruit, Jalapeno, a small hot thick-walled variety and Poblano with large medium hot heart-shaped fruits. Some of the hottest chilli varieties include Habanera and Puerto Rican Rocatillo. Sweet varieties include Sweet Banana with a 25 cm long yellow fruit.

Capsicums include the chocolate-coloured Sweet Chocolate, Golden Calwonder and the bush capsicum that can grow for up to five years in the tropics.

CARE AND MAINTENANCE

After transplanting, plants can be slow to start growing and then will suddenly begin to flower and produce fruit. Keep the soil moist and water regularly in dry weather, taking care not to saturate the soil as overwatering can lead to root disease. Feed plants once the fruit begins to swell with a liquid fertiliser every few weeks. Chilli and capsicum usually don't grow more than 1 m high so staking is usually unnecessary. Capsicums have a bushy habit. To encourage them to branch out pinch out the growing point when the plants are half a metre high.

Birds are apparently unaffected by the capsaicin in chilli although most mammals find it unpleasant.

HARVESTING AND STORAGE

Chilli and capsicum take about three months to grow. Ripe capsicum can be left on the plant for up to 10 days and then kept in the fridge for four to five days. It can be preserved by bottling or freezing.

Chillies can be picked when immature or left until fully coloured and slightly shrivelled. They can be dried or frozen whole. To make cayenne pepper select well matured chillies and dry them in the sun for three to five days. When completely dry remove the seeds and stems and grind the fruit in a spice grinder or pepper mill.

PESTS, DISEASES AND PROBLEMS

Watch for slug damage and aphids early on and protect from birds.

Plant rotation will minimise verticillium wilt and other soil-borne diseases. The most common disease is spotted wilt. Yellowish spots and rings appear on the leaves and fruit. It affects tomatoes as well. Remove and destroy all plants and use a spray for thrips.

Plants can also be affected by powdery mildew, target spot and blossom end rot. Target spot affects potatoes, tomatoes and eggplants as well. Dark brown spots appear on the leaves and the fruit rots. Usually caused by warm humid weather, it is carried by diseased seeds. All plants will need to be removed and destroyed.

Blossom end rot affects capsicum and tomatoes and looks like a brown sunken mark on the fruit. Caused by not enough calcium in the soil, it can be prevented by liming the soil before planting, avoiding using too much fertiliser and by adding a lot of organic matter to the soil to help prevent waterlogging.

COMPANIONS AND SUCCESSIONAL SOWING

Do not grow chillies or capsicum where related species of the family Solanaceae such as tomatoes and eggplants have recently been grown. In a crop rotation they should be treated as a fruit crop and follow legumes. After them plant a leafy crop.

SEED SAVING

Although the flowers are self-pollinating they also readily cross-pollinate by insects so carefully isolate plants intended for seed saving with fine netting. When the fruit is ripe, scrape out the seeds, dry them for a few days and store them in a cool, dark place.

CARROTS

The domesticated carrot (*Daucus carota* subsp. *sativa*) originated in Afghanistan 5000 years ago and was purple. It is thought to have been brought to the West by Arab traders in about the 10th century. The modern orange carrot was bred by Dutch growers in the 16th century, but it was not until World War II that the popularity of the carrot reached its peak when, facing a glut of carrots, the British Government attributed the RAF's increasing successes to carotene, which was believed to help night vision. People eagerly tucked into carrots believing this would help them see more clearly in a blackout. Today, heritage carrot seeds are readily available and purple, yellow and red carrots can be grown at home.

WHERE TO GROW

Carrots can be a challenge to grow. They are not suited to all soils. Deep, stone-free sandy loam is ideal. If you have heavy or clay soil you need to add coarse sand to improve the texture. The soil needs to be well draining. Overly rich

to put a cup of dry river sand in a plastic bag and add the seeds, shake well and dribble the mixture along the drill or broadcast sow. Cover the seeds very lightly with soil or compost, vermiculite or seed-raising mix and pat it down with your hands. Water lightly. A sprinkling of grass clippings makes a good mulch. Germination is often slow taking two to three weeks for seedlings to appear. Keep the seeds moist until germination and then water weekly.

VARIETIES

Carrot cultivars can be small or stumpy, slender, broad, long or short. Top Weight, Western Red, Paris Market and Royal Chantenay have long tapering roots; Majestic Red is a 30 cm long carrot, bred in Australia. Shorter varieties are good in deep containers and include Early Chantenay and Baby, which are finger-sized and mature early. Short, quick-maturing summer carrots include Amsterdam and Nantes. Larger slow-growing types, like Autumn King and Berlicum, are for winter harvests.

soil and soil containing too much compost and manure can result in forked, flavourless roots. Carrots like a sunny bed that was fertilised for another crop during the previous growing season. They can be closely spaced and so are good for a small space.

WHEN TO PLANT

- In cool climates sow from early September to February. Sowings from late autumn to winter may run to seed without producing any roots, or fail to germinate in cold soil.
- In temperate areas sow from July to March.
- In the subtropics, sow them year round.
- In the tropics sow carrots in the dry season.

SOIL PREPARATION

Carrots do not need fertilisers. Don't add manure to soil before sowing carrots or sow them immediately after a green manure crop. Before sowing carrot seeds make sure the area is completely weed free and stone free and dig it over deeply. Rake it flat and then saturate the plot the day before sowing. The ideal pH is 6.5–7.5.

HOW TO PLANT

Carrots are grown from seed sown directly into the garden, as their roots must not be disturbed. Create 2 cm deep drills, 20 to 30 cm apart. Scatter the seed thinly along them. Carrot seed is small and difficult to handle. A good idea is

CARE AND MAINTENANCE

When the seedlings are 5 cm high, thin them to 2 to 3 cm apart (eat the removed seedlings) and then thin again to 5 to 7 cm apart when the tops are about 15 cm high. Make sure the soil is weed

free while the carrot seedlings are young. Mulch between the rows to prevent weeds. Planting companions like garlic, leeks or onions between the rows is another way to cover the soil and prevent weeds. Water carrots well in dry weather.

HARVESTING AND STORAGE
Most varieties take three to four months to harvest from seed. You can start harvesting whenever your carrots seem big enough. Always twist off the tops of carrots as soon as you pull them up and take them inside, the sun causes the leaves to draw moisture from the roots, drying them out. Main crop varieties may be left in the ground over winter and dug as required.

PESTS, DISEASES AND PROBLEMS
Pests and diseases in carrots are rare. It is, however, not uncommon to have problems growing carrots. Stones, clumps of dirt or bulky organic soil may cause forked, misshapen roots. Cracked or split roots may be caused by heavy rain after a dry spell or over-fertilising. You can help avoid this by piling earth over the crowns, or tops, while they are growing. Green tops on carrot roots are caused by sunlight on exposed crowns.

Carrots with a pale colour are usually the result of strongly acid soil or excessive nitrogen in the soil. Add lime to soil, avoid nitrogen fertilisers and add some potash to increase colour intensity. Some varieties are quite pale anyway.

Seedlings can burn off in hot weather so try to avoid this by keeping the soil moist.

Birds and native animals can be interested in carrots. Lengths of bird wire bent to form tunnels over the crop is one means of protection, poking wooden skewers in the ground around the crop is another.

Seedlings which get water stressed or are subject to cool weather during early spring growth may bolt. Remove bolters to prevent them from encouraging others. Excessive leaf growth indicates too much nitrogen in the soil, again avoid nitrogen-rich fertilisers, like poultry manure.

COMPANIONS AND SUCCESSIONAL SOWING
Onions and leeks are traditional and hugely beneficial companion plants to carrots; others include chives, lettuce, garlic, peas and tomatoes. Avoid dill.

Grow root crops after leafy green crops or fruit crops like tomatoes and before legumes.

> 'Our vegetable garden is coming along well, with radishes and beans up, and we are less worried about revolution.'
> ~E.B. White

CAULIFLOWER

'Cauliflower is nothing but a cabbage with a college education' according to Mark Twain. Perhaps he was referring to the many transformations cauliflower (*Brassica oleracea* var. *botrytis*) has had from wild cabbage to the cauliflower eaten by the Romans by 600BC. What we eat today is the flowers of the cabbage suspended at the bud stage.

WHERE TO GROW

Often quite difficult to grow, cauliflowers take up a lot of space for a long time and can fail if there is any check to their growth. They need an open, sunny position in the garden with fertile, moisture retentive soil. Cool to cold climates are best for growing cauliflowers but they can be grown successfully in mild temperate areas. They are not suitable for the tropics.

WHEN TO PLANT

◆ In cool and temperate climates, when to sow or plant depends on which season the variety is to be harvested. Cauliflower needs low temperatures for the flower heads (curds) to form and is sown or planted from spring all the way through to mid-summer for a winter harvest. Cauliflower can also be planted in winter for mini caulis and early summer varieties, which are better for small gardens.

SOIL PREPARATION

Cauliflower is a heavy feeder and as such must have rich, moist soil. Dig a barrow-load of manure and/or compost and a handful of complete or general organic fertiliser or blood and bone into the bed before planting. They will grow across a wide range of soil pH (6.5–8).

HOW TO PLANT

Cauliflowers are 'late' or 'early' varieties depending upon when they are due to be harvested. Late varieties are larger and take longer to grow. They need more space in the garden and are planted about 90 cm apart. Earlier, smaller varieties will need about 50 to 70 cm between them and about 60 cm between rows. Sow seed thinly 10 mm deep in a seedbed or seed box in rows 7–10 cm apart. Transplant after hardening off, when the seedlings are between 7 to 15 cm high. When

transplanting the seedling be very careful not to disturb the roots and make sure to plant it up to the first set of true leaves, so that the leaves are resting on the ground. Extend the harvest by sowing two different varieties of different maturity.

To produce mini caulis, sow closer together—these are easier to grow and the soil needn't be as rich.

VARIETIES

There is a wide range of cauliflower available, suited to different growing seasons and varying in the length of time to mature. It is usually white but you can get purple, light green (Broccoflower) and orange cultivars. Mini caulis take 10 to 12 weeks to mature while large caulis like Phenomenal Early can take 14 to 24 weeks.

CARE AND MAINTENANCE

When plants are half-grown, hill them slightly by pushing soil up around the stem and firming it to prevent the plant being blown over by the wind. Water regularly and, as they are hungry plants, give them a handful of a complete fertiliser every two to three weeks, a mulch with manure, or liquid feeds. A seaweed solution is particularly beneficial. Surround them with a thick mulch to prevent them from losing moisture.

The heads are easily discoloured by sunlight, rain or frost. Protect them by loosely tying the leaves together over the developing heads with string or pegs, or break the midrib of the outer leaves and bend them over, tuck them in around the head.

HARVESTING AND STORAGE

Harvest when the curds are well developed and solid and before they start to turn yellow and soft. Store in the fridge or blanch and freeze.

PESTS, DISEASES AND PROBLEMS

See the section on broccoli as they have the same pests and diseases.

COMPANIONS AND SUCCESSIONAL SOWING

Plant cauliflower with other members of the brassica family as their requirements for feeding and watering are the same.

Cauliflower will grow well with dwarf beans, beetroot, celery, cucumber, onions, marigold, nasturtium, rhubarb and aromatic herbs (sage, dill and chamomile). Avoid growing it with climbing beans, tomato, capsicum, eggplant or strawberry.

In a crop rotation, plant cauliflower after legumes and follow it with a root crop.

CELERY

Wild celery was used as a food and flavouring by the ancient Egyptians, Chinese and Romans. The Greeks crowned victors of the Nemean Games with garlands of its leaves and made funeral wreaths from them.

Celery seed has a strong diuretic effect and is said to relieve symptoms of gout, arthritis and rheumatism. The blanching celery we use today was first cultivated in Italy.

WHERE TO GROW

Celery (*Apium graveolens*) is a cool season plant, which needs quite a lot of attention to be grown well. It needs to be grown quickly and requires enormous amounts of water. A biennial, celery is usually grown as an annual. Grown in sun or partial shade, the soil needs to be well-drained and the position protected. Celery grows in most soils, but does best in rich, moist soil.

WHEN TO PLANT

- In cool zones, sow seed in October and November and plant seedlings from December to March and again from August to November.
- In temperate zones, sow seed from late winter to early spring and again from late summer to autumn.
- In the subtropics, sow seed from April to August and plant out seedlings six weeks later.
- In the tropics, sow seed during the dry season.

SOIL PREPARATION

Unless the bed was enriched with manure the previous season, add well-rotted compost and/or manure and a handful of potash to all soils. If your soil is acidic, treat it to a good dose of lime or dolomite.

HOW TO PLANT

Celery seed is difficult and slow to germinate. Nurseries sell seedlings. If growing from seed, soak the seed overnight in warm water and as the seed is so small it is a good idea to mix it with some sand. Sprinkle seed over the surface of the seed-raising mix or garden drill and cover very lightly with more mix. Use a garden sieve if you have one. Keep moist at all times. It should take around three weeks to germinate. You can later prick out the seedlings into small seedling pots. Alternatively, you can sow seeds into biodegradable pots to plant straight into the garden once the seedlings have been thinned and hardened off.

Plant seedlings with 25 cm between them and in a block pattern to help encourage the stems to grow longer and fleshier. Make sure that the little bulbous swellings at the base of the plant are at

soil level and not buried beneath the soil. Liquid feed seedlings every couple of weeks.

Chinese celery is also quite difficult to germinate, especially in high temperatures. Leave the seeds uncovered and in sunlight and keep the soil moist. Chinese celery can grow up to 1 metre tall. It has a stronger flavour than ordinary celery but produces over a long period of time.

VARIETIES

Some cultivars can be red stalked, some can be stringless. Varieties include Golden Self-Blanching, Green Pascal, Tall Utah, French Dinant and Dutch Soup Celery d'Amsterdam. Soup or Asian celery is a variety that is used for its leaves and narrow stems—it is easier to grow but not crisp.

CARE AND MAINTENANCE

Celery needs lots of water, indeed it is almost impossible to overwater. Mulch well to help keep the soil moist. When watering, try to do it at ground level to reduce fungal problems. Celery likes a liquid feed; this can be worm juice, weed tea, shop-bought plant food or liquid manure, every couple of weeks.

Excluding light from the stems produces sweeter, paler stalks—this is called blanching. Do this by gradually hilling the soil around the plants as they grow. Alternatively, when the plants have grown to about 40 cm tall gather the stalks into a bunch and tie loosely with string or rubber bands or wrap the stems of each plant in thick newspaper or cardboard leaving the leaves exposed. Some varieties are self-blanching.

HARVESTING AND STORAGE

After blanching it takes two to three weeks for the stalks to be paler and ready to harvest. Harvest from mid-summer to autumn, before the plants begin to flower and the stalks become fibrous. Either lift the whole plant using a fork or harvest a few stalks at a time from the outside first by cutting them with a knife or giving them a gentle twist at the base.

PESTS, DISEASES AND PROBLEMS

Celery is mostly disease resistant, although septoria leaf spot can occur. Brown spots appear on the older leaves then spread to younger ones. Remove affected leaves and ensure to practice crop rotation. You may need to use an organic fungicide like Bordeaux or make a spray with one tablespoon cider vinegar and 1 L of water.

Snails and slugs like to hide in celery. Setting up beer traps or surrounding the plants with sharp sand or coffee grounds is usually enough to get rid of them.

Spray off leaf miners/hoppers or aphids with a jet of water or try a neem oil spray, or an organic insecticide or soap.

COMPANIONS
AND SUCCESSIONAL SOWING

Celery can be grown together with brassicas, leeks, onions, beans, spinach and tomatoes, which will shade it in the summer months. Avoid carrots, potatoes and corn. Plant it after a crop of cabbages, lettuce or kale.

CELERIAC

Celeriac is bred from the same wild plant as celery, but is grown for its large taproot rather than its stem. Sow seed in seedtrays undercover

Above: Celeriac.

at a depth three times the diameter of the seed in autumn in the subtropics and tropics and again in spring for another crop, and in spring in cool and temperate zones. Transfer the seedlings into individual pots and after the last frost plant out after hardening off. Celeriac needs a fertile rich soil in full sun.

Make sure to plant the crown, or stem base, at soil level with 30 to 40 cm between each plant. Celeriac is moisture-loving so keep the soil constantly damp.

As the plant grows, pull off the outer leaves when they start to grow horizontally to expose the crown to the sun. Leave celeriac in the ground until you want to harvest it. Varieties include Prinz, Alabaster and Monarch. Like celery, celeriac is popular with slugs and susceptible to celery leaf spot.

EGGPLANT

A cousin of the tomato and potato the origins of eggplant (*Solanum melongena*) are obscure. It probably hails from India or China where a fifth century text talks of it being used to make black dye. Eggplant is part of the deadly nightshade family and as such was known throughout Europe as the 'Apple of

Sodom' or 'mad apple', as it was thought to cause insanity and epilepsy. Botanically a fruit, technically a berry, early varieties were white and egg-shaped.

WHERE TO GROW

Adaptable to a wide range of soils, eggplant nevertheless flourishes in rich, free-draining soil. It is a warm season crop and grows best in frost-free tropical and subtropical regions. It will grow well in pots.

WHEN TO PLANT

Eggplant needs a long period of temperatures of well over 21°C to do well. In most areas, it is grown from late spring and summer.

- In cooler areas, sow seed in punnets undercover in October and November but don't plant out seedlings until the weather and soil warms up. A cloche or fleece over seedlings until the days are hot and as a protection from late frosts is a good idea.
- In temperate areas, sow seeds from September to December.
- In the subtropics and tropics sow seed from September to March and grow the plant year round.

SOIL PREPARATION

Add well-rotted compost and/or manure and after digging it in mound up the bed to ensure good drainage. Eggplants prefer slightly acidic conditions, a pH of 5.5, so you may need to lower the pH of your soil by adding sulphur in the form of iron sulphate and loads of compost or use pots if your soil is alkaline.

HOW TO PLANT

Eggplant seeds can take up to three weeks to germinate. Place the seedlings in a warm, sheltered position to harden off before transplanting. Thin out the seedlings so that they are 5 cm apart and plant them out when 10 cm tall, spacing them 50 to 70 cm apart. Disturb the roots as little as possible as you are doing this.

VARIETIES

There are a surprising number of varieties of eggplant available, ranging in colour from purple, lavender, green to white and varying in length from 10 to 25 cm. Some cultivars worth trying include Rosa Bianca, an Italian heritage variety with lavender and white streaks, Casper White with white fruit, or the more traditional dark purple eggplant Black Beauty, which is good for cooler areas.

CARE AND MAINTENANCE

Keep soil moist but take care that it is not too wet as the roots may rot. Dry soil may result in poor fruit production and splitting, so mulch around the plant to help retain moisture.

Give the plants a handful of a balanced fertiliser every six weeks or a fortnightly liquid feed to ensure good growth. As some eggplants can grow to a metre high they may need staking for support.

HARVESTING AND STORAGE

Although easy to grow, eggplants do take up to three months to reach harvest. They are ready to pick when firm and glossy and best harvested young before they have a chance to get bitter. Use secateurs or a knife to cut the fruit with a centimetre or so of stem. Store in the fridge for several days or deep-freeze.

PESTS, DISEASES AND PROBLEMS

Many of the pests that attack potatoes and tomatoes attack eggplant. These include leaf-eating ladybeetles that you can remove by hand.

If plants start to wilt they may have been attacked by nematodes—you can tell this by a knobbly growth on the roots. Dispose of the plant and grow marigolds for a season in the plot to kill the nematodes.

A yellowing of the lower leaves followed by wilting is symptomatic of wilt disease. Dispose of the infected plant.

Soft brown roots may indicate root rot, increase organic matter and improve drainage.

Seedlings that don't take off may have been cold checked and not have received enough warmth to thrive.

COMPANIONS AND SUCCESSIONAL SOWING

Eggplants are a good companion to capsicum and beans, as they have the same growing requirements and benefit from growing with marigolds, mint and tarragon.

Don't plant eggplants after tomatoes, capsicum or potatoes as the same diseases affect all of these plants. Make sure to rotate your planting by not planting a new eggplant crop in the same area for a couple of seasons.

Eggplants are a good crop to plant after legumes.

FENNEL

Florence fennel (*Foeniculum vulgare* subsp. *vulgare* var. *azoricum*) is an annual with an enlarged bulb-like leaf base which tastes of aniseed. It is indigenous to the Mediterranean where it grows wild and is one of the main ingredients in absinthe. It is a member of the umbellifer family, like carrots, parsnip and celeriac.

WHERE TO GROW

Grow fennel in rich, well-drained soil. It thrives in warm temperate climates, but can be grown in cool climates as well, although it dislikes frost. It likes a sunny position.

WHEN TO PLANT

♦ Sow seeds direct or plant seedlings in spring and again in autumn in cool and temperate zones. If seeds are sown too early a cold snap is likely to make fennel bolt to flower before developing a bulb.

● In the subtropics, plant Florence fennel in the autumn and in the dry season in the tropics.

SOIL PREPARATION
Heavy clay soils are not suitable for fennel. Well-rotted manure or compost should be incorporated during winter, if possible, before sowing or planting.

HOW TO PLANT
Fennel is best sown into the garden bed, as it resents root disturbance. If you start fennel in containers, biodegradable pots are preferable. Thin to one seedling per container and make sure to harden off before transplanting.

Germination of fennel seeds can be poor so sow enough to allow for this and thin seedlings to 30 cm apart. Sow seeds 1 cm deep in rows 30 cm apart and a fortnight later sow some more for a succession of crops.

VARIETIES
Some modern cultivars are now resistant to bolting, like Zefa Fino and Finale. Romanesco has traditional large bulbs but care must be taken in not sowing it too early.

CARE AND MAINTENANCE
Mulch around fennel with a 5 cm deep layer of compost and make sure to keep it well watered so the bulbs will grow. When the leaf bases or bulbs begin to swell you need to blanch them by drawing soil or mulch up around the bulbs or tying newspaper around them. Continue to do this throughout summer until they are ready to harvest.

HARVESTING AND STORAGE
About four weeks after earthing up the bulbs they should be large enough to start harvesting. Harvest the entire leaf base by cutting beneath it with a sharp knife. Leave the base of the bulb and roots in the ground and a new, smaller bulb should form. The leaf of Florence fennel can be used in the same way as the herb fennel. Fennel will keep for two weeks in the fridge.

Fennel is a traditional, natural flea repellent. Crush a handful of fresh fronds and rub them over the dog or cat or put handfuls under their bedding.

PESTS, DISEASES AND PROBLEMS
Fennel rarely has any pests or diseases although you may encounter slugs. (See Pests and Diseases section for more on slugs).

COMPANIONS AND SUCCESSIONAL SOWING
Fennel is good grown with legumes and onions in a crop rotation.

GARLIC

Garlic (*Allium sativum*) is an allium, which is part of the onion family. Most historians believe it is native to Siberia and spread from there more than 5000 years ago by nomadic tribes. In Ancient Egypt and some Middle Eastern cultures it was used as a currency and around 2500BC it was recorded that 15 pounds of garlic could purchase a slave. In the Balkans, garlic was rubbed on window frames and doorknobs to repel vampires. Garlic has been used medicinally throughout the ages to treat anything from arthritis and toothache to freckles and plague. In World War II it was mixed with water to disinfect wounds and prevent gangrene.

Garlic is easy to grow and hardy but it does need to sit in the ground for a lengthy period to reach a good size.

WHERE TO GROW
Garlic grows in an open site. It likes sun and must have a well-drained soil, as it will rot if waterlogged. It can be slotted in around other crops or around the borders of a garden. Garlic can be grown in all regions but it is tricky in the tropics. In the tropics you need to use a variety specially suited to a neutral day length, like Glenlarge, New Zealand Purple or Southern Cross and refrigerate the bulbs for six weeks before planting. The bulbs will only ever be small but the leaves make an excellent herb. Otherwise, grow garlic chives or society garlic, which does well in humid areas.

Garlic does well in containers.

WHEN TO PLANT

In cool and temperate climates garlic needs to be planted in mid to late autumn to produce large bulbs. Garlic is grown over winter. It needs short, cool winter days and then a warm spring for bulb formation. In areas where the winter is mild, a cold snap can be emulated by putting the bulbs in the crisper of the fridge for six weeks before planting.

SOIL PREPARATION

Garlic likes rich soil and one improved for a previous crop is ideal. If the soil hasn't been previously enriched add compost. Do not, however, add manure or blood and bone before planting garlic. Garlic loves sweet soil. The ideal pH is 6–7.5 and so most soils, particularly acidic ones, will benefit from a dose of lime dug in a month or so before planting the bulbs.

HOW TO PLANT

Garlic bulbs for planting can be bought at nurseries and online or from organic grocers. Don't buy supermarket garlic for planting as it is usually fumigated to prevent it sprouting.

Divide the bulbs into cloves (corms) and

peel the papery membrane, but not the base. Make holes 8 to 10 cm apart and about 8 cm deep. Pop a clove in each hole, pointed end up, and fill the hole with soil or sandy compost. Firm down the soil with your hands to help prevent the bulbs 'heaving', or being pushed from the ground, during cold weather. If you are planting in rows, space them 20 cm apart.

VARIETIES

There are two types of common garlic, softneck and hardneck. Softneck garlic contains all the common white varieties of garlic, those you can buy readily in the supermarket. Hardneck garlic has a sturdy neck and will cope well with heat but not humidity. There are many varieties of both, including Elephant (Russian), which is a mild giant garlic and purple and white skinned cultivars, Italian White, New Zealand Purple and the pungent Ramson's garlic.

Society garlic (*Tulbaghia violacea*) can be grown in the subtropics and tropics as a garlic substitute. Its dense clump of strap-like leaves can be chopped up and used as a garlic flavouring in food and its lilac flowers steeped in vinegar. It is grown in full sun but will also grow in some shade in light, sandy soil. Set the bulbs 20 cm apart and 1 cm below the soil surface. The clumps can be divided every two or three years by digging up and cutting the roots into sections.

CARE AND MAINTENANCE

Keeping the young shoots free of weeds is essential, as garlic does not like competition. Mulching will help this. Make sure to keep the mulch away from the bulbs though, as otherwise they may rot. Keep the soil moist but not over-watered. Under-watered garlic will often develop only a single clove and no side shoots.

Garlic shouldn't need to be fed as it grows. However, a top dressing of blood and bone applied in late winter or early spring will help to increase bulb size.

HARVESTING AND STORAGE

The tips of the foliage can be snipped and used at any time. Garlic itself is ready to harvest when the leaves begin to turn yellow and fall over, usually from January to March. To harvest, use a garden fork and gently lift it from the ground. If the skin on the bulbs is damaged the garlic will not store well.

To store garlic you need to harvest it on a sunny day and leave it in a warm place to dry out. Leave the stem intact and use it to plait or bundle the garlic together. Hang it in a dry, airy place. It should store for six or so months. Don't separate the cloves until ready for use.

PESTS, DISEASES AND PROBLEMS

Garlic can be attacked by nematodes (eelworms). Planting dwarf marigolds nearby will help prevent this.

If the leaves develop large yellowish spots the garlic may have developed downy mildew. Improving the air circulation and ensuring good drainage should help. See also the Pests and Diseases listing for Onions.

COMPANIONS AND SUCCESSIONAL SOWING

Garlic is a traditional companion for roses and fruit trees. It is also a good companion to silver beet, tomatoes and lettuce. Avoid beans or peas.

It is important to practice crop rotation with garlic. Grow garlic before potatoes, tomatoes, eggplant or capsicum. Grow it after peas or beans.

Put the biggest and best bulbs from the crop aside, in a dry airy place, to replant in the following season. As garlic adapts to local day length your own strain of garlic will develop over the seasons.

GLOBE ARTICHOKE

Not related to the root vegetable Jerusalem artichoke, the globe artichoke (*Cynara scolymus*) is a thistle. It originated in North Africa and the Mediterranean and has been under cultivation since ancient times. The globe artichoke is a very large attractive plant with beautiful blue flowers that attract bees. We eat the fleshy lower portions of the bracts and the heart or base of the immature flower buds. The florets in the centre of the bud make up the mostly inedible 'choke'.

WHERE TO GROW

Globe artichokes are easy to grow in cool and temperate zones in a sunny, well-drained, fertile spot. Growing up to 1.5 m tall and about 90 cm wide, globe artichokes take up a great deal of space, but are so attractive that they look fabulous in flower beds. They will happily tolerate coastal windy conditions. They are not suited to the tropics or sub-tropics as the high temperatures cause the flower buds to prematurely open and they receive an insufficient chilling time.

WHEN TO PLANT

Plant crowns in autumn and winter for a spring harvest, or offsets in spring.

SOIL PREPARATION

Globe artichokes grow in most soils with good drainage although you need to avoid heavy or wet soils. Growing them in a raised bed will assist with drainage. They are deep-rooted plants so dig the ground deeply then add compost and manure or a handful of blood and bone. Their ideal pH is 6.5–7.

HOW TO PLANT

The best way to grow globe artichokes is from crowns bought from a nursery or plant offshoots or root sections of older plants. Plant crowns 10–15 cm deep with 70–90 cm between plants as they grow into quite large plants. Otherwise you can purchase seeds and sow them in spring.

VARIETIES

Green cultivars include Green Globe, Vert de Laon and Imperial Star. Purple artichokes include Purple Globe and Violetta di Chioggia.

CARE AND MAINTENANCE

Other than keeping the plants well watered they need little care. Once growing, they like some nitrogen-rich fertiliser and some potash occasionally. Mulch to keep them moist. Removing the side buds will increase the size of the main head.

If globe artichokes are left to flower in summer, once they have started to die back cut them back hard to encourage new autumn growth.

After harvesting, you can leave the plant in the ground and grow it as a perennial for up to five years (making sure to leave room around it to grow). After five years the plant will need to be divided. In autumn pull it up, cut the roots into sections and replant in a new location. Globe artichokes can, of course, also be grown as an annual and pulled up after harvest.

To propagate, take suckers or offsets in autumn and winter by cutting through the roots between the sucker and the main plant and then dig it up. Cut off the large outer leaves and then plant the suckers into enriched well-limed soil.

HARVESTING AND STORAGE

One plant can produce up to 20 edible buds. Harvest them in spring and early summer.

Harvest the buds before they begin to open and the globe is still tight and heavy by cutting each bud off with about 3 cm of stem. After a bud is cut the plant produces new buds that are smaller. Flower buds that have started to open are inedible—the edible heart will have formed into a spiny 'choke'. These buds should be allowed to open to reveal immense bright blue flowers.

Before eating the 'heart' at the stem, remove all of the fibrous 'choke'. The heart is exposed after peeling off the tougher outer bracts.

PESTS, DISEASES AND PROBLEMS

Pests and diseases rarely affect globe artichokes.

However, a very hot spell of weather while the buds are forming can cause bitter and tough artichokes.

Wilting plants may indicate verticillium wilt. Poor drainage is often the cause.

Aphids, leaf miners, slugs and snails can be prevented with a soap spray and a barrier around the plant like sharp sand or coffee grounds.

A plant that fails to thrive may be infected by root knot nematodes. Knotty-looking and distorted roots are a symptom. The plant will need to be entirely dug up. Grow marigolds for a season in that bed.

JERUSALEM ARTICHOKE

The Jerusalem artichoke (*Helianthus tuberosus*) is neither an artichoke nor from Jerusalem. It is a member of the sunflower family with a tuberous root like a potato. It is this root which has a vaguely artichoke flavour that you eat. A native of North America, it was cultivated by Native American Indians (who called them sunroots) and first known to the West as the Canadian potato.

This is an easy, hardy vegetable to grow. It can, however, become difficult to eradicate so it is a good plant for a forgotten corner of the garden. Plants grow two or so metres high in clumps and produce small yellow flowers.

WHERE TO GROW

Jerusalem artichokes grow in most soil types and from cold, temperate to subtropical regions.

They grow in full sun or part shade and do well in freely draining soil.

WHEN TO PLANT

Plant in winter or spring from tubers you can buy online or from nurseries or local organic stores.

SOIL PREPARATION
Give the ground a good digging over and fertilise it by adding compost or manure.

HOW TO PLANT
Position the tuber with the dark growing bud or eye facing upwards. You may need to 'green sprout' the tubers to develop the eyes. Spread the tubers out on a tray or shelf in the shed and leave them for four to five weeks. The eyes will develop short stubby roots.

Plant 15 cm deep with 50 to 60 cm between tubers and 1 m between rows.

VARIETIES
Jerusalem artichoke varieties can be white or purple skinned and include Fuseau and Dwarf Sunray.

CARE AND MAINTENANCE
In summer, pinch out the flower buds as they form. The tubers are ready four to five weeks after the buds appear but can be left in the ground until winter. Mulch with hay or straw and water regularly in dry weather once the shoots are sprouting. Adding some potash when the shoots are around 20 cm tall will help to develop flavour.

The clumps can easily become congested and so every couple of years it is a good idea to lift them with a fork, separate and replant them.

HARVESTING AND STORAGE
About five months after planting you should be ready to start harvesting. See potatoes for how to harvest tubers.

You can postpone harvesting until the plants have died down and store the tubers in the ground, digging them up as you need them. Jerusalem artichokes will keep in a cool, dark place for two weeks.

PESTS, DISEASES AND PROBLEMS
Jerusalem artichokes are not normally affected by any specific pests or diseases.

KALE

From the Brassicaceae family, kale (*Brassica oleracea* var. *acephala*) is an extremely hardy, easy-to-grow biennial plant. It is known as *boerkool* in South Africa, *chou vert* in France and *calvero nero* in Italy. Kale is believed to have been cultivated from the early Middle Ages from wild kale in the Mediterranean or Atlantic parts of Europe. Kale is reasonably new to Australian kitchens. It grows and tastes not unlike silverbeet. Like silverbeet, it has a long growing period, cropping through winter, spring and summer.

WHERE TO GROW

Kale grows in all climates and although it prefers full sun it will tolerate some shade. The site, however, must be well draining. Kale is frost and snow tolerant so it makes an excellent vegetable to grow throughout winter. Kale is excellent in pots.

WHEN TO PLANT

- Plant kale seedlings year-round in cool climates and in all but the hottest months in warm climates.
- Sow seeds in containers or the garden in early spring for a summer crop and in early autumn for a winter crop in temperate climates.
- Sow or plant kale from March to July in the subtropics.
- In the tropics, sow or plant kale during the dry season.

SOIL PREPARATION

Kale likes a slightly acid to neutral soil with a pH of 6.5–7. Enrich any soil with compost or manure to aid in moisture retention.

HOW TO PLANT

Kale is easily grown from seed. To save space in the garden you can sow seeds in seedtrays, and then transplant them to the vegetable patch

when they are 10 to 15 cm high. Alternatively, sow two to three seeds every 40 cm into shallow drills in the garden and lightly cover with soil. Thin out later to the strongest plants, leaving 60 cm between them.

When planting seedlings, plant them deeply making sure that the plant's lowest leaves sit just above soil level.

VARIETIES

Kale can be curly, blistered, dark green or purple. Red Winter has purple stems and ruffled foliage, Squire is very curly, Cavolo Nero or Tuscan kale has a distinctive tall form, Red Russian is heat and cold tolerant and grows up to 1 m tall and Half Tall Scotch is shorter with curly leaves.

CARE AND MAINTENANCE

Ensure to water kale well in dry weather and mulch around the plants to retain moisture. Kale benefits from a regular feed of liquid plant food or fish or seaweed emulsion. Kale is one of those winter vegetables that is often tastier after frost.

HARVESTING AND STORAGE

Some fast-growing varieties can be harvested as soon as seven weeks after planting, although individual leaves can be harvested after four to six weeks. Harvest as you would silverbeet; just twist the leaves off, as you need them. Most kale can be progressively picked for six months or more. The more you pick kale the more new growth you encourage. To harvest the whole plant, cut it off at the base. Pull up the roots to avoid any root rot infection and compost.

PESTS, DISEASES AND PROBLEMS

Grey aphids and cabbage white butterfly can be a problem. Hose off aphids with a strong jet of water or spray with pyrethrum. To remove bugs before eating pour boiling water over the leaves in the sink. See the section on broccoli for dealing with pests.

COMPANIONS AND SUCCESSIONAL SOWING

Kale grows well with other brassicas, especially cabbage. Silverbeet, spinach, lettuce, garlic and onion make good companions. Mint, dill, sage and nasturtiums will all act as deterrents to cabbage white butterfly. Avoid strawberries or beans.

The best bed to grow kale in is one that has had a nitrogen-enriching pea or bean crop or a green manure crop previously grown in it. After kale, grow a root crop.

Remember to avoid growing brassicas in the same bed each year as practising crop rotation reduces the risk of pests and diseases.

COLLARD GREENS

Collard, or borekale, is another cool season brassica that is very similar to kale and grows in the same way. Easy to grow, they are more heat-tolerant than kale.

Below: Curly kale may need to be staked.

KOHLRABI

Another brassica, 'kohl' is German for cabbage and 'rabi' means turnip, which perfectly describes the taste of kohlrabi (*Brassica oleracea* var. *gongylodes*), although the texture is crisp and juicy. It is easy and fast to grow. It can be harvested almost all year round and grows well in containers.

WHERE TO GROW

Kohlrabi is very hardy. It will grow in relatively poor soils but prefers a sunny, well-drained site.

WHEN TO PLANT

- Sow seed or plant seedlings in cool and temperate areas from January to May and again from August to December. Sow successively at four to five week intervals. Kohlrabi tends to bolt in cold weather.
- Sow seed or plant seedlings in the sub-tropics and tropics from March to August.

SOIL PREPARATION

Prepare the soil by digging in a handful of lime or dolomite, if you haven't already done so for a previous crop, and a bucketful of well-rotted compost and/or manure.

HOW TO PLANT

Sow a few seeds in clumps directly into the garden about 10–15 cm apart with 30–40 cm between rows. Cover the seeds with about 5 mm of soil and lightly mulch over the top, then water gently.

After the seedlings have germinated thin them so that only the strongest remains in each clump. Kohlrabi can be transplanted easily from seedbeds or pots.

VARIETIES

There are white, green and purple cultivars available, including Early Purple with a flattish round bulb and purple stems and Purple Vienna, an heirloom from the 1860s.

CARE AND MAINTENANCE

Grow kohlrabi quickly by regular watering and liquid feeds of seaweed or liquid plant food every few weeks. It is important not to hill or push up the soil around the plants as damp soil can rot the bulbs.

HARVESTING AND STORAGE

Kohlrabi takes from seven to 10 weeks to be ready for harvest. The new leaves are edible as a green. Harvest the swollen, above-ground stem when it is the size of a tennis ball—any bigger and it starts to turn woody.

Cook kohlrabi or eat it raw grated in coleslaw. Store in the fridge for up to two weeks. Peel and blanch for two minutes then freeze.

PESTS, DISEASES AND PROBLEMS

Control caterpillars, cabbage white butterfly and aphids. Otherwise, they are a tough and disease-resistant crop.

COMPANIONS AND SUCCESSIONAL SOWING

Kohlrabi should not be grown with tomatoes, eggplant, mustard, strawberries, capsicum and chillies or runner beans. It is compatible with onion, beets, celery and herbs. It can be grown in a crop rotation with roots, so is good to plant after leafy greens and before legumes.

Below: A young purple cultivar of kohlrabi.

LEEKS

A member of the Liliaceae family, leeks (*Allium ampeloprasum* var. *porrum*) are unknown in the wild. They were first introduced into Britain by the Romans. They became the national emblem of Wales in commemoration of the Welsh victory over the Saxons in 640 AD, where Welsh soldiers wore leeks on their helmets to distinguish them from the enemy.

Leeks are a cool season vegetable and will withstand the harshest cold. They are a very hardy crop and suffer few problems, taking up very little space.

WHERE TO GROW

Leeks like at least six hours sun a day and a sheltered spot in free-draining soil.

WHEN TO PLANT

● In cool, temperate and subtropical zones, leeks can be sown or planted throughout autumn for a spring and summer harvest and again in spring after the last frost.

Successive plantings every four to six weeks will ensure an ongoing harvest.

- In the tropics, you can sow from late autumn to early winter.

SOIL PREPARATION

Leeks like a well-composted soil with a neutral pH. Work compost, cow or sheep manure into the soil quite deeply. Add a handful of dolomite per square metre to an acidic soil. Leave it to settle for a couple of weeks if possible before sowing. If you don't have time for this, then ensure you water it in well.

HOW TO PLANT

Raise leeks as seedlings in seedboxes or trays. When seedlings are 20 cm tall transplant them. Separate the seedlings into individual plants and plant them into holes 15cm apart in rows 30–40 cm apart. Make the holes with your finger or a thick stick and drop one seedling into each hole—make sure two-thirds of the seedling is below soil level. Rather than fill the hole with soil, water it regularly so that soil is gradually deposited around the leek seedling.

The traditional method of growing leeks is to plant them at the bottom of 20 cm-deep trenches. Fill the trench with soil as the plant grows so that the leaf bases are covered in soil to increase the white portion. If the seedling flops over upon being planted it will right itself in a few days.

VARIETIES

Varieties include Elephant, Autumn Giant, Musselburgh and perennial clumping or multiplier leeks, which are a better option for the tropics and subtropics.

CARE AND MAINTENANCE

Leeks need regular watering and benefit from a seaweed tonic every two to three weeks. Mulching is essential in warm climates. If you are not growing them in a deep trench, as the leek grows draw up soil against the lower stem so that the bottom of the leek is blanched. Alternatively, you can make a newspaper cuff for the stem and pile dry soil up around it to prevent soil getting into the leaves.

HARVESTING AND STORAGE

Leeks take up to four months to mature. They can be left in the ground and picked as required. To harvest use a knife to cut the stems off below ground level. If you leave the root base in the ground it will produce a crop of new seedlings, which can be dug up and transplanted to form a new crop cycle.

PESTS, DISEASES AND PROBLEMS

Control aphids and thrips by spraying with homemade garlic spray, pyrethrum or horticultural soap.

COMPANIONS AND SUCCESSIONAL SOWING

Grow leeks mixed with onions, carrot and celery. The flowers from leeks left to go to seed attract beneficial insects.

Leeks can be grown after the summer crops of pumpkin, zucchini and sweetcorn. They can be followed in a crop rotation by broad beans or peas.

LETTUCE

Picking fresh lettuce (*Lactuca sativa*) leaves from the garden as you need them is one of the most rewarding parts of vegetable growing.

Most likely to have originated from Asia Minor and the Mediterranean, lettuces have been consumed for millenia. The Romans believed they had a soporific effect and ate them at the end of a meal, while to the ancient Egyptians they were an aphrodisiac, made obvious by the tendency of lettuces to shoot upwards and exude a milky substance when they bolt. The 'lac' in their Latin name means milk. Lettuce is a cool season crop but regularly eaten in the warmer months so some care needs to be taken to grow them for summer harvest.

WHERE TO GROW

Lettuce will grow in full sun in winter, but will need partial shade in the summer months, particularly in hot areas. In really cold weather use a cloche over plants to coax them along. Lettuce needs a well-drained soil.

Lettuce is a great vegetable to interplant amongst other slower growing crops or flowers, or in any spare space in the garden, as it is very fast to grow and doesn't take up a lot of room. Lettuce is excellent in pots and hanging baskets but must be kept well watered.

WHEN TO PLANT

- In temperate and subtropic zones you can grow lettuce year round. In all other zones, it is important to grow lettuce according to the seasonal planting instructions on the seed packet, as different types can be grown in different seasons. Some lettuce types will bolt in hot weather.
- In the tropics, the cooler months are the best time for lettuce, and loose-leafed or oak lettuces are far more reliable than large hearting varieties.
- Sow small batches of several varieties in punnets or a seedbed every few weeks throughout the year to ensure an ongoing harvest.

SOIL PREPARATION

Lettuce will grow in most soils except poorly drained ones. It does best, however, in humus rich soil, that is slightly acidic to neutral soil with a pH of 6.5–7. Add half a barrow load of manure and/or compost to each square metre. Dig it in well and rake the surface smooth.

In pots it is critical to use a good potting mix and add in some compost, worm castings or coconut coir to hold moisture.

HOW TO PLANT

Lettuce grows easily from seed, either sown directly into the garden in drills or into punnets. Cultivate the soil then scatter seed, which is very small and fine, over the surface. Lightly press seed into the surface of the soil or simply water the soil. The seed of some varieties (those with white seeds) doesn't need to be covered by soil or compost as it needs light to germinate. Burying any variety of lettuce seed too deeply is one of the main reasons seed fails to germinate. When seedlings are a few centimetres high, start thinning to about 25 cm between plants (you can eat the thinnings or transplant them elsewhere). Keep the soil moist until the seedlings are established.

Above: Mesclun, a variety of salad greens growing together.

Once the temperature is over 30°C lettuce seeds won't germinate.

For seedlings, space plants about 25 cm apart, in rows 30 cm apart. Firm the soil around the seedling and water it in well. Mulch around the seedlings to help preserve moisture. In hotter months and in the tropics, seedlings may need to be shaded until they are established.

VARIETIES

Lettuces have either a compact form or are loose-leafed.

Iceberg and crisphead have solid heads. They are not suitable for the tropics and varieties include Great Lakes and Superior.

Butterheads are hearted, with soft leaves. More heat tolerant, they make good summer crops. You can pick individual leaves as needed ('cut and come again'). Types include Green and Red Coral, Green Mignonette, Royal Oakleaf and Buttercrunch.

Cos and Romaine types have crisp leaves, are very hardy and bolt resistant. Loose hearted and upright, they do better in cooler weather and over winter. Harvest outside leaves as required or the whole lettuce. Sow them only 15–20cm apart to force an upright growth. You may need to tie up cos to blanch the insides and prevent bitterness. Types include Baby Cos, Little Gem, Cos Verdi and Crispmint.

Other leafy salad greens include non-hearting lettuces whose individual loose leaves can be picked over many weeks. They are the easiest to grow, as they are heat resistant. They include:

Corn salad, also known as lamb's lettuce, is a useful autumn and winter season salad in temperate zones and grows well in winter in the subtropics. Harvest a few leaves or the whole plant. Leave one plant to go to seed for a crop the following year.

Landcress is a hot, mustardy biennial that self-sows once established.

Mizuna and mitsuba are mustardy flavoured dense leaves from Japan.

Mustard and cress can be sown densely in any season. Cover the seedling tray with a piece of cardboard to aid germination.

Endive is a cool season salad plant, it may need to be blanched or it will be too bitter. Simply overlap the heart with the outside leaves and secure them with a peg or string. Blanching should take from five to 10 days in summer, longer in winter. Endive can also be snipped when young for leaves as required. Sow in situ from early summer.

Chicory has slightly bitter leaves and is frost and drought tolerant. Older plants can be cooked and eaten as a vegetable.

Mesclun mix is a mixture of different salad seeds. You can buy mixed seeds or make up your own by including non-hearting lettuce, rocket, mizuna, mustards and baby spinach. Simply sprinkle mixed seed over the surface of soil or in a box, water gently and keep damp. Begin cutting off leaves with scissors from three weeks.

CARE AND MAINTENANCE

All lettuces have shallow roots and so need plenty of water. It is critical to grow them fast by regular watering or they will become bitter. To ensure they don't dry out, you may have to water lightly twice a day in dry weather. Every couple of weeks water your crop with seaweed or fish emulsion, weed tea, worm juice or liquid compost.

Mulch seedlings with pea straw, lucerne or sugar cane mulch to help prevent them from drying out. Lettuce may bolt in hot weather or when it is not watered enough.

In cool climates, to grow lettuces through winter you will need to enclose them in a cloche or plastic bag to provide some warmth, otherwise you may find their growth stalling.

HARVESTING AND STORAGE

Three weeks or so after sowing you can start harvesting baby leaves of non-hearting lettuce by breaking them off, outer ones first. In eight to 10 weeks full heads can be harvested. Harvest hearting lettuce while the heads are still rounded. Simply pull the plant from the ground.

It is best to pick lettuce as you need it, or refrigerate for a couple of days.

PESTS, DISEASES AND PROBLEMS

You may need to net lettuce to protect it from birds.

Slugs and snails can be pests. Protect seedlings by popping cloche bottles over them or setting beer traps.

Wilting lettuce indicates a lack of water or too much hot afternoon sun. Transplant it to a shaded spot or cover the crop with some shade

cloth or the like. Rotting lettuce may be caused by overly wet, warm soil and humidity.

Failure to germinate may indicate the seeds were sown too deeply or were too old and had lost their viability.

Seed stalks may form when temperatures warm up or the plant starts to age. Harvest the crop before all of it bolts.

COMPANIONS AND SUCCESSIONAL SOWING

Lettuce does well with cucumber, carrots, radish, strawberry, beets, brassicas and onions.

Avoid growing lettuce with parsley, celery and potatoes.

Chervil planted nearby is an old remedy for protection from aphids.

As a leafy green, lettuce will follow a fruit crop, like capsicum, and can be followed by a root crop. Lettuce, though, can usually be planted wherever it can be popped in as it is fast growing. It makes a good crop to grow between slower growing crops to help keep weeds down. As a rule, avoid growing them too often in the one spot.

SEED SAVING

Seed saving from lettuce plants is easy as they are self-pollinating. If left to flower a lettuce plant will often self-sow. Simply leave a plant to flower and produce its fluffy seed. When it has done this pull up the whole plant and hang it upside down in an airy dry place. When the flower head has dried out rub it between your hands over a bowl. Shake the bowl, skim off the fluff from the top and collect the seed. Store the seed in a dry, cool dark place.

MICROGREENS

Microgreens or microherbs are tiny seedlings cut off when four or more of the true leaves have grown. These are the leaves that grow after the first seed leaves. They are quickly grown over 10 to 14 days, snipped off at soil level and then re-sown. Grow your own microgreens from a bought seed-mix or make up your own using a mix of any leftover seeds, including lettuce, mustard, Asian

greens, rocket, endive, beets, spinach, basil, coriander, chicory, silverbeet, kale, chervil, parsley, cress, sorrel, radish and shallots.

Microgreens are best grown in a large seed tray filled with 2 to 3 cm of seed raising mix, or a blend of potting mix, cocopeat, vermiculite and sieved compost. Soak seeds for a few hours or overnight. To sow the seeds, moisten the seed raising mix, sprinkle them on top and pat them down with your hands. Cover them with a few millimetres of potting mix or compost and then water, preferably with a spray bottle. Covering the tray with plastic wrap, a plastic shopping bag or sheet of glass will aid germination. Take it off once the shoots are through. Keep the tray moist and in a sheltered, sunny position.

Microgreens can be grown in any container or garden bed or even without potting mix and on a sheet of moist paper towel on a saucer in a well-lit kitchen. Care needs to be taken to not let them dry out. To harvest snip the little plants off at soil level. They are only harvested once. A fresh batch of seeds can then be sown over the top of the roots.

You can also use grains for microgreens, taking care to soak the seeds in water before sowing. Suitable grains include sunflower, linseed or flax and buckwheat.

MUSHROOMS

Mushrooms are a fungus, that is, a plant which, lacking leaves, has no chlorophyll and so is unable to manufacture its own food. Instead it relies on other organisms. There are many varieties of mushrooms available in kits to grow at home. Mushrooms, of course, also grow in the wild in fields, forests and woodland areas especially in autumn—but many are poisonous, so if you go mushrooming be sure to know what you are looking for.

WHERE TO GROW
Mushrooms are relatively easy to grow at home provided you get the ambient conditions right. They need to be indoors or under shelter out of direct sun, like in a cellar, cupboard or garage, or a very shady cool part of the garden. They prefer a fairly constant temperature, high humidity and darkness.

WHEN TO PLANT
Anytime of the year.

HOW TO PLANT
The easiest way to grow mushrooms is to buy a kit from a nursery or hardware store. The kits include inoculated mushroom compost, a live mycelium or 'spawn' and a growing box. Follow the instructions on the kit. If the compost looks mouldy and white it is ready to use, if not, close the box and leave it for seven to 10 days. Add the 'spawn'. Water a couple of times a week, keeping the compost moist but never wet (a light water spray is ideal).

Mushrooms start forming after two to three weeks and take about four weeks to mature.

Materials or 'substrates' on which to grow mushrooms outside include logs, untreated sawdust or wood chips. The fungus breaks the substrate down to compost in the process of digesting it as food.

Another method of growing mushrooms is to pare back turf by a shady, damp hedge or tree and mix in mushroom spawn with the soil, then re-cover with turf.

VARIETIES
There are several types of mushroom, including buttons, caps and flats.

CARE AND MAINTENANCE
Keep moist at all times.

HARVESTING AND STORAGE
Mushrooms mature quickly and need to be harvested regularly. Twist and pull each mushroom out.

Once the harvest is finished put the remains in the compost, add it to the garden as mulch or grow a quick crop of lettuce or Asian greens in the tray.

Store mushrooms in brown paper or cloth bags in the crisper. Asian mushrooms should be put on trays and wrapped with plastic wrap.

ONIONS, SPRING ONIONS AND SHALLOTS

Onions are part of the Liliaceae family. They do not exist in the wild. The ancient Sumerians first planted onions more than 5000 years ago, while the ancient Egyptians had about 8000 medical uses for them, including as an inhibitor of blood clotting, and often placed onions in the thorax, pelvis or near the eyes of mummies. In later times, in Ireland, the juice of onions mixed with honey was said to cure baldness!

WHERE TO GROW

Onions are easy to grow in cool and temperate climates; however, they need a cold winter to thrive. Because onion seed germinates better at low temperatures, in warm areas put the seed in the fridge for a fortnight before sowing. In the subtropics the winter does not get cold enough to grow many types of onions. Grow shallots instead, which can be bought from the local greengrocer and chilled in the crisper in the fridge for a couple of weeks before planting; this gives them a chill period to help encourage growth.

Onions are an excellent plant for intercropping into any available spaces, especially between brassicas or carrots, or for growing along the edges of the patch.

WHEN TO PLANT

Onions come in three varieties—early, mid and late season, according to when they are to be planted and the hours of sunlight needed for their growth. Early season onions are planted in late autumn, mid season are planted in early winter and late season varieties are planted in late winter, spring or early summer. A common failure with onion growing is sowing a variety in the wrong season. For a continual harvest, make successive sowings of all the varieties.

- In cold climates, plant early, mid and late season varieties from April to September.
- In temperate climates, you can grow all varieties of onions, planting early onions from March to May, mid-season onions from June to July and late-season onions from late winter on.
- In the subtropics, if you want to try to grow onions plant early and mid-season varieties only, in March and April.
- In the tropics, spring onions, shallots and leeks are better options and are planted at the beginning of the dry season.

SOIL PREPARATION

Onions need a pH of 6.5–7.0 so add lime prior to planting if the garden hasn't been limed in the past 12 months. They will need well-drained soil, enriched from a previous crop. Don't add manure or blood and bone prior to planting. Do not use poultry manure, as onions need only a low nitrogen fertiliser, otherwise you will get bushy leaf growth and mushy bulbs.

HOW TO PLANT

Onions are easy to germinate from seed. Rake the soil well and dampen it. Thinly sprinkle the seed in rows that are 6 mm deep and 10–15 cm apart. Cover the seed lightly with soil, compost or sand and press it down. Keep moist until germination, which can take up to several weeks.

After they have germinated thin out the seedlings to 10 cm apart. The thinnings can be planted elsewhere. Make sure the seed you use has not expired as onion seed has only a short viability. Alternatively, grow your own seedlings by potting seeds up and growing them under cover.

Onions can be bought as seedlings in groups known as 'sets'. To plant onion sets make rows 2 to 3 cm deep and 20 cm apart. Gently drop the sets into diluted liquid seaweed or a compost tea and separate them into individual plants. Then lay the onions in the row, 7 or 8 cm apart and backfill by pushing the soil back to cover the roots. The seedlings won't stand up automatically but will soon right themselves. Make sure not to plant the seedling too deeply (as you would for leeks) just cover the roots and the base of the stem.

VARIETIES

Onion bulbs vary considerably in shape and size and are white, red or brown. Early season varieties include the heirloom Early Barletta and Lockyer Gold, which is good in the subtropics. Hunter River White is good for temperate zones.

Mid-season varieties include Gladalan Brown, which is an Australian cultivar, Sweet Red, Red Shine and White Spanish.

Late-season varieties include Creamgold, great for cool climates, Brown Spanish and Red Brunswick.

CARE AND MAINTENANCE

Onions grow slowly and do not compete well with weeds so keep the bed well weeded, especially whilst they are still seedlings. They need to be watered regularly as they are shallow rooted. However, make sure to avoid mulching up to the stems of onions, as this will cause rot. Onions planted in rich soil will not need additional fertiliser.

HARVESTING AND STORAGE

You can, of course, start harvesting your onions whenever they are large enough to use. Most, however, take from six to eight months to be

ready for harvest. As a rule of thumb onions are ready when their tops become dry and fall over. If this doesn't happen bend the onion tops above the neck to encourage the bulb to swell. This also aids curing for storage. To harvest loosen the soil underneath with a fork and lift. Spread the onions in the sun or dry them off in an undercover airy space to cure. Store in a well ventilated area. Brown onions tend to store better than white.

Leave some onions to go to flower, these are beautiful flowers and are excellent for attracting beneficial insects. You can then collect the seed in early autumn to save for the next crop.

PESTS, DISEASES AND PROBLEMS

If onions fail to thrive the soil may need liming.

Onions may suffer fungal or bacterial diseases if grown in heavy, poorly draining soil. Downy mildew is a fungus producing pale spots on older leaves followed by a white furry covering usually caused by damp weather. The plant may outgrow it as the weather dries up. Improve soil drainage and air circulation. It also affects leeks, garlic and shallots. Dusting the plants with some wood ash may act as a

Above left: Shallots.

Above right: Spring onions.

Below: Salad onion.

remedy. For other remedies see the Pests and Diseases section.

Onion thrips are a small grey insect that infest the leaf base turning the leaves blotchy. Use an horticultural fleece to keep them away or spray with pyrethrum.

If onions start to rot and become covered in a white fluffy fungus, this is caused by white rot. Remove the diseased onions and throw them away. Do not replant onions, shallots or leeks in the same bed again for a couple of years.

Overwatering, hot weather and too much nitrogen in the soil can cause thick stems but no bulb. Sown at the wrong time onions will bolt prematurely.

Failure to germinate is usually caused by old seeds, which have lost their viability.

COMPANIONS AND SUCCESSIONAL SOWING

Onions are good companions for carrots, beetroot, silverbeet, lettuce, strawberries and tomatoes. In fact, try to plan to plant alternate rows of onions and carrots. Avoid peas and beans.

In a crop rotation scheme plant onions after a leafy green crop and before a legume crop.

Try to ensure that the bed doesn't have another onion crop for at least a couple of years.

SPRING ONIONS

Many varieties of common onions can be used as spring onions. You can also buy 'spring onion' or 'shallot bunching onion' seed. Sow both varieties direct in spring through to autumn. They should be ready for harvest in eight weeks.

Spring onions will tolerate some shade. Sow thickly in rows 5 to 10 cm apart. It is not necessary to thin them. Spring onions are good in pots. Once you have used the shoots, replant the roots with a couple of centimetres of stem and they will reshoot.

SHALLOTS

Shallots are less demanding than onions and are easier to grow. Plant them in open sun or shade. It is not necessary to enrich the soil if it was fed for the previous crop. Plant them from sets or seeds in early spring, or autumn to winter in mild areas. Make a small indentation in the soil and pop each bulb on.

Space them 10 to 15 cm apart in rows 30 cm apart. Don't bury the bulbs—merely press them

into the soil to about half the bulbs depth. The tip of the bulb should be at ground level. Hill up the soil on either side of the row to blanch the lower parts of the stalk. Water shallots in dry weather and harvest when the leaves are dying back, each shallot should have increased to 10 or more bulbs.

PARSNIPS

Parsnips (*Pastinaca sativa*) are native to the Mediterranean. Unsurprisingly, they are a relative of the carrot. The nut-like flavour of homegrown parsnips is far superior to flaccid shop-bought ones and so worth the trouble you have to take to germinate them. Traditionally, parsnips were used to treat toothache and stomach problems and fermented into beer and wine. Today they are fed to pigs to produce Parma ham.

WHERE TO GROW

Parsnips are a hardy, biennial root vegetable grown as an annual that need a long growing period, anywhere between four to nine months, but take up little space. They like an open sunny position with good drainage and a friable soil. Parsnips grow in all climate zones and are frost tolerant.

WHEN TO PLANT

- In cool zones, sow seed from August to February. Seeds sown late in autumn and winter will often fail as they won't germinate in cold, wet soil or they will produce small roots and run to seed prematurely.
- In temperate zones, sow seeds from July to March for an autumn and winter harvest.
- In subtropic and tropical zones sow seed from February to September.

SOIL PREPARATION

It is important that the soil for parsnips is not too rich. Too much nitrogen in the soil causes forked roots. Soil that has been manured or composted for a previous crop is perfect provided it is loose, friable and free of stones. Dig the soil to about a spade depth and rake it flat. Parsnips like a pH of 6.5 to 8 so add a handful of dolomite or lime to acidic soil.

HOW TO PLANT

Parsnip seed is notoriously fickle and can be hard to germinate. You will need to buy fresh seed each season to make sure that it is viable as it deteriorates rapidly. Parsnip seeds are also slow to germinate, taking up to four weeks. One trick to help to remember where it has been sown is to sow parsnip seed mixed with radish. The radish will be ready to harvest when the parsnip is just starting to peep through.

Sow seed where it is to grow, by marking out furrows about half a centimetre deep. Space rows 30 cm apart. Cover seed with fine compost or vermiculite or seed-raising mix and water gently. Keep the bed damp until the seeds emerge. Thin them out a month later to about 7 to 10 cm apart.

VARIETIES

There are long and short-rooted cultivars. Hollow Crown is good for cool climates, Guernsey is a French heirloom. Melbourne White Skin and Cobham are also worth a try.

CARE AND MAINTENANCE

Parsnips are slow to grow but require very little attention. You might protect seeds with a cloche in cold areas, as germination is so slow.

Once they are out of the seedling stage, cut back on watering to encourage the root system to develop. They do not need any fertiliser or feeding, as this will encourage the tops rather than the roots.

HARVESTING AND STORAGE

Leave parsnips in the ground until they have had a frost or a couple of weeks of cold weather. Cold weather stimulates parsnips to convert starch to sugar increasing their sweetness. They are also best left to store in the ground until needed. If you do want to take them inside remove the tops and store in an airy cupboard, or for several weeks in the fridge. They can be blanched and frozen.

The early foliage can be cooked and eaten as a green like silverbeet or raw in salads.

Leave some parsnips in the ground to flower as their flower is beautiful and attracts beneficial insects.

PESTS, DISEASES AND PROBLEMS

Forked roots indicate too much nitrogen in the soil or soil that is too compacted.

If carrot fly attacks parsnips use a homemade garlic spray. Interplanting parsnips with onions is a way to avoid carrot fly.

Canker is a fungus that is avoided by practising crop rotation.

If summer crops suffer from mildew, use a milk spray to control.

COMPANIONS AND SUCCESSIONAL SOWING

Parsnips do well with beetroot, silverbeet and kale.

As it is important to grow them in a soil that is not too rich in nitrogen, they are a perfect crop to plant straight after brassicas, which are nitrogen hungry.

SALSIFY

Salsify, also known as oyster vegetable, is another root vegetable. It is, however, a member of the lettuce family. Its edible roots taste similar to oysters. It is a biennial and if left to flower in the second year its purple flowers will attract beneficial insects. Salsify takes up very little space and is grown from seed, which, like parsnip, has a very short viability. Scatter seed in well-draining soil that has been deeply dug, in a sunny spot in early spring for an autumn harvest. Roots can be left in the ground over winter and lifted as required.

To cook the roots you need to remove the thick skin. If the flesh is cut a milky liquid will seep out. The roots need to be put straight into water with lemon juice or vinegar to prevent discolouration.

Black salsify or scorzonera is another hardy root crop which has black-skinned roots with white flesh. It grows the same way as salsify. The young shoots can be eaten as can the flower buds in the second year.

PEAS

Peas (*Pisum sativum*) are another of the nitrogen-fixing plants that help to replenish soils by converting atmospheric nitrogen into a form other plants can use. According to Norse myth, Thor, the hammer-wielding god of thunder, gave peas to humans as a punishment, by sending dragons to fill up all of the wells on earth with peas. Some missed the wells and landed on fertile soil. To placate Thor, humans only ate peas on his day, Thursday.

WHERE TO GROW

Peas are quite adaptable, but optimally like loose, well-drained soil in a sunny site. They have trouble germinating in cold, wet soil.

Peas will grow in a container but will need compost and/or manure or worm castings added to the seed-raising mix to add the rhizobia bacteria necessary for nitrogen fixation.

WHEN TO PLANT

Peas will grow in all climates in the cooler months.

- In cool areas, sow seeds from June to October. While they are sown in the cooler months, frost can still damage the flowers and young pods so you may need to protect the young plants overnight in areas prone to frost.
- In temperate areas, sow from March to August.
- In the subtropics and tropics, sow seeds from March to July.

SOIL PREPARATION

Soil does not need nitrogen-rich fertilisers (chicken manure, complete garden food) added to it before planting peas. Add some compost or cow manure to give the soil a good structure, a handful of potash and treat acid soils with lime to bring the pH to between 6.5 and 7.5, as peas dislike acidity. Water the bed and leave it to settle for a few days.

HOW TO PLANT

Grow peas from seeds sown directly into the garden. Shop-bought seedlings may not thrive. Sow seeds in two parallel lines, 60 cm apart. Space the seeds 5 cm apart for dwarf varieties and 15 cm apart for larger climbing varieties and 3 cm deep. Cover with soil. Water the seeds once with liquid seaweed or water and not again until the seedlings emerge a week or two later. This helps to minimise the chance of the largish seeds rotting. Sow more seeds in a couple of weeks to extend the cropping time. Germination of pea seeds can be helped by soaking the seeds overnight in a jar of water with a pinch of Epsom salts.

VARIETIES

Peas are climbing plants, growing to 2.5 metres tall, or dwarf bushes which grow to about 75 cm high. Varieties include sugar snap peas, of which Honey Pod is an excellent cultivar for cooler climates. Snow peas are vigorous climbers and more tolerant of heat than other varieties. Of the shelling peas, Greenfeast is an heirloom, Telephone and the purple-podded 'Dutch' are suitable to a wide range of climates and by growing a wide variety you can harvest over a long period.

CARE AND MAINTENANCE

Peas need supports. They climb by using small tendrils that wrap around anything they come into contact with. If you stroke the tendrils lightly on the underside they will start to turn towards that side within a couple of minutes. The supports need to be thin enough for the tendrils to wrap around and are best put in place while the plants are still small. Twigs popped next to each plant are ideal for dwarfs, while a row of netting, wire mesh or string tied between stakes is a good support for climbers. Twigs placed in the ground next to the seedlings will encourage them up to the netting.

Don't overwater peas but try to keep soil moisture consistent especially while the plants are flowering and the pods filling out.

HARVESTING AND STORAGE

Peas are ready to harvest from six to 12 weeks after sowing. Snow peas are ready to pick when the peas are just starting to form in the pods. All other peas are ready once the pods have swollen with peas. Peas are best when they are young. Pick pods from the bottom of the plant first and then move upwards as the lowest are the most mature. Harvest peas every couple of days to prolong flowering and production.

The tips of young plants can be picked and eaten in salads. Peas can be blanched and frozen.

PESTS, DISEASES AND PROBLEMS

Birds and mice are partial to peas.

Peas are prone to fungal diseases like powdery mildew. See the section on Pests and Diseases for ways to deal with it.

If the peas in the pod are small and fail to grow or flowering ceases the plant may have been water stressed. Mulch around the plant to help preserve water but be careful of putting mulch against the stem which will cause stem rot.

Thrips, caterpillars, mites and aphids might be a problem but are easily controlled by soap sprays.

Peas may be prone to root disease if they do not have good drainage. Very wet weather may cause root rot and pod and leaf spot. Brownish spots on leaves and pods and blackish purple streaks on stems are caused by a fungus and you will need to dig out the plant and destroy it. Provide good air circulation between plants

and avoid over-fertilising plants with nitrogen fertilisers to minimise fungal leaf diseases.

COMPANIONS AND SUCCESSIONAL SOWING

Good companion crops for peas include beans, carrots, cucurbits, corn, turnips and potatoes. Avoid onions and garlic.

It is ideal to plant peas where you have previously grown leafy greens or brassicas, or a root crop. After peas, the best use of the nitrogen-enriched soil is to plant a fruit crop like tomatoes or cucumber, or a leafy green or brassica crop.

SEED SAVING

Because peas are self-pollinating seed saving from them is easy. Simply allow the pods to develop to maturity and leave them to dry naturally on the bush. Once they are brittle, shell them and store them in a sealed glass jar in a cool dry environment until the next sowing season.

Below: Snow peas.

POTATOES

Potatoes (*Solanum tuberosum*) were first cultivated in the Andes between 3000 and 7000 years ago, where the Incas used raw potatoes to knit broken bones and carried potatoes to prevent rheumatism. The Spanish conquistadors took potatoes back to Spain with them in 1570 but many felt its membership of the deadly nightshade family bespoke its creation by witches or devils. The potato, nevertheless, went on to become the third most cultivated crop in the world.

Home-grown potatoes come in an enormous selection of varieties and are infinitely tastier than shop-bought ones.

WHERE TO GROW

Potatoes are easy to grow but take up a fair amount of space. They grow best in cool, mild regions and like full sun and slightly acidic soil (with a pH of 5–5.5). In hot areas, they will tolerate some shade. Wherever they are grown good drainage is essential.

Crop rotation is essential with potatoes so ensure to leave a couple of years between potato crops in the same garden.

You can grow potatoes in pots as long as they

are big and provide enough room for the tubers to swell inside the pot. The pot also needs to be well draining. No-dig gardens are also ideal for potatoes. Potatoes can be grown in old bins with the end cut out and old tyres stacked up, in hessian bags or grow-bags, available from nurseries, as long as the plant can be 'hilled-up' to allow enough growing space for the tubers at the roots.

WHEN TO PLANT

Potatoes can be planted in spring for an early to late summer crop in cool districts, temperate zones and the subtropics and in the tropics in April and May. In cool districts an additional crop can also be planted in summer for a late autumn harvest. However, note that they are frost tender. When planting bear in mind that potatoes do not like being planted into cold wet soil.

SOIL PREPARATION

In the garden potatoes are excellent planted after a green manure, but do not plant them in recently limed soil. To prepare for a potato crop fork plenty of cow or sheep manure and/or compost into the soil, you can also add some mineral rock dust if your soil is reasonably poor.

Below: A large section of this garden has been devoted to potatoes.

HOW TO PLANT

Potatoes are grown from small tubers called 'seed' potatoes. Buy these from nurseries, produce stores or online, ensuring they are certified 'disease-free' (be warned that potato seedlings bought from nurseries may not grow into decent crops). When you get these, in late winter or very early spring, they need to be 'chitted' or 'green sprouted', that is, exposed to light prior to planting to encourage shoot development. Place them out on trays or in egg cartons with the end with the most eyes facing up. Put them in a warm, light place out of direct sunlight until shoots start growing. This can take four to five weeks. The skins will turn a greenish colour and the eyes will develop short stubby shoots. Allow them to develop 1 cm long shoots. Discard any that develop spindly shoots as they may have a viral infection and any that are shrivelled, soft or damaged.

In hot or dry climates, potatoes are often sprouted in seed trays filled with potting mix.

Before planting, any large tubers can be cut into smaller pieces as long as each piece has at least one 'eye' or shoot, and it is the size of an egg.

Potatoes can be planted into individual holes or into trenches. To plant them in holes make each hole 10 to 15 cm deep and 35 cm apart and put the seed potato in the bottom with the

shoots pointing upwards, cover the seed with soil mixed with compost but do not fill the hole completely. Once the shoots appear push soil around them. As the plant grows, continue to drag soil up around the shoots and continue 'earthing up' the plant with a mulch of spent straw, hay, compost, wilted comfrey leaves or grass clippings or soil. This is to exclude sunlight and prevent green potatoes. When a potato tuber is exposed to sunlight it turns green by producing chlorophyll and elevated levels of a protective chemical, known as glycoalkaloids, which can cause food poisoning.

To plant potatoes in trenches, dig a trench 10–20 cm deep (with 60 to 80 cm between trenches) and 30 cm wide and fork in a good layer of manure and/or compost or a fertiliser high in phosphorous like chicken manure, and cover it with a few centimetres of soil, or wilted weeds or grass clippings. Lay the seeds along the trench shoot side up, with 30 cm between them. Cover with 10 cm of soil and water them in. As with potatoes grown in holes, cover emerging shoots with soil and as the crop grows continue 'hilling up' with soil or mulch, leaving only a small amount of foliage showing at the top. The hilling will help with drainage and should create an irrigation trench between the ridges of plants.

NO-DIG POTATO GARDENS

Potatoes grow beautifully in no-dig systems. Lay the potatoes on the soil in the spot you want to grow them 30 cm apart with their shoots pointing up. Cover them with a good thick layer of straw, hay, pea straw or leaf mould and a thin layer of manure and organic fertiliser like blood and bone. Water each layer as you go. Continue to cover the potatoes until they are buried at least 40 cm deep in layered material. Add additional material as the potatoes begin to shoot through. After about four weeks of growth cover the tops with a final layer of mulch.

POTS

The pots must be deep. Spread a 10 cm-deep layer of compost mixed with soil or potting mix on the bottom and space the seed potatoes 30 cm apart, with the shoots pointing up. Add a 10 cm layer of mulch (grass clippings, sugar cane, hay or pea straw) or compost over the top and water. As the shoots begin to peep through cover them with more compost or mulch, continuing to do this until the container is full.

VARIETIES

There are over 1000 varieties of cultivated potatoes in the world. Their flavour will often vary depending on where they are grown so it can take some experimenting with types to see which ones best suit your soil. Different varieties also vary enormously in their productivity.

Generally each tuber should produce between eight and 20 potatoes. Cultivars can be pink, purple, yellow or red skinned with cream or yellow or even purple flesh.

A few of the varieties available include Kipfler, Spunta, a white-fleshed prolific potato, Purple Congo, a finger-sized potato with deep purple skin and flesh, Toolangi Delight, with rounded tubers, purple skin and white flesh and Dutch Cream, which has cream-coloured flesh.

CARE AND MAINTENANCE

Potatoes need to be kept moist, particularly while the tubers are forming, about three weeks after planting. Check that the soil feels cool and moist; a lack of water is one of the reasons for a small yield. Regular feeding with liquid seaweed will help improve yield. The longer you can keep potatoes actively growing the larger the tubers will become. It is, of course, essential to keep earthing up the crop, but otherwise no additional care and maintenance should be necessary.

Make sure early potatoes are not at risk of frost by covering the foliage with straw or mulch overnight.

HARVESTING AND STORAGE

Potatoes sown in spring should be ready for harvesting from December to February. You can begin harvesting a few tubers about four weeks after flowering by 'bandicooting' under the plant, that is, feeling around in the soil to find young tubers, while leaving the remainder to grow on.

When foliage starts to die back it is unlikely more tubers will form and you can start harvesting. You don't have to harvest all of your potatoes at once; they can be left in the ground to mature and use as you need them. Use your hands or a garden fork to gently lift the potatoes from the ground. Allow them to dry in the sun for 15 to 20 minutes so that the skins can harden for storage. Do not wash the potatoes if you are going to store them. Store disease-free tubers on trays in a cool dark place, or in hessian or brown paper bags.

Mature potatoes store better than new potatoes whose thin skins can damage easily.

PESTS, DISEASES AND PROBLEMS

Do not confuse the natural withering of the haulm or top of the plant as it matures, with a disease.

Rot can be caused by poorly drained soil or overwatering.

Root-knot nematodes can affect potatoes. You can help avoid these by not growing crops in the Solanaceae family (eggplant, capsicum, chilli or tomato) one after the other in the same soil. Marigolds planted amongst the crop are an excellent companion to check nematodes.

Potato scab can occur in alkaline soil and where the soil gets too dry. To avoid this, ensure the soil pH is not above 6 before planting. Add compost to lower soil pH and keep water up to tubers for the first month they are forming.

Leaf-eating beetles and slugs are attracted to Solanaceae crops. Squash these by hand or apply a homemade soap spray or pyrethrum.

Late or Irish blight is a fungus that blackens the foliage and makes the crop smell rotten. The tubers get small blackish shrunken spots and brownish blotches. Dig up the plants and throw them out.

COMPANIONS AND SUCCESSIONAL SOWING

Potatoes are good companions for beans, brassicas, sweet corn and peas. Avoid growing with tomatoes or cucurbits.

Save some mature tubers for planting next season provided they don't have any diseases. They can have green bits on them. Check that the skins are dry and firm and store them in shallow boxes in a cool, well-ventilated shed.

Do not plant a new crop where potatoes or other Solanaceae have been grown in the previous season and try to leave a number of years between crops. Plant a legume crop after potatoes to re-enrich the soil.

PUMPKINS

A member of the Cucurbitaceae family along with zucchini, squash, gourd and cucumber, pumpkins are technically a fruit. They originated in the Americas and were a critical staple for native North Americans, who dried strips of pumpkin for sustenance throughout the winters. The American pilgrims quickly took to cultivating pumpkin and the first pumpkin pies were made by hollowing out the shell, adding milk, cream, eggs and spices, then baking them whole.

WHERE TO GROW

Pumpkins grow on trailing vines and are very easy to grow. They do, however, take up a lot of space. Vines can be trained over fences or pagodas, clotheslines, paths or sheds provided they can support the weight of the fruit. Some of the bushier varieties like Golden Nugget can be grown in containers, but most are too vigorous.

Pumpkins need full sun and well-drained soil. They can be grown as one of the 'three sisters' (corn, beans, pumpkins) in a patch where they wind their way around corn stalks, acting as a groundcover to shade the corn's shallow roots, while the corn acts as a trellis for beans, which, in turn, fix nitrogen into the soil to nourish the corn and pumpkins.

WHEN TO PLANT

Pumpkins love warmth. Plant pumpkin in spring after the last frost as it is not frost tolerant.

- In cool climates, it is a good idea to sow seeds indoors or undercover in a warm place so they can be planted out immediately after the last frost. Cover the pots with a plastic bag to retain warmth, removing it as soon as the seed has germinated.
- In temperate zones, plant or sow outside from spring to early summer.
- In frost-free and tropical areas, pumpkin can be grown all year but it is often best

if grown from April to July to avoid fungal problems in the humidity.

SOIL PREPARATION

Pumpkin vines are greedy and need a rich soil so plenty of compost and/or manure should be added before planting. Do this over a large area, ensuring plenty of nutrition for the runners the plant will put down. Good drainage is critical and a sure way to achieve this is to plant the seedling or seed in a raised bed, or on top of a mound of soil. They do best in slightly acidic to neutral soils (pH 5.5–6.8).

HOW TO PLANT

Pumpkin seeds need a soil temperature of 20°C for germination to occur. Seedlings can be raised by sowing seeds individually into small pots and planted out when the plants are sturdy. To plant pumpkin seedlings or seeds make a mound or ridge of compost and soil. Sow four seeds together, 2 cm deep. Place the seeds on their sides to prevent them rotting. Cover seeds with a thin layer of soil and firm down with your hands. Dig a shallow moat around each mound or alongside each ridge for watering. Water the ground well. If you plan to grow more than one vine leave 60 cm between mounds. Mulch around the seeds or seedlings to keep the ground moist. Once the seedlings appear choose the strongest and snip the other three off at the roots.

Below: Bees generally act as pollinators for pumpkins.

VARIETIES

There are many varieties. Golden Nugget is the best choice for small gardens and pots. Atlantic Giant has a massive fruit. The traditional Jap suits the tropics. Butternut can be successfully grown Australia-wide as can Beaudesert Blue, Queensland Blue and Jarrahdale, a Western Australian variety. Australian Butter is an heirloom and Jack Be Little grows dozens of tiny pumpkins.

CARE AND MAINTENANCE

Pumpkins need regular watering in summer and in dry or windy weather, particularly once the fruit begins to swell. They also benefit from a supplement of liquid fertiliser or liquid manure or side dressings of manure in late spring and again in mid summer. Mulch around plants to retain moisture.

Pumpkins produce both male and female flowers that can be eaten as you would zucchini flowers. Bees and insects generally act as the pollinators. However, if there are not enough bees around or high temperatures over 30°C have affected fruit formation, you might have to do it yourself. Simply pick off a male flower. This is the one without the bulge at the base. Remove the petals then dab the pollen on to the stigma of the female flower, the flower with the swollen embryo fruit at its base. Gently squeezing the female flowers also aids pollination in wet weather.

When the runners on the plant are about 3 m long pinch off the tips. This encourages side branches, which produce the female flowers and contains the wandering habit of the plant.

HARVESTING AND STORAGE

Pumpkins take from three to four months to mature and ripen. The best practice for harvesting is to let the pumpkins fully mature and harvest after the vine has died (before frosts arrive). When ripe, fruit should feel hard and heavy and make a hollow noise when tapped. To pick, use a knife or scissors and cut the fruit off with a 10 cm piece of the stalk still attached. Store off the ground in a cool, dry, well-ventilated place for between two to six months. Toast the seeds to eat.

If pumpkins are still on the vine by the time the first winter frosts set in, make sure to cover them at night. Harvest them soon thereafter and if they are for storage, set them in the sun during the day for a few weeks before storing.

Above: Vibrant orange pumpkin with a leaf-eating lady beetle nearby.

PESTS, DISEASES AND PROBLEMS

Leaf-eating or 28-spotted lady beetles eat pumpkin leaves—handpick them off.

Powdery or downy mildew on the leaves can be prevented by watering in the morning only and spraying with a solution of one part full-cream cow's milk to 10 parts water. Some

mildew-eating lady beetles (watch for their yellow and black bands) will also help control mildew.

See Zucchini, Cucumber and Squash for other potential pests.

COMPANIONS AND SUCCESSIONAL SOWING

A good companion to corn and beans, pumpkins don't like potatoes or tomato.

Root crops, such as carrots, beetroot, parsnips, onions and garlic, will grow in a crop rotation after pumpkin.

SEED SAVING

It is easy to save pumpkin seed. One month after harvesting scoop the seed from the flesh, wash it in a sieve and leave it to dry. Store it in a cool dry spot away from sunlight. When saving seed make sure it is from one variety of pumpkin that was grown in isolation.

RADISH

The origins of radish are obscure, although the popular consensus is that it originated in either China or India. We do know radish (*Raphanus sativus*) was highly prized by the Egyptian Pharaohs, while the ancient Greeks served them on dishes of gold in their sacrificial offerings to Apollo. They are quick and easy to grow, germinating in as little as five days.

WHERE TO GROW

Radishes can be grown anywhere. In summer they like a light shade. Because they are so fast to grow they are good to plant in alternate rows between slower growing crops like lettuce. The radish is grown and harvested while the lettuce is still growing. They can also be sown to mark out a dividing line between slower germinating seeds.

WHEN TO PLANT

Radish can be sown year round in all climates.

SOIL PREPARATION

Radishes like a soil rich in organic matter, which retains moisture. If the bed was manured for a previous crop this is ideal. They like a pH of 6.5, so add lime if necessary.

HOW TO PLANT

Radish seeds must be sown directly into the garden, they do not transplant. You can broadcast sow or sow them in rows 6mm deep and 5mm apart. Sow the seeds in rows 15 cm apart. Thin to 3 to 5 cm apart when they grow their second leaf. For a continual harvest sow again every four weeks.

VARIETIES

Radishes can be small, pink, red, white, round or elongated. Mooli or daikon radishes are a summer to autumn crop. Red Turnip, Cherry Belle, French Breakfast and the globe shaped Salad Crunch are worth a try.

CARE AND MAINTENANCE

For crisp, juicy radishes grow them quickly with plenty of water and a liquid feed every couple of weeks. In hot weather, mulch around radishes with compost to keep the soil moist and in winter mulch over radishes with straw to protect them from frost.

HARVESTING AND STORAGE

Some radishes can take as little as three weeks to be ready to harvest. Other long-rooted radishes can take up to two months. Radish gets old and tough quickly so harvest as they become ready by pulling them straight from the ground. They can be stored in the fridge, trimmed of the green ends, in a plastic bag for a couple of weeks. Mooli radish can stay in the soil for several weeks; its top can be harvested to eat in mid to late summer. The green tops of baby radishes can also be cut and eaten as a seedling-cutting crop.

PESTS, DISEASES AND PROBLEMS

Radishes are not affected by any serious diseases, although cabbage white butterfly is one pest to watch out for.

COMPANIONS AND SUCCESSIONAL SOWING

Leave one radish to flower. It will then produce pods that can be picked and stored in a dry place for planting out for the next crop. Radish flowers are also good for beneficial insects.

Radishes can be slotted anywhere into the garden. They do, however, tend to make particularly good companions to carrots, beans, lettuce and parsnip.

Horseradish (*Armoracia rusticana*) is a perennial herb from Eastern Europe, which has been grown for medicinal purposes since early times. It is best grown as an annual. The plant is very attractive and can grow up to a metre high—it is the long taproot that you want though. Grow horseradish in full sun in deep sandy or loamy soil. Dig manure or compost deeply into the soil, to a depth of 30 to 40 cm. Horseradish is propagated from root cuttings in late autumn or winter. Simply take 15 cm sections of the roots of an established plant, space them 30 cm apart at an angle in the soil and cover the thick end with a couple of centimetres of soil. When the shoots appear cut them back to two or three. Horseradish can be invasive, so you may want to restrain it. The roots should be left to harvest from late autumn to early winter. Dig them up. Grate and use horseradish in a cream or mayonnaise, or preserve it chopped up in a jar of white vinegar. Store unused roots in sand for future use.

Daikon or white radish is a Japanese radish best grown as a cool season crop. Sow in autumn in cool regions and in spring and autumn in temperate and tropical regions, in cool shady spots. Sow seeds directly into the ground, 1 to 2 cm deep, in drills 4 cm apart. Thin the seedlings so that they are 10 cm apart, although large-rooted varieties will need about 40 cm between them. As the seedlings grow cover the stems with soil. Don't let the soil dry out. Daikon should be ready to harvest in eight to 10 weeks.

ROCKET

Rocket, also known as arugula, rucola or roquette, is native to the Mediterranean, Turkey and Jordan, where it grows wild. In ancient Rome, it was used to concoct an aphrodisiac and was later banned from European monasteries as it allegedly inflamed lust.

WHERE TO GROW
Rocket is very easy to grow. It grows in full sun in the cooler months, but likes a light shade in summer. The soil should be well drained. Rocket grows well in pots and is great added to a mesclun mix of other salad greens.

WHEN TO PLANT
In all climates rocket can be sown directly into the garden from late winter to early summer and again from late summer to autumn. Sown in the middle of summer rocket has a tendency to bolt. Make successive sowings, every few weeks, for a continual crop.

SOIL PREPARATION
Rocket will grow in any soil but does best in fertile soil enriched with manures or compost or a complete plant food fertiliser.

HOW TO PLANT
Grow rocket from seed, as it is extremely quick and easy to germinate and has a tendency to bolt if grown from seedlings. Broadcast sow seed thinly in wide rows or blocks, sowing 1 cm deep and thin to 15 cm apart as the seedlings grow.

VARIETIES
Varieties include tall rocket, London rocket, Mediterranean rocket, Dame's violet and wild rocket with a more deeply indented leaf. Wild rocket is listed as a weed in South Australia.

CARE AND MAINTENANCE
Rocket must be grown quickly so it needs to be well watered and will benefit from a liquid fertiliser every seven days. Keep the patch weed free. Rocket is notorious for running to flower at the onset of hot weather or if it suffers from water stress. Pick off the flowers as they appear, to prolong the crop. The flowers are edible.

HARVESTING AND STORAGE
Rocket can be harvested in as little as three weeks. Pick or cut the leaves, as you need them.

The more you pick the more that grow. Cut the foliage back and give the plant a soluble feed to encourage a new flush of growth. As it gets older the taste becomes more bitter.

PESTS, DISEASES AND PROBLEMS

Rocket can suffer from flea beetles and caterpillars. Simply squash these by hand or use Dipel (a biologically friendly caterpillar spray that's safe to use on edible plants).

Snails and slugs like to feed on rocket and should be squashed or trapped with beer traps.

COMPANIONS AND SUCCESSIONAL SOWING

Rocket will grow happily next to lettuce and herbs. Make sure to rotate your crop, avoid planting rocket where brassicas have just been grown.

SEED SAVING

Saving rocket seed is easy. Simply cover the plants after flowering with stockings or paper bags tying them up with string, to catch the seeds as the pods open or cut off the stems with pods and hang them somewhere upside down in a paper bag until the seeds dry. Rub the seeds from the pods and replant. Plants can also be left in the garden to self seed.

SILVERBEET

A close relative of beetroot, silverbeet (*Beta vulgaris* var. *cicla*) is also known as beet, perpetual spinach, Swiss chard, strawberry spinach and sea kale beet. Silverbeet originated in the Mediterranean and was one of the vegetables Aristotle wrote about in his fourth century BC treatises on nature and plants.

WHERE TO GROW

Easy to grow as long as it has free draining soil, silverbeet likes a sunny position but will tolerate some shade. It is a good option for coastal gardeners, as it will tolerate salt-laden winds.

Silverbeet will grow well in pots.

WHEN TO PLANT

- In cool and temperate climates, sow silverbeet from early spring right through to mid autumn.
- In the subtropics, silverbeet can be sown and grown year round.
- In the tropics, avoid growing silverbeet in summer, as it is prone to fungal diseases, instead sow it from April to July.

Silverbeet is a good winter crop, but will go to seed in spring in hotter areas. In cooler climates it is a biennial.

SOIL PREPARATION

Silverbeet likes a soil rich in organic matter so add a couple of bucket loads of compost or manure to every square metre and a handful of a nitrogen-rich fertiliser, like chicken manure pellets, to prepare the soil. If your soil is particularly poor, silverbeet will benefit from a dose of trace elements, added in accordance with the instructions on the packet.

HOW TO PLANT

Silverbeet is easy to germinate from seed. Sow seed in punnets four weeks before you are ready to transplant them. Silverbeet seedlings transplant well. To sow seed directly into the garden bed dig it over well and rake it smooth. Make narrow seed drills 5–10 mm deep and 40 cm apart. Sow the seeds finely, cover them with soil and firm down with your hands. When the seedlings start to appear thin them out to 30 cm apart.

VARIETIES

Fordhook Giant has dark glossy leaves and a white stem. Lucullus has pale smooth leaves. Five Colour, or rainbow chard, is an heirloom with different coloured stems, including vivid crimson.

CARE AND MAINTENANCE

Water silverbeet regularly, particularly in warm weather. Give it frequent side dressings of a nitrogenous fertiliser, like poultry manure or a liquid feed, every two to three weeks. Mulch around the plants to help them to retain water. Cut away any flower stems that appear, this will help prolong the harvest.

HARVESTING AND STORAGE

Silverbeet can be harvested over a long period of time. It is an excellent winter crop, but will crop year round in most areas. Harvest it regularly to encourage more growth. You can start harvesting from about eight weeks after planting. Gently twist the leaves at the base of the plant. Don't cut them as the cut can increase the risk of fungal diseases. If you pick the entire plant, cut off the stems at ground level and leave the roots to re-establish a new plant. You can also rejuvenate an old plant by taking all the leaves off and leaving it to reshoot. If you have a number of plants take a few leaves from each every time you harvest, picking from the outside first.

PESTS, DISEASES AND PROBLEMS

Birds may try to eat the seedlings so protect them with wire netting or cloches.

Snails love silverbeet and can often be found deep in their stems. Pick them off and establish beer traps or use snail bait. Beet leaf miner may be a problem, a greyish yellow fly about 1 mm long whose larvae produce white lines in the leaf. The best method to get rid of them is to squash them and leave the corpses lying about.

Beet leaf rust is a fungal disease where brownish spots develop on leaves, which can be reduced by picking all diseased leaves off and avoiding overhead watering. Creating more space to improve air circulation around the plants will also help to prevent rust. See the Pests and Diseases section.

Silverbeet tends to bolt when the weather gets hot—regular harvesting helps prevent this.

COMPANIONS AND SUCCESSIONAL SOWING

Silverbeet does well with brassicas, onions, garlic and beetroot. Avoid runner beans.

In a crop rotation, plant silverbeet as you would other leafy greens, that is, after a green manure or legume crop. Root vegetables follow on well after it.

SPINACH

Thought to have been first cultivated in ancient Persia, spinach (*Spinacia oleracea*) or English spinach, was taken to China sometime before its first mention in 226 AD and is still known in China as 'Persian green'.

WHERE TO GROW

Spinach needs a rich, well-drained soil with a pH of 6–7. Grow it in full sun in winter but in summer provide a light shade. It is frost tolerant and grows well in containers.

WHEN TO PLANT

Spinach is a cool season vegetable and runs to seed in warm weather.
- In cool climates, sow spinach seeds from late summer right through to early spring.
- In temperate zones, sow seeds from early autumn to early winter.

- Spinach can be grown in autumn and winter in the subtropics but is generally unsuitable for the tropics.

To ensure a continuous harvest sow successional crops as the previous sowing is just starting to germinate. Spinach is a quick growing crop and can be ready to harvest in as little as five weeks.

SOIL PREPARATION

Spinach likes a rich fertile soil so add compost and/or manure or pelletised chicken manure before planting.

Add a generous handful or two of lime or dolomite for every square metre a week or two before sowing, if possible. This is criticial if your soil is acidic. Spinach loves lime. If you don't have time, water in the lime well before planting.

HOW TO PLANT

Soak seed for a few hours or overnight before sowing. To sow directly into the garden make rows 30 cm apart and 1 cm deep. Sow the seed, spacing it 15 cm apart and cover it with compost, soil or vermiculite. Seeds can also be germinated in punnets and planted out as seedlings. Make sure to keep the soil moist.

Don't transplant seedlings or buy them as they are very likely to bolt.

VARIETIES

There are many varieties of spinach from small to large-leaved varieties. English and Winter Hybrid have medium-sized leaves, while Winter Queen and Summer Supreme have large leaves, the latter being reasonably heat tolerant. Native Spinach is a drought-hardy native, which can be harvested for months. New Zealand spinach (known as Warrigal Greens) will grow in hotter and drier conditions than other spinach.

Alternatives for the sub-tropics and tropics include Ceylon or Malabar spinach and Egyptian spinach, also known as Huauzontle. Malabar spinach is a warm season annual, easy to grow in most parts of Australia. It is a vigorous vine and can grow up to 2 m, so will need a trellis or support. It can be grown in a large pot. It is sown in spring and summer and harvested in summer when other spinach has finished. Full sun and well draining rich soil is all it needs. Pick out the flowers to prolong harvest and eat the new leaves and stems.

Kangkong or water spinach is an Asian spinach, which also grows well in the tropics. It must be grown in a very moist spot or even a pond.

Orach, also known as mountain spinach, has young red leaves, which fade to green as they get older and can grow to 1 m high. Sow from early spring to autumn; it is also suitable for temperate zones.

CARE AND MAINTENANCE

Regular watering is essential for spinach. Mulching around the plants will help preserve moisture and keep dirt off the leaves. Side dressings of a nitrogen-rich fertiliser or liquid feeds every 10 to 14 days help the spinach grow quickly.

HARVESTING AND STORAGE

When the plants are big enough start picking the outside leaves as you need them. Spinach is best cooked immediately after picking but will keep in the fridge. Harvest the outer leaves continually to prevent bolting.

PESTS, DISEASES AND PROBLEMS

Spinach is relatively pest and disease free although prone to bolting if water stressed in hot weather.

COMPANIONS AND SUCCESSIONAL SOWING

Since it likes a light shade in warmer months spinach is a good crop to interplant amongst taller, slower growing vegetables and so makes an ideal companion to broad beans. It will also grow happily beside lettuce. Grow it after a legumes or fruit crop and before a root crop.

SWEDES AND TURNIPS

Swedes (*Brassica napus* var. *napobrassica*) and turnips (*Brassica rapa* var. *rapa*) are cool season vegetables with the same climatic and cultivation requirements. Turnips were the first vegetable successfully grown in Australia by the First Fleet colonists. They are hardy root crops with a long growing season.

WHERE TO GROW

Swedes and turnips like cool damp conditions with good drainage. They will withstand mild frosts and some shade. For the most part, they won't do well in the tropics.

WHEN TO PLANT

- Swedes can be sown from late spring to mid-summer in cool and temperate regions.
- Turnips can be sown all year round in cool and temperate climates and subtropical regions.
- If trying them in the tropics, sow from May.

SOIL PREPARATION

Both vegetables require plenty of organic matter in the soil. A garden bed composted for a previous crop is ideal. If it hasn't been, then add some manure and/or compost and, if it is an acid soil, add lime. Swedes and turnips like a pH of 5.5–7.5. Let the soil settle for a few days before planting.

HOW TO PLANT

Swedes and turnips must be grown from seed sown directly into the garden. You cannot transplant them. Firm down the soil and make drills 2 cm deep and 35 cm apart. Sow the seed thinly along the drills. The seeds should germinate within a week. When the seedlings are small thin them so they have 20 cm between them.

VARIETIES

Swedes can have yellow or white flesh and purple or brown skin. Marian, a cultivar, has some resistance to clubfoot and mildew. Champion has a purple top.

Turnip cultivars include Orange Jelly, a golden-fleshed Italian heirloom, White Globe, a more traditional variety and Golden Globe, a heritage cultivar dating back to before 1888.

Japanese turnips are sown in spring and autumn and are very fast growing. White-fleshed, they are eaten raw or in salad.

CARE AND MAINTENANCE

Turnips and swedes are fast growing. Water regularly in hot and dry weather as they have a tendency to bolt or turn woody.

HARVESTING AND STORAGE

Harvest swedes from autumn as soon as the roots are large enough. Gently pull them from the ground or use a garden fork.

Leave them in the ground and dig them up as you require them or store in boxes in a cool place.

Harvest turnips as you need them, anything from five to 10 weeks after sowing. The young leaves can be eaten raw as greens in salads, or steamed or stir-fried.

If turnips grow too large they become fibrous.

PESTS, DISEASES AND PROBLEMS

Boron deficiency, clubfoot and downy mildew can all strike turnips. See the Pests and Diseases section on how to deal with these.

COMPANIONS AND SUCCESSIONAL SOWING

Both turnips and swedes do well with peas, but avoid kohlrabi, potatoes or mustard.

Grow them as a root vegetable in a crop rotation, after brassicas and before cucurbits.

SWEET CORN

- In cold climates sow seeds from October to December.
- In temperate zones sow seeds from August to January.
- In the subtropics, sowing can start in September and continue until March.
- Sow all year in the tropics (in the wet season protect the seedlings and crop from pests by fencing it and covering with a shade cloth).

Corn (*Zea mays*) has been grown in the Americas for millennia. Indeed, the native Americans taught the pilgrims to put a fish in the growing hole with the corn kernels they planted—as the fish decayed it provided a rich fertiliser for the growing plant. The sugars in the kernels convert to starch as soon as the cobs are picked, so the corn you eat fresh from the garden at home is far superior to shop-bought corn.

WHERE TO GROW

Corn is adaptable to all climates. It does, however, have a number of non-negotiable requirements, foremost among them being a heavily enriched soil. It needs to be well drained and planted in a position receiving maximum sunlight. Corn also needs a water-retaining soil. It is a tall slender plant that must be grown in a block so be mindful that it will need space and may cast shade on underlying plants.

WHEN TO PLANT

Sweet corn is a warm season, frost tender crop. It is important that plants receive a warm start. Seeds germinate best when the average soil temperature is 20°C or higher.

SOIL PREPARATION

Sweet corn has extensive roots that can penetrate into the subsoil and is a hungry and thirsty plant so you need to prepare the ground for it carefully. The soil needs extra deep cultivation to at least a shovel depth. Add a 5 cm layer of cow or sheep manure and a sprinkling of pelletised poultry manure and a handful of potash to encourage flowering growth. Fork in everything as deeply as possible. Rake the surface, water deeply and leave to mature for a few days.

HOW TO PLANT

Corn is best planted close together in short rows that form a block as it is pollinated by the wind. Avoid planting an extra long single row.

Make sure the soil is damp for planting (not waterlogged). Create four or five rows 2.5 cm deep using the edge of a rake, with 35 cm between rows. Sow the seeds 20 to 30 cm apart, two in each spot. Cover the seeds with soil and firm down.

Give the seeds a good watering but don't water again until the shoots appear in about 10 days. The relatively large seeds of sweet corn can absorb enough moisture to carry them through to full germination. While the plants are still small, thin any overcrowded seedlings. Pick out the weakest of each pair of seedlings when they're about 15 cm high and cut them off at the roots.

It is best to sow direct where the corn will grow. This always produces stronger, more productive plants than bought seedlings. If you do sow seeds in seed trays transplant them when they are 10 cm high. Plant seedlings deeply and later earth up around the stems.

Only grow one variety of sweet corn at a time as cross-pollination between different types can produce starchy kernels similar to field maize. To grow a succession of crops sow the next batch when the first plants are about 15 cm high.

VARIETIES

There are many varieties; best amongst them are the heritage cultivars, many of which produce three cobs per plant instead of the one or two that modern hybrids produce. These include Golden Bantam, Hawaiian, True Blue and True Gold.

CARE AND MAINTENANCE

Sweet corn pollinates itself with the help of wind and gravity since both male and female flowers are on the one plant. The male flower has tassels that sprout upwards from the top of the plant, which produce the pollen. The female cob forms down the stem and grows long silks. These catch the pollen as it falls down towards them. As the male flowers mature you can assist pollination by gently shaking the stems early in the morning to release the pollen.

Seedlings are susceptible to wind damage so mound up the soil around the stems as they grow to stabilise them. The secret to good corn crops is regular deep watering, especially once the first immature ears appear. Once established, corn grows rapidly so increase the amount of water and give it weekly feeds of fish emulsion or a liquid plant food. Before it is

too tall mulch it well with mushroom compost, hay, sugarcane or compost to help keep the soil moist. Use as much mulch, as high around the plant as you can.

HARVESTING AND STORAGE

Cobs are ready for harvest usually two or three weeks after the flowers appear and when the silks have shrivelled and begun to turn brown. If you prick a kernel and it releases a thin slightly cloudy liquid it is ready to harvest. Pull the cob down and off the stem husk or use a knife to cut the cob away from the stem. Eat as soon as possible after harvesting as corn starts to lose its flavour quickly after picking. Corn can be blanched and frozen whole or as kernels.

PESTS, DISEASES AND PROBLEMS

The main reason sweet corn seeds fail to germinate is overwatering or saturated soil causing seeds to rot.

Corn earworm is a caterpillar-like insect that nests in the ears and destroys the crops. To prevent this cut the tips and silks off the husks once they have started to dry out.

Corn is vulnerable to aphids and fungus if it is planted late in the season. See the Pests and Diseases section. Insufficient watering causes cobs without kernels.

COMPANIONS AND SUCCESSIONAL SOWING

Pumpkin, squash, zucchini, cucumber and beans love to grow alongside corn. Pumpkin or squash can be planted and allowed to delve in between and even grow up the corn stalks. Climbing beans can be sown next to corn to use the stalks as a climbing support.

Corn should follow a legume or be sown with them. Potatoes are a good intercrop around the bottom of corn. Carrots and daisies nearby are said to help ward off pests.

SWEET POTATOES

Only a distant relative to the potato, the sweet potato (*Ipomoea batatas*) or *kumara* in Maori, is native to the tropical parts of South America, where it was domesticated at least 5000 years ago. In 1493, Christopher Columbus took sweet potato back to Europe with him. Known as the 'Spanish potato' it became a favourite of Henry VIII after it was included in Catherine of Aragon's dowry. He had it made into confectionery and set a prize for the first English gardener to grow it successfully. No one could.

WHERE TO GROW

Sweet potatoes grow in warm humid climates. They require four to six months of warm daytime temperatures. In cool areas you will not produce any significant harvest, particularly as sweet potatoes are intolerant of frost.

Sweet potatoes grow as a groundcover with tubers growing underground and need a lot of space. They have a tendency to take over the garden. Sweet potatoes will grow in a rich, friable soil. Good drainage is essential.

WHEN TO PLANT

- In cooler regions, you can try to grow sweet potatoes by planting cuttings or tubers at the beginning of spring. You will need a long, hot summer for success.
- Plant sweet potato throughout the year in warm climates, although spring is generally the best time.

SOIL PREPARATION

Add compost and/or manure and an organic fertiliser, like blood and bone, to the bed and sprinkle potash through at the recommended rate. Don't use poultry manure or other fertilisers that are high in nitrogen, as these will encourage leaf growth at the expense of tubers. Unless your soil is very sandy mound it up or make ridges 15 cm high to prevent the tubers rotting.

HOW TO PLANT

Sweet potatoes are grown from tubers or cuttings. If you have access to existing plants take 30 cm long cuttings, known as slips, from them. Remove the lower leaves along the stem, leaving a couple only at the top and place them lying down in a box of potting mix or along a ridge in the garden. Cover over the stems leaving just the top leaves above the soil. Mulch and then water regularly. After a couple of weeks the cutting should root and it can be planted in the garden. Plant slips 40 cm apart in rows 90 cm apart and water.

You can also propagate sweet potatoes by sprouting tubers. Buy some sweet potatoes from a local organic grocer or from a seed supply company. Slice them lengthwise and place in a pot of clean wet sand or potting mix. Cover with 10 cm of soil or sand. Keep moist in a warm position. When the shoots are about 15 cm long transplant them into a garden bed.

VARIETIES

Sweet potatoes can be white, yellow, orange or purple. Marguerite, White Maltese and Porto Rico are all yellow fleshed and Sweet Gold has orange flesh.

CARE AND MAINTENANCE

Like potatoes, sweet potatoes need to be mounded up with soil or mulch over the tubers, to prevent them being exposed to the sun. Trim back some of the plant's leaves to encourage the tubers to grow. Keep the bed well weeded, as sweet potatoes don't like competition. Regular watering helps prevent the potatoes splitting.

HARVESTING AND STORAGE

Sweet potatoes take around 5 months until they are ready for harvesting. They must be harvested before the first frost, when the vines have started to yellow. Lift mature roots with a fork, two or three potatoes will be at the base. Lay them out in a sunny, dry place for a couple of hours to allow them to dry out. Sweet potatoes store well for four or five weeks in a dry, ventilated place.

PESTS, DISEASES AND PROBLEMS

In the tropics sweet potato weevils can be a big problem, especially if the sweet potatoes have been left to grow for too long in the one location. These are 6mm long, blue and orange bugs that lay their eggs in the roots. If your plants are attacked by them dig up the crop and dispose of it. Don't plant a replacement crop in the same patch.

Rats and grasshoppers are attracted to sweet potato.

COMPANIONS AND SUCCESSIONAL SOWING

Grow sweet potatoes with other root crops, beetroot, parsnips and salsify. Dill, thyme, oregano and summer savoury help confuse and repel sweet potato weevil. Avoid growing sweet potato with melons or pumpkin, which will compete for space.

Always rotate sweet potato crops to prevent weevils.

TOMATOES

Lycopersicon esculentum, the botanical name for tomatoes, means 'tasty wolf peach'. Tomatoes first grew wild in South America and were introduced into Europe during the early 16th century. As a member of the nightshade family they were initially deemed a poisonous plant and used only as an ornamental.

WHERE TO GROW

Tomatoes need at least six hours of full sunlight a day and warm temperatures. They are large plants and can grow anywhere from 60 cm to 2 m tall and 60 cm wide. Therefore, they need a lot of open space. Tomatoes are good in large pots, particularly cherry tomatoes.

Provided the drainage is good, tomatoes will grow in any soil, including poor soil. They do, however, prefer a slightly acidic soil with a pH of 5.5–6.5. Tomatoes do particularly well near a fence or brick wall where they get reflected heat.

WHEN TO PLANT

- In cool and temperate areas sow seeds in punnets under cover in a dry, warm place towards the end of winter to get a head start. Sow seeds in the garden after the last frost in spring. Seedlings are best left to be planted out from early November when the weather has warmed up, until the end of January.
- In the subtropics, sow seed in trays in August to plant out seedlings from October to January.
- In the tropics, sow or plant during the dry season. Sow seeds in a seed tray undercover in May, to plant out in June and July.

SOIL PREPARATION

Prepare soil by deeply digging in a large load of compost and/or cow or sheep manure. Fork in some potash to aid flower set and fruit development.

HOW TO PLANT

Tomatoes are very easy to germinate from seed. In cooler climates give the seeds some extra warmth by using a heat bed or place the seed tray in a foam box and use an overhead lamp, or put the tray on the top of the fridge. Once the seedlings are large enough to handle they can be pricked out into pots and gradually hardened off outside.

You can also sow seeds directly into the garden. Thin them out when they are big enough, leaving the strongest seedlings.

Spacing is important as tomatoes need good air circulation and lots of sunlight. Tall growing varieties need about 60 cm between them and 90 cm between rows. Bushy types need about 50 cm between plants and 45 to 60 cm between rows.

Make a hole in the soil and plant the seedlings deeply, up to the first leaves. Firm down the soil around the stems with your hand. Cut off any foliage touching the ground and water plants in with liquid seaweed. Lightly mulch with hay, straw or sugarcane, being very careful to keep the mulch away from the stem.

A good idea to help watering is to dig a small trench, like a moat, around each plant. Fill the trench when you are watering. This will help root

growth and prevent water getting on the leaves.

If your drainage is not great sow tomato seeds or plant seedlings in mounds or ridges 10 cm above the soil surface.

Staking

All tall growing varieties of tomatoes need staking. Gently push three 2 m tomato stakes evenly around each plant on planting. As the leaders (the main stems) grow, use soft gardening ties or old stockings to tie the stems to the stakes. Make a figure of eight with the tie circling the leader and the stake. Keep doing this as the plant grows. Smaller varieties need only two stakes.

Some varieties like Grosse Lisse, Surecrop and Sweet Bite can grow more than 2 m high and spread widely. Each of their four or five major branches will need its own stake.

Bush tomato plants grow less than 1 m high but spread in the same manner as vine varieties. They generally don't need to be staked or pruned. Short stakes can, however, be used to keep fruit off the ground or thick layers of straw can be put under the plant for the fruit to rest on.

VARIETIES

There are hundreds of cultivars of tomatoes, many of them wonderful heirlooms with vastly superior flavour. In cool climates, it is advisable to plant the smaller varieties such as Apollo or grow cherry tomatoes to ensure that the fruit ripens before the first frost.

Rouge De Marmande is good in cool and temperate climates and is disease resistant. Green Zebra is an heirloom which will actually fruit in frost. Tigerella has orange stripes.

Cherry tomatoes are the easiest to grow and often don't require staking. Unlike other tomatoes, they can be grown in semi-shade. They are good for the tropics and cool zones. Varieties include Tommy Toe and Yellow Pear, Sweet Bite and Baby Red Pear.

CARE AND MAINTENANCE

Tomatoes need lots of water and the soil must be kept consistently moist. Plants that become water stressed are prone to black scabs or blossom end rot. The best time to water tomatoes is in the morning when it is still cool. Wet foliage at night encourages mildew so try not to shower them with water; instead, direct the hose under the plant and water around the roots.

Once flowering begins, give tomatoes a handful of potash around the base and start fortnightly feeds of fish or seaweed emulsion, a liquid fertiliser for flowering and fruiting plants, a couple of handfuls of blood and bone or cow or sheep manure. Don't use fertilisers high in nitrogen, as these will create leaf growth at the expense of fruit.

As the tomato grows, keep attaching it to stakes with soft ties so it won't blow over.

Pollination

Tomatoes, like the other members of their family, capsicum, chillies and eggplants, are self-pollinating; both the male and female parts exist in the same flower. The trick with pollinating is that the female part (the pistil) is located above the male flower parts, which produce the pollen. The wind usually is sufficient to help pollination but in overly hot temperatures or cool, cloudy conditions the female part may have trouble being pollinated and the flower will drop off. Aid pollination yourself by gently tapping the stem below the flower clusters with a pencil each morning or hold an electric toothbrush against the stem. It is also an excellent idea to encourage 'buzz pollinator' bees into the garden. See the section on bees for how to attract buzz pollinators.

Pruning

There is no need to prune smaller bush tomatoes but large varieties should be restricted to four or five main stems. Do this by 'pinching out'. As the plant grows you need to pinch out the little side growths, known as laterals. These are the little leaf growths that grow out from between the main stem and the branches. With your fingertips, pinch them out to help keep the tomatoes compact. The leading tips of the major branches are left to continue to grow and climb.

Tomatoes ripen by temperature so don't constantly cut off leaves as this will expose the fruit to the sun. Once the fruit has set you can remove some of the leaves below the last one to aid air circulation around the plant. This will help the fruit to ripen and reduce the risk of fungal disease.

Above: Pinching out a lateral.

HARVESTING AND STORAGE

Tomatoes are best left to ripen on the vine for as long as possible. However, should they suffer from bird or animal attack cut the fruit off and put it on a sunny windowsill or in a brown paper bag with an apple or banana to ripen it. To harvest, cut the stem at the joint above the fruit. Harvest all fruit before the first frost comes. If unripened fruit is still on the vine dig up the whole plant and hang it upside down undercover and the fruit will continue ripening.

Store tomatoes in the crisper but take them out of the fridge to get to room temperature before eating.

PESTS, DISEASES AND PROBLEMS

Aphids, whitefly and mites can be controlled with horticultural soaps or yellow sticky tapes.

Fusarium and verticillium wilts are soil-borne fungal diseases that work their way up the stems. Rapid wilting is followed by the plant dying. Don't plant tomatoes or family members again for several years in a spot where plants have suffered from wilt.

Adding dolomite to the soil before planting will prevent blossom end rot.

Fruit fly is a problem in New South Wales and Queensland. These bright green flies lay their eggs into maturing fruit. The eggs hatch as

maggots. If fruit fly is a local problem cover the ripening fruit with fine mesh exclusion bags and set up oil-based baits near the plants (on a stake or nearby fence). These baits lure the female fruit fly to feed on the protein in them. The baits contain insecticide so the fruit fly dies before any eggs are laid. See the Pests and Diseases section for how to make homemade baits.

Tomato grubs can be picked off by hand or sprayed with Dipel or neem oil.

COMPANIONS AND SUCCESSIONAL SOWING

Tomatoes love to grow with basil. They also grow well with asparagus, carrots, brassicas, onions, garlic and parsley. Don't grow them with potatoes or kohlrabi.

Crop rotation is crucial with plants in the tomato family. Allow a break of three years if possible. Plant tomatoes after a legume or green manure crop. Root crops can be sown once tomatoes have finished.

SEED SAVING

Scoop out the pulp from ripe fruit and allow it to ferment for a day. Rinse the seeds in a sieve under running water and press out excess pulp. Spread the wet seed over some paper towel and dry well at room temperature, and then cut the paper towel into sections and store in an airtight jar up to four years. The seeds can be planted out on the paper towel, which will decompose.

WATERCRESS

Ideally grown in running water, watercress (*Nasturtium officinale*) can be grown in a pot plunged into a pond or a water barrel. You can plant watercress in a container provided you water it daily, or in a damp part of the garden year round in temperate and subtropic regions. In the tropics grow it in winter.

Watercress can be grown in shade or part-shade. It likes an alkaline soil enriched with compost or manure. If grown in the sun it gets tough and peppery.

It is easily propagated from a shop bought bunch. Simply place 10 cm cuttings in a glass of water and roots will form in seven or so days and then plant out.

Alternatively, sow seed in spring or autumn. Water daily. Feed watercress with liquid compost or seaweed every few weeks.

Pick leaves as you want them. Pinch out any flowers to encourage leaf growth and prolong the harvest.

ZUCCHINI, CUCUMBER AND SQUASH

Zucchini, cucumber and squash are all cucurbits and have been staple food crops for centuries. The Roman emperor, Tiberius, is said to have demanded a cucumber at his table everyday and had them cultivated to be able to survive winter. The Romans used them to treat scorpion bites and to scare away mice. The humble zucchini travelled from the Americas to Italy where it was cultivated into what we eat today. Cucurbits have the same growing requirements. They are interesting plants as each individual plant has separate male and female flowers. The male flowers contain the pollen, while the fruit is produced by the female flowers.

WHERE TO GROW

Cucurbits need full sun and a rich well-drained soil, high in nitrogen. They are good in pots and can be included in an ornamental garden. Trailing cucumbers can be trained to climb up netting or canes or over paths. Pop a couple of seeds on the compost heap and grow a crop while the compost breaks down underneath. Cucurbits are all vigorous plants that grow to be quite large. Where space is limited some compact cultivars are available.

WHEN TO PLANT

Cucurbits are warmth-loving plants and suffer from even a hint of frost.

- In cool climates, sow seed undercover in peat pots in October and plant out or sow seed directly into the garden in December and January.
- In temperate zones, sow seeds undercover in punnets in September and plant them out when the soil has warmed up and frosts have passed from November to January. Seeds can be sown directly into the ground in summer.
- In the subtropics, you can start seed in individual biodegradable pots undercover in August and plant out seedlings or seeds directly into the garden from October to March.
- In the tropics, plant seeds or seedlings from April until the end of August.

SOIL PREPARATION

Cucurbits are greedy feeders that like a neutral soil (pH 6–7). Apply lime if your soil is acidic. Incorporate lots of organic matter into the bed before planting.

HOW TO PLANT

All cucurbits are exceptionally easy to grow from seed and resent root disturbance so it is best to sow seed directly into the ground. The best way to plant cucurbits is in a mound. Simply mix well-rotted manure and/or compost with soil and hill it up into 20 cm wide mounds. Sow three seeds 10 cm apart into each mound and thin to the strongest seedling when they have sprouted by cutting the two weaker ones just below the soil surface.

If the weather hasn't warmed up place them under a cloche for protection and added warmth. Dig a shallow moat around each mound or alongside each ridge of plants to aid watering. Generally space mounds for cucumbers 60 cm apart and zucchinis and squashes 70 cm to 1 m apart. Check the seed packet for more specific spacing recommendations. Overcrowding the plants reduces air circulation, which may cause fungal diseases.

If starting seedlings off undercover use biodegradable peat pots or old toilet rolls and plant the seedlings out in the pots.

CONTAINER GROWING

Compact cultivars grow well in large tubs. Provide a good quality potting mix, adding a shovel full of compost or manure. Place the pots in a sunny spot with good air circulation and protected from hot afternoon sun in warm regions. Give the plants a fortnightly feed of a liquid fertiliser or compost tea and always make sure to water the plant well in hot weather. Cultivars for pots include Yellow Button squash, Green Button Hybrid squash, Spacemaster cucumber and Midnight F1 zucchini.

VARIETIES

Squash varieties include the pale green Bennings Green Tint bush squash, Sweet Potato Squash which is a striped heirloom with dark yellow flesh, Green Button squash and Spaghetti squash, which can be eaten like the pasta.

Zucchinis include Black Jack F1 with dark green fruit, Costa Romanesque, an Italian mildew resistant type and Black Beauty, a dark green prolific cultivar.

Cucumbers include Lebanese and Gherkin Pickling. Apple cucumbers include the heirloom Lemon and Burpless cucumbers, which are thought to prevent burping.

CARE AND MAINTENANCE

All cucurbits need a regular and consistent supply of water while they are growing. If they wilt they are in need of more water. Mulching around the plants will help retain moisture and keep the fruit clean. In spring and again in summer give them a liquid fertiliser or side dressing of manure.

Pinch out the terminal bud, (the bud at the end of the main stem), to encourage the plant to produce side branches. On lengthy runners snap off a leaf partway along and bury that section of the stem. It will develop roots at the nodes that will supply developing fruit with additional water and nutrients.

Train trailing cucumbers up netting, a string trellis or pyramid stakes for support. When the plant reaches the top of the support, nip out the growing point. 'Ridge' cucumbers grow along flat ground, nip out the growing point when five to six leaves have formed to encourage bushy growth.

Pollinating

Open pollinated varieties of cucurbits require pollination, mostly from bees and insects. In North America and Europe professional growers import beehives into their fields just before flowering. A scarcity of bees, high temperatures which can make pollen sterile, or irregular watering, can cause poor fruit set and fruit drop. If this is the case you may need to hand pollinate. Pick two male flowers, these are the first flowers to develop on the vine and have slender stems. Peel back the petals and brush the pollen from the styles of both the male flowers against the pistil inside the female flower. The female flower has a slight swelling at the base of the petals and develops further along the vine.

HARVESTING AND STORAGE

Harvesting can start whenever you think the vegetable is large enough. Cut the vegetable from the plant or gently twist. Regular harvesting encourages more flowers to form. Store cucurbits in the crisper of the fridge.

Zucchini flowers can be picked and eaten—a good use of the male flower after pollination. A zucchini left to grow on the vine will, in the space of a couple of days, grow into a marrow, an enormous woody vegetable and quite unpalatable.

PESTS, DISEASES AND PROBLEMS

Fungal diseases are the most common, especially powdery and downy mildew, which looks like white dusty spots on the tops of the leaves. While this is a natural part of the breakdown process of plant senescence (the dropping of leaves as the plant dies) it can decimate crops if it attacks too early. Simply cut off the diseased leaves. Common in cool wet weather, the fungal spores are spread by the wind. Infected seedlings will usually die. To prevent infections make sure to water the plant from the bottom, not overhead, or use a drip watering system. Ensure drainage is good and

that the plants are grown sufficiently far enough apart for good air circulation.

Seaweed sprays encourage vigour and mulching will help restrict the spread of spores from the soil. Resistant varieties of all cultivars are available.

Fruit fly can be a pest. See the Pests and Diseases section for information on how to deal with this.

COMPANIONS AND SUCCESSIONAL SOWING

Beans, lettuce, peas, sweet corn and sunflowers are good companions for zucchini and cucumber. Avoid potato.

Zucchini and squash grow well with beans, cabbage and lettuce. In a crop rotation, root vegetables will follow cucurbits. All cucurbits will benefit from being planted after a green manure crop.

Planting thyme, borage and lavender nearby is helpful for attracting bees.

Choko (*Sechium edule*)—plant a single choko on its side with the narrow end jutting just above the ground in a warm, sunny well-drained spot beside a strong trellis or fence. Mulch thickly, water regularly and fertilise with manure and compost in early spring and summer.

Bittermelon (*Momordica charantia*) grow like cucumbers; harvest them while small and tender. Best suited to the tropics and subtropics bittermelon can also be grown over a long hot summer in temperate zones.

SEED SAVING

Seed saving is difficult as they have a habit of cross-pollinating.

Below: Apple cucumber.

GROWING HERBS

'Let food be your medicine and medicine be your food.'
~Hippocrates

Herbs are easy to grow and require a lot less attention than vegetables. Their uses range from culinary to medicinal and in the garden they are often exceptionally good companion plants, both warding off pests and attracting beneficial insects. Herbs are either annuals, grown for only one season and planted again each spring, like basil, coriander and dill, or perennials, that is, living for several years and generally dying back in autumn to re-grow in spring like chives, marjoram, mint, thyme, tarragon, sage and rosemary. Parsley is a biennial herb, growing over two years.

Most herbs prefer full sun, although some, like chives, mint, coriander and dill, will tolerate a light shade. They all need excellent drainage and most require a moderately rich, friable soil.

Herbs make excellent potted plants and many will grow indoors on a windowsill provided they get enough sunlight.

BASIL

Also known as common or sweet basil or St Joseph wort, basil is from the Lamiaceae family, which includes mint. Its scientific name, *Ocimum basilicum*, is Greek for 'kingly herb' and it is said to have grown around Christ's tomb after the resurrection. The ancient Romans believed people should curse as they sowed basil to ensure germination. In Western Europe from the 16th century, it was thought to belong to the devil.

POSITION

Basil must have full sun and a well-drained soil. It is a summer plant that needs lots of warmth.

Basil is excellent in pots and is a good herb to place around your windows as it repels flies. Make sure to use a good-quality potting mix, add in some organic matter on planting and keep well watered.

WHEN TO PLANT

Basil is a tender plant and easily killed by frosts. In the tropics, you can plant basil all year long. In all other zones you can sow seeds undercover into pots in early spring and germinate in a warm sunny location. Alternatively, sow seed directly into the garden in late spring but only after the soil has warmed up. Basil likes a soil temperature of over 20°C.

Don't plant out your seedlings until the danger of frost has passed. Seedlings planted too early fail to thrive. In cool and temperate zones wait until November or December. Basil can then be planted throughout summer.

SOIL PREPARATION

Basil likes a rich soil with lots of organic matter added in prior to planting. It likes a pH of 5.5–7.

HOW TO PLANT

Basil is easy to propagate from seed. If sowing seeds direct do so fairly closely together and thin out the plants after germination. Basil seeds germinate quite slowly. If you sow them into a seedtray, covering it with cling wrap, a sheet of glass or a cloche will aid germination. Remove the plastic or glass once the seeds have germinated. Once seedlings are long enough to handle, prick them off into small pots and harden off in the sun prior to planting. Do not plant the stems of seedlings below soil level as they may rot.

Space plants 25–30 cm apart with the same space between rows. Make a hole 5 cm deep and pop the seedlings in, backfilling with soil. Firm down the soil around the seedlings.

If you buy potted seedlings, buy the smallest ones as basil has long roots and dislikes being transplanted.

VARIETIES

There are many varieties of basil available. Common basil is Genovese; other large leaved sweet basils include Lettuce Leaf and Mammoth. Greek basils are small leaved. Ararat is green and purple. Lemon scented basils include lemon basil, Sweet Dani and Mrs Burn's Lemon. Spicy basils include Oriental Breeze, Cinnamon and Blue Spice. There are liquorice basils and Thai and Vietnamese basil with ornamental lavender flowers among many others.

CARE AND MAINTENANCE

Whenever you pass your basil plants, pinch out the white flower heads to prolong the harvest and encourage bushy growth. Water well in dry weather in the morning, as basil hates being wet overnight. This minimises the chance of dampening off and prevents root rot.

Before the first frosts you can dig up basil plants and pot them into compost and take them inside to a sunny window sill to grow through autumn and winter.

HARVESTING AND STORAGE

Harvest basil regularly to encourage growth and stop the plant going to seed. Pick off leaves as you need them.

Blanch and freeze basil in ice cubes or dry the leaves. To dry, cut the bushes at the bottom of the stem and hang them out of direct light, then store the leaves in an airtight container. Microwaving the leaves will also dry them.

PESTS AND DISEASES

Basil has no serious pests or diseases. Sometimes the fungal disease fusarium wilt can attack plants causing sudden wilt. The only solution is to pull them out but do not compost and don't replant basil in contaminated soil.

COMPANIONS

Basil is a natural companion to tomatoes, chilli and capsicums as it acts as a pest repellant. Basil is a good crop to grow after peas or beans, as it likes the enhanced nitrogen that they leave in the soil.

BAY

The bay tree (*Laurus nobilis*) is a long-lived, slow-growing evergreen tree. The Roman emperor, Tiberius, always wore a crown of bay laurel when thunderstorms were raging, as he believed that it would provide protection from the gods of thunder and lightning. In folklore, a bay tree in the garden keeps away evil. The death of a bay tree was considered a portent of evil times; when Rome fell to invasion in the fourth century all the bay trees were reputed to have died.

POSITION

Bay trees grow in full sun but will withstand some shade. They like a rich, well-drained, moist soil. They are low maintenance trees to grow and can reach 15 m in height.

Bays are excellent in pots but make sure you use a big deep pot and enrich the potting mix with compost.

WHEN TO PLANT

Plant bay at any time.

SOIL PREPARATION

Bay trees prefer deep soil, so work compost and/or manure into the soil to a depth and width double that of the purchased pot.

HOW TO PLANT

If you are transplanting your bay or planting out a potted bay into the garden disturb the root system as little as possible. Bays are easy to train into a fan or espalier.

Bay seeds take up to six months to germinate. Plants can be propagated from cuttings from semi-ripe wood; these will take three or more months to form roots. See section on Figs on how to propagate.

CARE AND MAINTENANCE

The ornamental plants cherry laurel and mountain laurel are easily confused with the bay but the leaves of these are poisonous if ingested.

As bay trees can grow to be enormous they should be pruned to keep in check. They are also notorious for suckering so watch out for suckered plants cropping up. Dig these up.

HARVESTING AND STORAGE

Pick the leaves for use at any time. Leaves can be dried out in the sun and stored in an airtight container. Bay leaves strewn around the pantry are a common method for deterring moths.

PESTS AND DISEASES

Bays are generally trouble free. They may be attacked by scale so if you see small insects infesting the underside of leaves and stems, remove them by rubbing them off with your fingers or spraying with a garlic spray or horticultural oil.

If grown without adequate ventilation or light, bays can develop grey mildew. Treat this with sulphur while the plant is wet with morning dew.

CHIVES

Chives (*Allium schoenoprasum*) are part of the onion family and have been known as a culinary herb for the past 5000 years. The Romans believed chives relieved sunburn and were beneficial for people with low blood pressure. In European folkloric traditions, they were said to ward off evil and disease if hung around the house in bunches. In the garden, chives are invaluable as the sulphur in them repels unwanted insects, while the mauve flowers are immensely attractive to bees.

POSITION

Chives are a perennial herb which will grow in full sun, but will appreciate some shade in summer. They will grow in partial shade but will not be as vigorous. They are excellent in pots, as they grow in a dense clump. Chives like a rich fertile soil so add manure or a nitrogen-rich fertiliser before planting.

Like most herbs, chives like a well-drained soil, with a pH of 6 to 7.

WHEN AND HOW TO PLANT

Sow seed directly into the garden or undercover in early spring and again in early autumn. Seeds should germinate in 10 to 14 days. In cool zones, start the seed off under a cloche. Fully grown chives can be divided by digging up the plant and carefully cutting the roots into pieces, then replanting. Do this in late summer or autumn.

VARIETIES

Garlic chives, (*Allium tuberosum*) also known as Chinese chives, have a slightly garlicky taste.

Common chives may also be known as onion chives.

CARE AND MAINTENANCE

Chives will appreciate an annual application of manure or a nitrogen-rich fertiliser in spring or summer, spread around the base of the plant. To rejuvenate them they can be cut back in winter when they start to die down. In cool climates they will die back in winter, to re-appear in spring.

HARVESTING AND STORAGE

Cut the leaves as you need them. They can be frozen.

To soften garlic chives before eating, blanch them in boiling water.

Chives are one of the *fines herbes* in French cuisine, together with tarragon, chervil and parsley.

PESTS AND DISEASES

Chives may be prone to rust. See the Pests and Diseases section.

COMPANIONS

Chives will help ward off mildew and as an insect repellant are traditionally grown under fruit trees. Carrots, onions, parsnip, strawberry and other herbs will benefit from growing with chives.

CORIANDER

Also known as Chinese parsley or cilantro, coriander (*Coriander sativum*) was found in the tombs of Tutankhamen and other Egyptian pharaohs. It is mentioned in the Bible and is one of the bitter herbs traditionally eaten at Passover. Cultivated for its foliage, roots and seeds, it is used to flavour gin.

POSITION

Coriander needs a spot in full sun with good air circulation in light fertile soil.

WHEN AND HOW TO PLANT

Coriander is best grown as a cool season crop in warm areas as it runs to seed quickly in hot weather. During summer you may need to use a shade cloth and frame to create a mini greenhouse to shade coriander.

Add some compost or manure to the soil before sowing.

As coriander seedlings tend to bolt it is better to sow seeds directly into the garden rather than transplanting seedlings. Do this from late spring to early autumn, every four weeks, for continuous supplies. Space the seeds 2.5 cm apart in a drill 2.5 cm deep. Lightly cover with

soil then water in well. Germination should take two to three weeks. You can assist germination by rubbing the seeds in your hands before sowing or soaking them in water for 24 hours.

VARIETIES

Include Spice, which is good for seeds and Santo, which is slow to bolt.

CARE AND MAINTENANCE

Weed around plants regularly. Water stress will cause coriander to bolt so ensure that they are watered regularly. Feed the plants with seaweed fertiliser or a liquid plant food every few weeks to promote growth. Coriander will benefit from a cloche or cover when the weather cools.

HARVESTING AND STORAGE

Start picking the leaves once they are large enough to encourage new growth to develop. For seeds, leave the plant to flower. Harvest the seeds when they have turned brown. Pull up the plant and hang it upside down covered with a paper bag to catch the seeds.

The flowers of coriander are good for attracting beneficial insects and are said to repel aphids. Coriander can be used in a spray to repel spider mites and aphids—boil one part coriander leaves with one part water for 10 minutes. Strain and spray.

PESTS AND DISEASES

Late crops are susceptible to mildew and fungal leaf spot. See the Pests and Diseases section for remedies.

COMPANIONS

A good companion for all brassicas and chervil, avoid planting coriander with fennel.

DILL

Below: A coriander plant left to dry in order to harvest its seeds.

From the Norse word *dylla* meaning to soothe or lull, dill (*Anethum graveolens*) was traditionally used to treat digestive disorders and flatulence, hiccups, insomnia and indigestion. It is still the main ingredient in gripe water. Indigenous to southwestern Asia and southern Europe it has been cultivated in these regions since ancient times.

POSITION

An annual plant, dill likes full sun and well-drained, moist soil.

WHEN AND HOW TO PLANT

Dill hates being transplanted so direct sowing into the open ground is the best method. Sow seeds direct in spring after the last frost and keep them moist until they germinate. Thin plants to about 45 cm apart once the seedlings appear. To get a head start, sow seeds in early spring into peat pots. Cover them with perlite or vermiculite and they should germinate in five to 10 days. Plant the entire pot into the garden when the seedling is 6 or 7 cm tall.

VARIETIES

Hercules, Tetra Leaf and Ducat are slow to bolt, strongly flavoured varieties. Dwarf varieties include Fernleaf and Bouquet. If you are growing dill for its seed try the heirloom variety Long Island Mammoth.

MAINTENANCE

Dill requires no special care, although some of the larger varieties may need staking.

HARVESTING AND STORAGE

Harvest the leaves as required. To dry them spread the leaves thinly on paper and allow to dry or microwave them to help retain their colour and fragrance. Store the dried leaves in an airtight container in a cool, dry place. Fresh leaves can also be frozen in ice cube trays. To harvest the seeds, leave the plant to flower and when the heads have dried pick them off.

PESTS AND DISEASES

None.

COMPANIONS

Another good repellant of cabbage white butterfly, dill makes a valuable addition to the vegetable patch, especially planted around cabbages.

MARJORAM AND OREGANO

Oregano (*Origanum vulgare*), also known as wild marjoram or pot marjoram, is very similar to sweet marjoram (*Origanum majorana*) but with a sharper flavour. Both are grown and propagated in the same way. Both were known in ancient Greece, where they originated, as 'Brightness of the Mountain'. Both oregano and marjoram have long folkloric histories—among other things, they were believed to be an antidote for poisons, a repellent of snakes and a balm that when put on to a loved one's grave gave peace to the departed spirit. There is an old wives' tale that if you anoint yourself with oregano before sleeping you will dream of your future spouse.

WHEN AND HOW TO PLANT

Both are perennial herbs but often grow as annuals. Oregano can be invasive so it may need to be restrained. Sow seeds in spring or autumn and space plants 20 cm apart. They grow to about 30–40 cm tall. Alternatively, buy seedlings. Both are extremely tough herbs but still like full sun in well-drained soil.

The only thing to watch is that you do not overwater once the herbs are established. In spring, cut back old growth to give the herb a new lease of life.

HARVESTING AND STORAGE

To harvest, pick the foliage fresh as you need it. The flavour of both herbs is enhanced if they are dried. Simply hang bunches in a dark warm place for several days. When dry and the leaves are crisp, rub them off the stem and store in an airtight container.

PESTS AND DISEASES

Marjoram and oregano are resistant to both pests and diseases.

COMPANIONS

Both oregano and marjoram grow as good companions to most vegetables including all brassicas, peas, carrots, silverbeet and eggplant. As they are perennial, they also sit well in a bed of asparagus.

MINT

In Greek myth, two strangers came upon a village where they were ignored by all but an elderly couple who offered them a meal. Before serving the meal, the couple rubbed the table with mint to clean it. The two strangers were the gods Zeus and Hermes in disguise. As a reward for their hospitality, the couple's home was turned into a temple. Mint went on to become a cross-cultural symbol of hospitality. The early Romans strewed banquet halls and temple floors with it and to this day in the Middle East mint tea is offered as a welcome drink.

POSITION

Mint likes a rich acidic soil, in partial shade to full shade, but what it loves most is a very damp area to grow in. As always, add compost or manure before planting.

WHEN AND HOW TO PLANT

You can buy small plants or take root or stem cuttings or divide clumps of mint from existing plants. Seeds for some varieties are available.

VARIETIES

There are some 600 varieties of this hardy perennial with a range of flavours and fragrances. They include apple, pineapple, chocolate, lime, spearmint, curly mint, peppermint, water mint and pennyroyal.

CARE AND MAINTENANCE

Mint can be invasive so you may want to grow it in pots.

Alternatively, grow mint in permeable sacks with drainage holes cut into them or in containers planted in the soil. Simply make drainage holes in the bottom of the container, fill with soil and compost so no part shows and plant the mint inside.

Cut mint to ground level in autumn and divide it every two to three years.

PESTS AND DISEASES

Some varieties are prone to a rust fungus. Remove any severely affected plants and, as a last resort spray with sulphur or zineb. See the entry on Silverbeet for dealing with rust.

Mint flea beetle can attack some bushes. The minute golden beetle causes shot-holing damage on the leaves. The leaves then look like they have been riddled by shotgun pellets. Use a chilli and garlic spray (see the Pests and Diseases section on how to make this spray), ensuring to reapply it frequently.

HARVESTING AND STORAGE

Pick mint fresh as required, or dry the leaves in a warm, airy place away from direct sunlight. Store the dried leaves in an airtight container and use as required.

COMPANIONS
Mint is a great companion to cabbages and tomatoes.

PARSLEY

Native to the Mediterranean, parsley (*Petroselinum crispum*) has been grown for more than 2000 years. The ancient Greeks used it for fodder for their chariot horses. In English folklore, parsley seeds, notoriously slow to germinate, were believed to go to the devil and back seven times before germinating. Furthermore, only the wicked, or in some folkloric legends only witches, were able to grow it.

POSITION AND SOIL PREPARATION
Parsley will grow in full sun to partial shade and is good in containers as long as they are at least 20 cm deep. It likes a well-composted, well-drained and moist soil. In acidic soil, add some lime or dolomite before planting.

WHEN TO SOW
Sow parsley in spring and summer for a summer harvest and late summer to early autumn for a winter crop, which you may need to grow under cover. Most parsley are biennials, that is, in the second year they produce flowers and seeds rather than edible leaves.

HOW TO PLANT
Parsley seed can take anywhere between three to eight weeks to germinate. With its hard outer casing it can be slow and difficult to propagate unless you soak it overnight in warm water before planting into trays. Another sowing trick is to pour boiling water over the seeds once they are in the seed drills then cover very lightly with soil.

On transplanting seedlings into the garden, space them 25 cm apart.

VARIETIES
There are several varieties of parsley including curly, Italian flatleaf and Japanese mitsuba.

CARE AND MAINTENANCE
Water parsley regularly to prevent it from bolting to flower. If flower stalks emerge cut them out to frustrate bolting. You can give parsley a boost with an application of fertiliser or liquid feed. Parsley will self-seed producing its own renewed crop. Or you can easily save seed by letting the plant go to flower and the seeds dry.

PESTS AND DISEASES
Parsley suffers from few problems. It may get a leaf miner in the foliage. Pick off the leaves with the telltale squiggly lines and destroy. Slugs love parsley so you may want to place a beer trap or a ring of used coffee grounds, sawdust or sharp sand around seedlings.

Yellowing leaves indicate a lack of water and nitrogen, give the plant a feed of a nitrogen-rich fertiliser to give it a boost.

HARVESTING AND STORAGE
Harvest leaves from around the outside of the plants leaving the new growth in the centre. To collect seed, hang bunches of ripening seed heads upside down in paper bags to dry.

dry soil. It will grow well in soil with a pH of 6–7.5. If the soil pH is below 6, add lime to the soil. Mulching with ground-up eggshells to add lime is an old-timer's trick.

Rosemary grows well in containers placed in a bright and sunny spot. As good drainage is essential, use a porous clay pot and a good potting-mix with some coarse sand added. Be careful to keep the soil moist but not wet. One trick for successfully growing rosemary in pots is to make sure that the pot is just big enough for the roots to fit.

PROPAGATION

Rosemary is easy to propagate. From early autumn to spring make a tip cutting by cutting a sprig of new growth, about 15 cm from the top of the bush. Then strip the leaves from the bottom 4 cm. Dip the tip into rooting hormone (honey does the same job) and pot it into some wet propagating sand to root. This process will usually take about six weeks.

Layering is another method of propagation— simply pin down the lower rambling branches of an existing herb to the soil until they root, and this will ultimately form a new plant.

COMPANIONS

Plant parsley with tomatoes and roses to help deter insects.

ROSEMARY

Rosemary (*Rosmarinus officinalis*) is a perennial evergreen shrub. Sometimes known as Mary's Mantle, it is said that when the Holy Family was fleeing Herod's soldiers, Mary spread her blue cloak in a field and the white flowers of rosemary turned blue in her honour. In ancient folklore, rosemary was called Elf Leaf and bunches were hung around houses to keep thieves and witches out and prevent fairies entering and stealing infants.

Rosemary is a popular remedy for combating general fatigue and depression and is said to enhance memory and concentration by increasing blood flow to the head.

POSITION AND SOIL PREPARATION

Rosemary likes full sun but will grow in semi-shade; it must, however, have excellent drainage and generally seems to grow best in light sandy,

VARIETIES

There are many different varieties of rosemary, whose form can vary from rounded bushes to prostrate or columnar. Flowers may be pale to deep blue, violet, mauve, pink or white.

Tall growing bushes include Tuscan Blue, Erectus and Portuguese Pink, semi-prostrate forms include Lockwood de Forrest, Fota Blue, Shimmering Stars and variegated leaf forms include Genges Gold and Silver Spires.

CARE AND MAINTENANCE

Give rosemary a trim before the onset of spring and after it has flowered, trimming any long and straggly branches to stimulate new growth and to shape the plant. Mulch the plant with coarse gritty sand or small pebbles as organic mulches near the stem can cause stem rot.

PESTS AND DISEASES

Overwatering rosemary may cause root rot. A browning of the root tip is a symptom of this. Rosemary can also suffer from fungal wilt. A regular light trim will help prevent this by allowing for better aeration. It can also sometimes be susceptible to infestations of scale, mealy bugs and spider mites. See the section on Pests and Diseases.

HARVESTING AND STORAGE

You can snip leaves anytime. Bunches of rosemary can be hung up to dry in a well-ventilated place. When it is completely dry, strip the leaves off the stem and store them in an airtight container.

COMPANIONS

Rosemary can be grown with parsnips and potatoes and does well with lavender planted in a border.

SAGE

Common or garden sage (*Salvia officinalis*) is native to Mediterranean regions and the Dalmatian coast. It has a long history in herbal medicine, including as an aid to reduce perspiration and menopausal hot flushes. It has a reputed ability to colour grey hair. Sage remains a popular anti-inflammatory remedy for sore throats. It is a perennial herb, growing up to 90 cm high and 50 cm wide.

POSITION AND SOIL PREPARATION

Sage will thrive in a sunny spot but will tolerate some light shade. It will grow in any soil, including sandy malnourished soil, as long as it is well drained. It prefers alkaline soil so add lime at recommended rates to acidic soil before planting.

Like most herbs, sage does well in pots. Keep it thriving by giving it a seasonal feed of compost, manure or a balanced fertiliser, or water it monthly with a compost tea and pick the leaves frequently to promote more growth. Keep the soil only slightly moist at all times although don't allow it to dry out fully.

WHEN TO PLANT

Plant sage in spring or, in early summer, propagate a cutting (see Rosemary for how). Sage can also be grown from seed.

VARIETIES

There are many varieties of sage including Common, Berggarten, Purpurea and Tricolour. Three-leafed sage is native to Greece and Turkey and Clary sage is added to liquors.

CARE AND MAINTENANCE

Sage likes a gentle pruning in spring or after flowering to encourage bushy growth and to stop it becoming woody and the leaves unpalatable. It will die back a bit in winter and the leaves will become smaller. Sage does not like heavy fertilising or overwatering. During winter mulch plants with straw or leaf mould.

Replace the plants every three to four years as the quality of the flavour starts to deteriorate.

HARVESTING AND STORAGE

Harvest fresh leaves and flowers as you need them. Leaves can be dried before flowering. Spread them out in a well-aired place to dry and store in an airtight container.

PESTS AND DISEASES

If you find caterpillars or slugs on sage pick them off by hand. Sage can be susceptible to root rot and fungal diseases.

COMPANIONS

Sage is an excellent companion for brassicas as it acts as a deterrent to cabbage white butterfly. It also grows well alongside carrots and parsnips.

TARRAGON

Cultivars of tarragon include French and Russian tarragon. French tarragon is a perennial herb once reputed to cure dragon bites. Its Latin name, *Artemisia dracunculus*, means little dragon.

Russian tarragon (*Artemisia dracunculoides*) is coarser with paler leaves and a more bitter taste, although its flavour improves the longer it is grown.

POSITION

French tarragon is cold hardy and drought-resistant. It is, however, susceptible to humidity and easily infected with fungal diseases. Therefore, it is important to avoid overhead watering. It needs full sun in cooler climates but a shady position in hot climates. To grow French tarragon in the tropics, when it is time to divide the roots refrigerate them for a couple of months before replanting. Winter tarragon is overall a better option for the tropics.

WHEN AND HOW TO PLANT

Take tip cuttings in spring and early autumn or dig up the plant and divide its roots. See Rosemary for how to propagate. Seeds can be sown directly into the garden into clumps 60 cm apart in spring or early summer.

CARE AND MAINTENANCE

In cold climates, French tarragon dies back in winter. Cut the plant to the ground after frost has killed off the top growth and mulch it well with straw or compost. It will grow back in spring. Otherwise, tarragon seems to thrive on neglect. Pick out flower buds as they appear to encourage leaves to grow.

Every two years, French tarragon needs to be lifted and the roots divided. Cut the roots into smaller clumps and replant in an enriched soil. After four years, plants need replacement as they start to lose their flavour.

PESTS AND DISEASES

Nematodes (eel worms) and fungal leaf diseases, especially rust, can be a problem. See the Pests and Diseases and Mint sections. In heavy soils, French tarragon can get root rot.

THYME

Originally a wild plant from the Mediterranean, there are an astonishing number of aromatic thyme (*Thymus vulgaris*) varieties now available. It has been used medicinally throughout the ages; indeed the highest praise one could receive in ancient Greece was 'to smell of thyme'. Pliny believed that when burnt, thyme puts to flight all venomous creatures. According to ancient Celtic folklore, a garden full of thyme will attract fairies. Thyme is a small, perennial woody herb.

POSITION

Thyme generally prefers full sunlight in well-drained soil and will tolerate dry conditions. While it will grow in any soil it prefers light, dry, even stony soil. If you have heavy soil add some sand before planting thyme.

Thyme will grow well in containers but add some sand to the potting mix to aid drainage and leave the pot to dry out between watering.

WHEN AND HOW TO PLANT

Thyme can be grown from seed sown in spring, summer or early autumn in clumps spaced 30 cm apart, but this is slow and difficult and germination is uneven. It is better to either get cuttings from someone's plant or buy small plants from a nursery.

VARIETIES

Garden or common thyme, also known as English thyme, is the principal culinary thyme. It has tiny white or lavender flowers. Varieties include Silver Posie, German thyme, winter and Provence Thyme, Black thyme, French thyme and lemon thyme which has lovely variegated lemon-scented leaves.

CARE AND MAINTENANCE

Keep thyme weed free. Trim it in spring to prevent it becoming woody and once every two or three years divide it by digging it up and cutting it into a couple of plants.

PESTS AND DISEASES

Thyme has no significant pests or diseases. However, substances leeched from the leaves of thyme inhibit surrounding plant growth and impede the growth of plants planted where thyme has previously grown. Soil will need to be fully enriched after thyme has grown in it.

COMPANIONS

Thyme is the perfect companion to lavender and is loved by bees.

GROWING FRUIT

Wherever you live in Australia you can grow fruit. Not only a step towards self-sufficiency, fruit-growing is adding something beautiful to your garden. Often spectacular trees, fruit follows highly perfumed blossoms. Fruit is, moreover, easy to grow and needs little attention once it is planted.

Fruit trees can be grown as feature trees in a garden or lawn, espaliered up a wall, trained into hedges, or can sit perfectly in large pots. All fruit trees and vines need at least six hours of sunlight a day and perfectly draining soil (see section on Irrigation and Watering). They need a soil rich in organic matter and nutrients, shelter from strong winds and a regular supply of water.

What you grow will depend on where you live. Some fruit trees, namely the deciduous ones like apples and stone fruit, need a cold winter with a specific number of 'chill hours' where the temperature gets below 7°C. Others have a 'low chill' and will grow in the subtropics. Fruit like mango, avocado and pawpaw need a subtropical or tropical climate.

How many trees you grow will depend not only on space but also on whether they need a cross-pollinator. Most apples, plums and cherries are not self-fertile and so another compatible variety will be required. Apricot, peach (except JH Hale), nectarines and mango as well as all citrus are self-fertile.

> Thought is the blossom, language the
> bud, action the fruit behind.
> ~Ralph Waldo Emerson

FRUIT FOR SMALL GARDENS

Even in a small garden you can grow fruit. Strawberries can be used as a ground cover, while rhubarb can be slotted in amongst the roses. Citrus trees are small and compact, while dwarf forms of many fruit trees can be purchased, including nectazee nectarines, pixee peaches and pinkabelle apples. These trees can grow in any small nook or in a large pot on a balcony. Trees can be fanned or espaliered. Multigraft trees, with several varieties of a fruit on the one tree, can be bought, or even ordinary trees can be kept small by giving them a good prune in summer.

ESPALIERED TREES

To grow an espaliered tree you are looking to flatten or fan the tree against an, ideally north-facing, wall or fence. This is done by evenly spacing the horizontal branches of the tree along a wire support attached to the wall. On planting, prune any branches that grow away from or towards the wall. Tie the remaining side branches to the wires. As the tree grows continue to tie the branches to the wires. Pinch out the tips of branches when they are big enough and rub off with your fingers any new shoots that grow outwards. In summer, this will need to be done every few weeks.

CONTAINERS

Fruit trees will grow well in large pots. Buy a tree grafted onto a dwarfing rootstock. Make sure to use a good-quality potting mix and add a couple of shovel loads of manure or compost and cocopeat if you have some to help retain moisture. Vigilance is needed in summer to keep the pot well watered and may mean watering it twice a day in some areas. If the tree gets too big give it a good prune during summer and try weighing down the branches by tying a weight to them to restrict growth.

BUYING A FRUIT TREE

Fruit trees are either deciduous or evergreen. The former are generally sold and planted during winter as bare-rooted trees and include apples, pears, cherries, figs, plums, apricots, almonds, walnuts and mulberries. 'Bare-rooted' simply means the trees are delivered to nurseries in batches that have been dug up from the ground in which they have grown. They will not be potbound as they have grown up in the ground. So when buying, the most important thing to check is the roots. Ensure that they are not broken and that the fine hair-like roots are healthy. The branches are not so important at this stage, in fact if you are not confident with pruning it is a good idea to ask the nursery staff to prune the tree for planting. The other thing to check is the graft. Make sure that this is strong and knitted together.

Evergreen fruit trees are sold in pots and include all citrus, olives and guavas. When buying, check that roots aren't growing through the pot or have been cut off. Don't buy any tree with lots of flowers or tiny fruit on it, as this is actually a sign of stress.

PLANTING A FRUIT TREE

It is best to prepare the ground for a fruit tree several weeks before you are ready to buy and plant it.

First, dig a hole up to 1 metre in diameter. The hole needs to be about 40 cm deep, going down into the subsoil. Soak it with water.

Secondly, into the soil you have dug out, mix a couple of buckets full of compost and, if you have any, some cocopeat. Don't add manure or fertiliser to this as it can burn the roots. If your soil is acidic, mix in a couple of handfuls

of dolomite or lime. Thirdly, drive two or three stakes into the outside perimeter of the hole.

To plant the tree, fill the hole with half of the soil mix and make a mound, so that it is at a depth where the top of the pot is level with the ground, or that the bare roots are comfortably spread over the mound and the graft is well above the soil level. If it is a tree that has grown in a pot, tease the roots out with your fingers. Fill the hole with the soil and give the tree a little shake up and down so that the soil filters around the roots. Secure the tree to the stakes using a soft tree tie in a figure-eight pattern around the stakes and trunk. Tread softly around the base of the tree, then spread some manure around the surface (not letting it touch the trunk) and then mulch with straw or hay to about 10 cm deep and give it a long, good watering.

If the nursery has not pruned the new bare-rooted tree for you then you will need to give it a prune.

PRUNING

Most fruit trees will produce some fruit whether they are pruned or not. The aim of pruning is to make the tree a manageable size and to assist the tree to produce a good-sized fruit. Essentially, deciduous fruit trees will need to be pruned when they are planted and again during their first winter and then again in their second winter to get the structure you want. Additional pruning thereafter will be more cosmetic and aim to increase the fruiting wood. To prune you will need a set of secateurs and loppers or a pruning saw, which need to be kept clean to prevent transferring diseases between trees.

The best shape for a fruit tree is one that is vase-like or open in the centre so light can get in. With your newly planted tree you now need to prune the main central limb till it is just above the first or lowest branch you chose to keep. Next look for three to four strong branches, coming out from the trunk, which will form the vase shape. Cut these back to one-third of their length. Then cut back all long spindly growths and cut off all other branches.

Pruning after the first year

The shoot on the end of each tip is called the terminal. This never fruits so is best cut off after five or six buds. Cut at an angle after the bud.

The branch that comes off the side of the shoot at an angle between 30 and 60 degrees is the lateral. This is the branch that develops the fruiting spurs for the next season. It needs to be left on the tree. The stubby growths are called the fruiting spurs. This is where the current season's fruit will develop.

Trees can also be trained into a pyramid shape. On planting, if you haven't bought a tree with a single leader only, the prune is radical. Cut all of the branches off and prune the remaining 'central leader' (that is the upright main branch) so it is one metre tall. In the following winter, select four main branches and remove all others. Prune the branches so that the lower ones are longer than the higher ones. In the following years select lateral branches one metre above the first branches to keep, and prune off the others.

After establishing the tree's shape, other than removing dead wood, cherries and plums need no other pruning. Apricots benefit from a summer prune after harvest as spurs bear for only a couple of years. Peach and nectarines need regular pruning as they fruit on the previous season's growth. The pruning here simply means cutting away about 50 per cent of the

1. Cut the main central limb to just above the first branch.

2. Choose three or four strong branches and cut back by one-third.

3. Cut off all other branches.

4. A vase-shaped tree.

previous year's growth and cutting off weak side-shoots.

Remove any old or dead wood that's cluttering the tree to encourage new growth. Apples and pears will thereafter simply need their side shoots shortened to leave three to four buds. Or simply tie down the vigorous growth so that it is horizontal.

To protect the tree from diseases make sure to cut out and dispose of any old rotten fruit and to compost the prunings.

PROTECTING FRUIT

Fruit, especially berries, will often require protection from possums, flying foxes, rats, mice and birds. Covering the crop with bird netting that reaches all the way down to the ground is often unavoidable. Some gardeners have had success with sonic and ultrasonic devices that emit the distress calls of target species.

Fruit bags and exclusion bags can be hung on ripening fruit. The traditional methods of visual deterrents like hanging shiny objects (old CDs are excellent these days) and fake owls, or wind chimes in the trees are worth a try.

A piece of smooth plastic sheeting tied around the trunk of the tree will make it impossible for possums to climb up.

HARVESTING FRUIT

Most stonefruits need to be left on the tree until they have ripened; harvest when they have changed colour and pass a taste test. Most apples will continue to sweeten after they have been picked. As a general rule, if fruit comes easily away from the stalk it is ready. Pears need to be harvested while they are still hard and left at room temperature inside for a couple of days before eating. Pick citrus when it is ready; don't leave it hanging on the tree.

STORING FRUIT

Some years will see a bumper crop and fruit might need to be stored, bottled, dried, frozen or made into jam. While apples and pears can be stored fresh for a number of months—as long as they are somewhere cold—other fruits can't. Apricots can be halved, stoned and placed in the sun to dry, but make sure they are covered at night. European plums, figs, cherries and berries can all be preserved. Otherwise, fruit is best enjoyed straight off the tree, warmed from the sun.

In an orchard there should be enough to eat, enough to lay up, enough to be stolen and enough to rot on the ground.
~James Borwell, 1740–1795

APPLES

Apples (*Malus domestica*) are beautiful deciduous trees with soft, pink buds opening to white flowers in spring. They are tough trees that generally love cool climates. Low chill varieties have been bred to tolerate milder climates. Most varieties are self-sterile and so you will need to plant at least two. They won't grow in the tropics. The domesticated apple has been traced to the wild fruit forests of the Tien Shan mountains of Kazakhstan. From there it journeyed, after the horse was domesticated, along the Silk Road to the West 7000 years ago. Apples were fed to the horses whose digestive systems were unable to digest the seeds. The apple soon spread across the world developing into 20,000 different varieties.

Note: Pear trees have the same requirements as apples.

POSITION

Best grown in an open site in full sun, apples will tolerate some shade. On windy sites they will need protection, like a windbreak. Most full-grown varieties will reach 6 to 8 m, although many varieties are available grafted onto dwarfing or semi-dwarfing rootstock. These take up little space and are easily trained as freestanding dwarf pyramid trees or espaliers. This reduces the mature size of the tree (usually up to a half) while allowing the fruit to remain full-sized.

Good air-circulation is critical to help reduce the incident of fungal diseases such as blackspot and powdery mildew.

VARIETIES

Apples can be early and late fruiting. Many heirlooms are available and, while most varieties require a cold winter, there are some varieties with a 'low chill' requirement and so are suited to the subtropics and warmer regions.

Most apples are not self-pollinating and will need a cross-pollinator. This means you need to grow at least two different varieties, which are compatible with one another and flower at the same time so insects can facilitate cross-pollination. Bonza, Fuji, Granny Smith, Kingston Black, Pinkabelle, Pink Lady, Red Delicious and Royal Gala all pollinate with Jonathon or other apples pollinated by Jonathon. Ornamental crab apples are small and will pollinate most apple trees, to a degree.

Self-pollinating apples include Beauty of Bath and Lord Lambourne. Partially self-pollinating trees include Golden Delicious and Jonathon.

Varieties suitable to subtropical climates with 'low chill' requirements include Tropical Anna, Tropical Sweet, Tropical Beauty and Golden Dorset, which all cross-pollinate with each other.

For small areas, Ballerina is a columnar-shaped apple that has a narrow, upright habit and is partially self-pollinating. Multigrafted trees are also good for small places. These are trees that have been grafted with two compatible cross-pollinating varieties. Dwarf varieties can also be purchased. Another space-saving trick is to plant two compatible bare-rooted trees in the one hole, placing the trunks side-by-side. Over time they will naturally graft onto each other and the competition between the trees is naturally dwarfing.

trim any circling roots with secateurs. Soak the roots in a bucket of very weak liquid seaweed for half an hour. Dig a hole and form a mound of soil and compost at the base of the hole. Put in a stake if necessary. Spread the roots evenly over the mound, making sure that the graft union remains above the soil level. Do not add fertiliser or manure to the hole, as it will burn the roots. Backfill the hole with soil and compost and then water it in with some liquid seaweed. Lastly, mulch around it being careful not to touch the trunk with mulch. The tree will need no extra fertilising until after the new leaves have formed.

PRUNING AND SHAPING

See the introduction of this section for general information on pruning and shaping fruit trees.

What you need to know before pruning apple trees is that most apples bear fruit on the short stubs, called spurs, which grow along old wood. Do not prune these off. Prune off any new shoots growing upwards, old or weak shoots, dead or diseased wood and old fruiting spurs. Then cut back last season's growth by two-thirds.

Bear in mind that apple trees won't suffer from neglect if you leave them alone.

To increase the size of fruit you can thin the small fruitlets (the clusters of four to five small fruits) from mid November on, leaving one per cluster.

WATERING AND FEEDING

In the summer months, water is critical to the development of the fruit and the trees will need a deep watering once a fortnight. In mid spring mulch thickly to beyond the drip line with compost, manure, organic fertiliser or worm castings and mulch over this with thick straw. Apple trees will benefit from a yearly application of gypsum for calcium and a dose of rock dust or trace elements. In the early years, keep weeds under control as they compete for nutrients. Grass can be allowed to grow up to the trunk of well-established standard trees.

If the tree is looking unwell, feed it with well-rotted manure or compost in early spring.

PREPARING THE SOIL

Apples need free-draining soil. They will tolerate a wide range of soil pH but prefer a pH of 6.5. If the soil is not very fertile choose an apple with a more vigorous rootstock.

It is always best to prepare the soil at least several weeks before planting by adding as much decomposed organic matter to the site as you have. This gives the soil time to break down the newly incorporated organic matter.

PURCHASING AND PLANTING

Apples are best planted during late autumn and winter while they are leafless and dormant. They can be purchased bare rooted or in pots. If the tree is to be freestanding, choose one that has multiple well-spaced branches. If you are going to espalier the tree against a wall choose one with a single leader.

Full-sized apple trees will need 4 metres between them, while dwarfs need 2 metres and Ballerinas can be planted even closer together.

To plant bare-rooted apples, remove compost from around the roots and trim any damaged ones. With potted trees tease out or

HARVEST

Apple harvest is from autumn to early winter. Full-sized trees will be ready for their first harvest three years after planting, dwarfs bear a little quicker. Peak production is reached after five to six years. Apples should crop for generations.

When the colour is rich and full and a few have fallen off the tree the apples are ready to harvest. Test this by gently lifting and twisting the fruit. If it comes away easily it is ready to harvest. Apples can be left on the tree to ripen.

PESTS, DISEASES AND PROBLEMS

Despite the following list most apples go on cropping prolifically year after year.

If the leaves have a black spot on them and there are black lesions on the fruit the tree may be suffering from blackspot or apple scab, a fungus that causes the leaves and fruit to fall. Rake up all fallen leaves and fruit as they contain over-wintering spores that will reinfect the tree. Mulch around the tree and spray it with copper hydroxide or activated potassium bicarbonate spray. Remove all mummified apples left on the tree after leaf fall, as these will cause re-infection, mulch and give the tree seaweed sprays.

White woolly patches are a kind of aphid and can be removed by soap spray or brushed off. Nasturtiums grown under the tree are said to hinder aphids.

The fungus, powdery mildew, looks like whitish-grey talc on the foliage and fruit. The fruit develops yellowish wavy patterns on the skin. In winter prune off any shoots that look dried out. For worse attacks you may need to use a sulphur spray.

Codling moths are small brown moths whose larvae burrow into fruit leaving little holes. The larvae pupate in white cocoons on or under the tree bark. If they are a problem in your area, in late spring hang sticky pheromone traps or wrap cloth or corrugated cardboard around the tree's trunk. Remove any cocoons. Trichogramma wasps are a biological control that can be brought in or try oil sprays to suffocate the egg and larvae. Exclusion fruit bags placed over the individual fruits are another way to protect them. Insect lights can also be used to attract the moths away.

Light brown apple moths feed on leaves and the surface of fruit. Sticky pheromone traps are a control. Hand removing the larvae and using exclusion bags over developing fruit will also help prevent outbreaks.

If fruit fly is a problem in your area, particularly in Queensland and New South Wales, then you must take early action. It is illegal not to. See the Pests and Diseases section for methods of dealing with it.

STORAGE

Apples will store for many months in the fridge or a cool dark cellar or shed in slatted boxes or vegetable crates or on shelves. Lay them in a single layer not touching each other, or individually wrap each in a sheet of newspaper or tissue. Polythene bags with small holes made in them will also keep apples fresh.

WHAT TO GROW UNDER APPLE TREES

Chives and other alliums and penstemon growing nearby are traditionally grown to deter pests. Stinging nettles nearby benefit the tree. Nasturtiums will help hinder aphids.

Flowers that will attract natural predators include gaillardias, phacelia, poached egg flower and lovage.

BERRIES

People have consumed wild berries since the Neolithic period. The Romans took cultivated raspberries to England and during the Middle Ages blackberries were used to make wine and blue dye. Medicinally, raspberry, particularly the leaves, was used in tisanes and teas for menstrual cramps and digestive problems. In medieval Germany, tying a piece of raspberry cane to a bewitched horse was thought to help tame it. Most berries like a cool winter, but will do well in all cool and temperate zones.

Care needs to be taken with blackberries. They are invasive and have been declared a noxious weed in most states. Blackberries need careful management to make sure they don't take over the garden.

RASPBERRIES

Raspberries (*Rubus idaeus)* are a member of the rose family.

They grow on long arching canes or stems and so are known as cane fruit. They are easy to grow and not particularly fussy.

POSITION AND PREPARATION

Raspberries prefer a slightly acidic well-draining soil that has been heavily enriched with compost or manure or blood and bone. If your soil is alkaline add iron chelates or sulphur before planting. What they are fussy about is having a support to grow up. A trellis or fence with three horizontal wires run along it will work. A simple support made from two posts or star pickets with two or three horizontal wires attached so the canes can be tied to the wires is easy to construct.

PLANTING AND HARVESTING

Plant canes in rows in autumn or winter in full sun. Constructing a ridge of soil 15 cm high, to plant along, will help drainage. Space the canes about 30 cm apart, with 1.5 m between rows.

You can harvest raspberries from summer to autumn by growing early, mid and late season cultivars. They can continue to crop for years.

CARE AND MAINTENANCE

Very little fertilising is needed for raspberries but heavy mulching with straw, hay and a and a layer of manure or compost is required. Water raspberries in hot dry weather.

The only thing you need to know about berries is that the new season's fruit will develop on canes produced in the previous season. At the end of harvesting you need to cut off at ground level all of the canes that had fruit on them. What will remain are the new young canes, which have grown at the base of each plant during spring and summer. Pull these to one side and tie them in a loose bundle. In winter, tie these onto the trellis, either individually or in bunches. If they are too tall bend the tops over and tie them onto the top of the trellis or cut them off. Beware that birds find berries irresistible and so the plants will need to be covered with bird netting as the fruit ripens.

BRAMBLEBERRIES – BLACKBERRIES, LOGANBERRIES, BOYSENBERRIES, ETC

Blackberries, loganberries, boysenberries, youngberries and silvanberries, among many others, are all known as brambles, although as most also grow on upright stems they are planted and grown like raspberries. They do, however, need about 1.5 metres between them.

CARE AND MAINTENANCE

All berries need to be kept weed free and well mulched. In spring, a light watering with two teaspoons of Epsom salts and two teaspoons of potash in a watering can will help with disease resistance. Berries may also need some protection, with a shade cloth, from hot afternoon sun.

PESTS, DISEASES AND PROBLEMS

Berries can become infected with the fungal disease botrytis that causes the fruit to turn grey and rot. To try to prevent this Bordeaux, a copper sulphate solution acceptable to organic gardeners, can be sprayed onto the dormant canes in winter. Sawfly caterpillars can also be a problem evidenced by chewed leaves. Spray the leaves with an horticultural soap.

BLUEBERRIES

Blueberries (*Vaccinium cyanococcus*) are native to North America where the Native Americans ate them fresh or dried all year round. They were so fundamental to their diet that they were attributed magical powers by most American tribes. Legend had it that during the time of starvation the Great Spirit sent these 'starberries' (so called for the star-shaped pattern on top of each berry—the base of its earlier flower) down from heaven to relieve the hunger of his children. During the American Civil War, blueberries were canned for the first time and fed to the Union Army. Blueberries are easy to grow in Australia; the only care that needs to be taken is to find a cultivar suitable to your area and to maintain a moist, acidic soil.

POSITION AND SOIL PREPARATION

Blueberries need a loose, friable, freely draining soil but will grow in full sun or part shade. They are an attractive flowering bush and can easily be grown amongst your flower garden or as a border plant. If you do not have an acid soil with a pH between 4.5 and 5.5 then blueberries should be grown in a large pot using a potting mix made

for azaleas and camellias. In the USA, commercial growers incorporate peatmoss into the soil when planting blueberries to help acidify it.

Before planting a blueberry bush incorporate as much organic matter as possible into the soil. It is advisable to add peatmoss, powdered sulphate and iron chelates at recommended rates as well. Mulch each plant preferably with pine or she-oak needles, sawdust or composted bark, which are all excellent acidifiers of soil.

VARIETIES

Northern Highbush is a cultivar suitable for cool temperate climates, while Southern Highbush and Rabbiteye are suitable for cool and warm temperate climates and the subtropics. Rabbiteye will need a cross-pollinator planted nearby. The other varieties are self-fertile but will generally fruit better if grown with a different variety. Space plants 1.5 m apart.

CARE AND MAINTENANCE

Blueberries need to be kept moist and weed-free. They are notoriously sensitive to salt and if possible it is advisable to water them with rainwater. They will crop two years after being planted.

Like all fruit they benefit from pruning and, like fruit trees, are best pruned into an open vase shape. Cut out branches that cross over others or touch the soil and after four years prune off any branches that no longer carry fruit. During spring mulch the plants with a 4 cm thick mulch of poultry manure.

HARVESTING

Blueberries do not sweeten after picking. The fruit takes a couple of weeks to ripen on the bush so leave the harvest until they are deep blue and come away easily. Like all berries they will need some form of netting to keep birds away.

CITRUS

Most citrus originated in Southeast Asia 4000 years ago. Oranges and lemons were introduced into Australia with the First Fleet in 1788. The citrus trees, together with other fruit trees, were procured in Rio de Janeiro and the Cape of Good Hope. Of course, it was the citrus fruit that Captain Arthur Phillip took with him on the voyage to Port Jackson that virtually eliminated scurvy—and lent the appellation 'limey' to British sailors.

All citrus trees are relatively easy to grow and have the added benefit of beautifully fragrant flowers. Citrus is excellent in large pots or can be grown as standard trees, dwarf trees or espaliered against walls.

BUYING A CITRUS TREE

Citrus trees are generally bought in pots and are available year round. You can plant them at any time of the year in temperate and tropical climates. In cooler climates the best time to plant is in spring.

When buying your tree don't buy a plant with a large number of mature or immature fruit. Masses of blooms and tiny fruits indicate that the tree is under stress and has been over-fertilised, is pot bound or neglected. These trees often remain stunted. If there is any fruit on the new tree remove it as you are planting it.

VARIETIES

In frost-free areas all varieties of citrus can be grown. Many are, however, frost tender and care needs to be taken to select a variety that is tolerant of frost.

Lemons are the most popular backyard citrus trees. In cooler areas, choose a frost resistant Meyer. In other areas Lisbon will grow into a large tree and Eureka will crop all year.

If planting an orange, Lane's Late Navel is quite frost-hardy. Joppa is a variety that came with the First Fleet. Valencia is frost sensitive.

More unusual citrus includes Seville or sour orange for marmalade making, Chinotto, another sour orange, Lemonade which is eaten fresh or used to make lemonade, Arnold Blood

Orange, Tangelo, a cross between a mandarin and grapefruit, Calamondin, a cross between a mandarin and cumquat and Pomelo, a little like a grapefruit.

Limes to consider include Tahitian limes, which can be grown in cooler districts, Kusaie and Rangpur limes. Kaffir lime is grown for its leaves and prefers the subtropics.

Wheeny and Marsh are common varieties of grapefruit. Wheeny is good for cool districts. For mandarins, an Imperial will grow in cool districts if provided with early frost protection, while Emperor and Honey Murcott (a cross with an orange) are good for warmer areas.

WHERE TO PLANT AND SOIL TYPE

For citrus trees to thrive the location and soil need to be right. They all require a warm, sheltered position in full sun and extremely well-draining soil. Citrus must be sheltered from strong winds as these are devastating to them. Any wind will seriously impede bees from pollinating the flowers. In coastal districts, to shelter them from salt-laden winds plant your citrus in a sunny corner close to a wall or provide a windbreak. Regularly wash the foliage to remove any salt. If you live in an area

with heavy frost, citrus will need to be provided with some protection from it.

The soil needs to be slightly acidic, with a pH of 6–8. If your soil is alkaline (with a pH of over 8) iron and other nutrients are not available to the tree. To acidify the soil water in iron chelates during spring and apply sulphur at recommended rates.

Citrus trees must have good drainage. Heavy clay soils and soils that remain saturated for several weeks after rain cause the feeder roots to rot and the eventual death of the tree. In poorly draining soils grow your tree in a pot or in a raised bed.

All citrus can be grown in large pots. Make sure to use a good quality potting mix and place the pot in a sunny protected position. You can buy some varieties that have been grafted onto dwarf rootstock, otherwise the pot itself acts as a dwarfing mechanism. Make sure to feed potted citrus every six weeks with a complete fertiliser or compost tea.

Before planting, dig lots of compost into the soil. See the section on Planting a Fruit Tree. After planting, mulch around the tree, making sure that mulch does not touch the trunk. Mulching with well-rotted manure is a good way to slowly feed the tree.

FEEDING

All citrus trees are heavy feeders—they need regular doses of nitrogen-rich fertiliser if they are to fruit well and sustain growth. They also benefit from an annual application of trace elements.

As a rule of thumb, fertilise the tree with a citrus or complete fertiliser around the drip line when the new spring growth appears, feed again monthly until the tree starts flowering and then stop until the fruit is setting. Always water the tree before and after fertilising.

Citrus trees will also benefit from an application of chicken or cow manure a few times a year. Potash, wood ash and liquid seaweed are also excellent to give citrus a boost.

PRUNING

All citrus responds well to pruning, but it is not essential. Citrus will often produce a new crop of flowers while fruit is still hanging on the tree. This should not stop pruning when it is needed. Once the danger of frost has passed in spring cut off any dead and diseased wood, any branches that touch the ground and any branches that cross or rub against one another. Citrus, lemons in particular, develop congested canopies over time. These will need a prune as any congestion can aggravate diseases and pests. Pruning forces the tree to form the new shoots on which the fruit forms.

Every few years radical pruning or skeletonising will reinvigorate citrus trees. Cut off all small branches and twigs until there are only a few bare branches left. Water the pruned tree heavily.

CARE GUIDE

Make sure to regularly water citrus throughout summer, especially from the time the flowers bud until the fruit is set. If the tree is allowed to dry out at any stage the fruit may drop off or split. Citrus is shallow rooted so make sure to mulch around it with a layer of compost and/or manure in spring, keeping the mulch well away from the trunk. This helps to retain moisture around the root zone and helps prevent the fruit splitting.

Don't plant around the base of citrus trees. They are shallow-rooted and other plants will compete for water and nutrients and may encourage potentially fatal stem rot diseases.

Above: Citrus displaying telltale signs of an iron deficiency.

For the first two years cut off all of the fruit as it forms so that the tree can develop a strong framework without diverting energy into producing fruit. Even with mature trees if a crop is particularly heavy thin or cut out some of the young fruit so the plant does not exhaust itself.

HARVESTING

Colour is no indication that citrus is ready to harvest. The best way to tell is by picking a piece and tasting it. To pick, use secateurs or your hand to twist and flick it off the stem. The longer on the tree the sweeter citrus will usually be, with the exception of mandarins.

Some varieties of lemon have thick pithy skins. If the fruit is placed in a box and covered for a couple of weeks the skins will get thinner and the flesh juicier.

PESTS, DISEASES AND PROBLEMS

Scale is a common pest on citrus. A sap-sucking insect, scale looks like minute brown or white lumps attached to the leaves, stems and fruit. Scale is often accompanied by a black fungus called sooty mould, which grows in the honeydew secreted by the scale. Ants are attracted to the honeydew and actively farm the scale for its production. They then spread the scale from plant to plant. To stop scale the movement of ants up and down the tree trunk needs to be halted. Do this by putting a grease barrier such as Vaseline, pawpaw ointment or a horticultural glue around the trunk. If an infestation is only small try rubbing off the scale with your fingers or hosing it off, otherwise apply an horticultural oil spray.

Fruit fly can be a problem. See Pests and Diseases section for ways of dealing with them.

Silver trails across leaves that then curl are caused by the citrus leaf miner, prevalent in late summer and early autumn. It is less important on mature trees as predators keep larvae in check, however, significant damage can be done to young trees. Use a horticultural oil spray to deter the moth from laying its eggs. Trim and destroy leaves with silver markings.

Bronze orange bugs or stinkbugs suck sap from the stem and fruit causing it to drop. You can pick out the bugs or shake the tree and they should drop off. Look for egg masses and squash them. Treating the tree with a horticultural oil spray in winter helps reduce populations.

The spined citrus bug is a little green bug that pierces the rind of fruit causing it to drop. Curling and chewed leaves are also symptoms. Pick off clusters of the bugs in winter and squash them or spray with pest oil.

The leaves of citrus may turn yellow. If the new leaves yellow first followed by the older foliage yellowing, the tree has a magnesium deficiency. Rectify this by watering the tree with two teaspoons of Epsom salts to 4.5 litres of water and reapply in a month's time if leaves are still yellow. If older leaves yellow the tree has a nitrogen deficiency. Apply a fertiliser high in nitrogen. If the old leaves yellow first followed by the new leaves also turning yellow or the leaves turn yellow with green veins, the tree has an iron deficiency. This is common in places with alkaline soil, like Adelaide. Water in or spray iron chelates at the recommended rates on the pack. After three weeks reapply if the leaves have not changed to green.

Most citrus dislike the cold and it's not uncommon for leaves—particularly on lemons and grapefruit—to turn to yellow in winter. A complete fertiliser at the first sign of growth in spring remedies this.

Citrus that produces masses of flowers and tiny fruit that drop off is generally stressed by neglect, or over-watering, over-fertilising or may be potbound if it is in a pot. Cut off all blossoms and fruit and prune any dead branches. Remove all new flower buds as they appear until the plant starts to grow new branches and leaves.

FIG

Known as the 'tree of life', the fig is one of the oldest domesticated trees. It was, of course, the fig leaf that Adam and Eve used as loin cloths after tasting the forbidden fruit from the Tree of Knowledge. Ancient Egyptians are recorded destroying the fig trees of their enemies, while Roman armies marched on a diet of dried figs. The fig, *Ficus Carica*, is a deciduous, large sub-tropical tree, which will grow well almost anywhere in Australia, apart from the tropics.

POSITION

Figs are tolerant of a wide range of soils, although prefer an alkaline one with an ideal pH of 6 to 7.5. If your soil is acidic, add lime before planting and reapply annually. Figs thrive in dry, hot areas but will also grow well in areas with a cool winter. They prefer full sun and require good drainage as they will not tolerate wet feet. Figs have reasonably shallow roots, but these spread quite far and so will compete with other trees planted nearby. Care needs to be taken not to cultivate around the roots.

VARIETIES

There are four types of figs. For the backyard, the common or Adriatic fig is the best choice as it is self-fertile. Varieties are either dark or light skinned. Black Genoa is a purple-skinned fig and good to eat fresh. Brown Turkey is harvested over a longer period and has brown skin. Of the light-skinned varieties Preston's Prolific is a cultivar from Victoria with thick, creamy skin and White Adriatic has a yellowish green skin and is good to eat fresh or dried.

San Pedro and Smyrna figs require pollination but not in the usual way, by wind or bees. Instead, they require a fig wasp from a Capri fig tree to pollinate them. This tiny wasp

lays it eggs in the fruit of the Capri fig and, covered in pollen, crawls into the San Pedro or Smyrna fig, whose flowers are enclosed within the fruit, and pollinates them. This was known to the ancients and is called caprification. Symrna figs enjoy a reputation for being the best-flavoured fig, particularly the cultivar Spanish Dessert, but you will need to grow the inedible Capri fig as well, to get fruit. So, if space is an issue, grow a common fig.

CARE AND MAINTENANCE

The fig is a deciduous tree and, like all deciduous trees, is best planted in winter. They require very little care. Mulch around the roots to help protect its shallow roots and the tree will benefit from a complete fertiliser or feed of manure every winter.

While figs like drier conditions than most fruit, they still require regular and consistent watering during fruit development. A good watering once a week should suffice in most areas.

Pruning

Usually when you buy a fig tree it will be a single stem. Depending on the height you may need to head it, or cut it off. Do this if it is any higher than 60 cm high. It will start to grow its branches as the season progresses. Select three or four of these to form the framework of the tree and cut off any others. Shorten the selected branches to allow further branches to develop. The tree should start to crop after two to three years.

Before pruning, you need to understand how the fruit of the fig develops. Figs are unusual in that they often produce two crops each season. The fruit sets on both the new and old wood and develops in the axils of the leaves. The first crop is called the breba crop. It develops on wood from the previous season and is harvested in early summer. The second or main crop sets on the new season wood and matures in late summer and autumn. In winter, a light prune will help to stimulate new wood growth. Every three years, a heavier prune will encourage the main crop. Always prune off diseased, overlapping and broken branches.

PROPAGATING

Figs are easy to propagate. In winter, take a 30 to 40 cm hardwood cutting and put it in a pot of coarse sand or sawdust, making sure to bury a couple of the nodes. In early autumn, transfer it to a pot of propagating mix until it takes root and after that plant it in the ground.

HARVESTING

Harvest figs once they begin to droop on the branch. This indicates full ripeness. Harvest them with a slight twist and then pull. The latex from the tree may cause skin irritation and so gloves might be required.

To dry figs, let them fully ripen and then spread them in the sun, turning frequently. Take them in at night. They may need a couple of days. Figs can also be dried in an oven on 130°C, with the door left open.

PESTS, DISEASES AND PROBLEMS

Figs are generally hardy, trouble-free trees. They can, however, be plagued by a few problems. If the fruit prematurely drops, the tree is most probably stressed. A lack of water may be the cause or a sharp, cool change in the weather.

If the fig is a Smyrna and is not pollinated, the fruit will abort and drop. Yellow leaves or the fruit failing to ripen also indicates the tree is stressed, either from too much or not enough water and a lack of nutrients. Ensure the tree is given a fruit and flower fertiliser or a good dose of manure annually.

Root knot nematodes can damage the roots, especially on sandy soils. The tree, particularly a young one, becomes stunted and yellows. There is nothing to be done but pull up the tree and grow a crop of marigolds or mustard as a bio-fumigant.

If you live in a fruit fly region, the usual precautions must be taken. See the Pests and Diseases section at the back of the book.

The fig blister mite is a whitish mite that enters the eye of the still-green fruit, causing rust-coloured dry patches. Throw out infected fruit. Use a horticultural oil or sulphur spray in autumn.

Powdery yellow-orange spots on the leaves that gradually enlarge, followed by leaf fall is usually fig rust. When the tree is dormant it will need to be sprayed with a copper-based fungicide. To prevent further outbreaks, take care to water the roots of the tree and not the foliage, and prune the tree to allow for better air circulation.

Anthracnose is a fungal disease affecting figs grown in coastal areas and humid conditions. Small brown and black spots grow into larger 'target' spots and the tree loses its leaves. Again, a copper-based fungicide is the only prevention.

Make sure to clean up all infected leaves and disinfect all garden tools.

Fig mosaic is a viral disease that causes a mottled pattern on the leaves and the eventual stunting of the tree. There is no cure and the tree will need to be removed.

MANGO

The mango (*Mangifera indica*) will grow in tropical and subtropical areas and may be grown in warmer areas if care is taken against frost at flowering time in spring. Mangoes are native to the Indian subcontinent where they are still revered both by Buddhists and Hindus.

Buddha is believed to have meditated under a mango tree and at Shravasti in India is said to have performed the instantaneous creation of a mango tree from a seed. In the Hindu religion, the mango tree is said to be a transformation of Prajapati, the Lord of Creatures. The leaves are used to decorate wedding rooms, as they are believed to symbolise fertility.

Mangoes and avocados are planted and cared for in the same way.

POSITION

Mangoes are large, evergreen trees that will cast a deep shade. They need all day sun in a sheltered position. For a good crop they must have a dry winter to initiate flowering, a lot of water in summer after the fruit has set and then another dry period for the fruit to mature.

Mangoes (and avocados) are not fussy about soil and, if anything, do better in soil that is not too rich. They are self-fertile.

VARIETIES

With some cultivars, Nam Doc Mai and Kensington for example, it is possible to germinate your own seedlings. Take the seed from a fully ripe fruit, place it in a pot with a mix of sand and peat moss and keep moist. Several shoots should appear. Pinch out all but the strongest and transplant the seedling when it is 20 to 30 cm tall.

Buying a grafted tree on dwarfing rootstock is probably the better option, however, as mangoes can grow up to 40 m tall. There are some 50 cultivars in Australia, the best known of which is the Kensington or Bowen mango. Glenn, Kasturi, and Tommy Atkins are others.

CARE AND MAINTENANCE

As mangoes can become very large, they need to be pruned to five to 10 main branches in the early years with a single trunk 1 to 2 m high. Thereafter they should not need any pruning, other than taking off diseased or overcrowded branches.

The tree needs only a small amount of a complete or organic fertiliser in summer when the fruit starts to form and again after harvest. Like all fruit trees, they benefit from about 10 cm of deep mulch that does not touch the stem.

The tree can be coaxed into producing more fruit by cincturing the branches. Choose a few main limbs and cut away a 3 mm-wide ring of bark right down to the hardwood. This upsets the flow of sap and forces the tree to initiate flowering above the cincture point.

HARVESTING

Mangoes are ready to pick when they are yellow or orange and smell sweet. They continue to ripen after picking.

The sap of the mango contains urushiol, a poison, which can cause dermatitis in some people.

Mangoes can be sliced or pureed and frozen.

PESTS, DISEASES AND PROBLEMS

Fruit fly can be a problem and in some areas baiting and spraying for it is mandatory. See Apples for notes on fruit fly.

The most common disease is anthracnose, a fungus that causes black spots on the fruit and leaves. Keep the tree healthy with mulches of compost and spray seaweed solutions and dig in some potash in late winter. Otherwise, a copper-based fungicide will need to be used as well.

The mango weevil is a large beetle found inside the seed of ripe fruit. The weevil won't hurt the tree so no control is necessary.

Scale infestations can be dealt with by natural predators or with white oil. See the Pests and Diseases section of Citrus for other ways of dealing with scale.

MELONS

Watermelon, rockmelon and honeydews are members of the Cucurbitaceae (cucumber) family. Watermelon has a long history originating most probably in the Kalahari Desert in east Africa and making its way up to Egypt where it has been cultivated since 2000 BC. Watermelon seeds were found in the tomb of Tutankhamen. They made their way to America with the slave trade and have traditionally been the gift Chinese and Japanese people take to give a host.

WHERE TO GROW

Melons need warm temperatures and a long growing season, up to four months. They need full sun, lots of space, as they are vigorous rambling vines, and rich well-draining soil.

WHEN TO GROW

- In cool climates wait until the weather has warmed up and be sure to choose a fast maturing variety.
- In temperate climates the time to sow is late spring.
- In the tropics, grow melons in the dry season.

SOIL PREPARATION

Melons need rich, friable soils. Soil that has previously had a green manure crop grown in it is excellent. If not, add plenty of cow or sheep manure or compost. Adding some rock dust will help enrich the ground. Avoid planting melons in beds where tomatoes, potatoes or eggplants have previously grown.

HOW TO GROW

Melons are grown from seed. Don't use the seed from shop-bought melons as these are usually hybrids and won't grow true to type. The best melons are the open-pollinated heirlooms available from online seed companies.

Melons grow best if the seed is planted directly into the ground where it is to grow. The seed germinates in about five days. If your growing season is short you could start the seed off in a peat pot but be very careful about

transplanting the seedling as melons resent any root disturbance.

Raise the soil into a mound or ridge about 1 metre square and 30 cm high. Sow seeds about two cm deep in three groups of three or four seeds each, about 30 cm apart. After a few weeks select the strongest seedlings and cut off the weaker ones, leaving only one seedling in each group.

VARIETIES

Rockmelon or cantaloupe varieties include Hale's Best, which is powdery mildew-resistant, and Planter's Jumbo. Greenflesh is a honeydew melon which can weigh up to 3 kg. Ein Dor smells like pineapple.

Watermelon varieties include Candy Red, a large variety weighing up to 14 kg. Sugar Baby is a small round early maturing fruit. Sweet Black Mountain is good for cooler climates, while Golden Midget is a small heirloom, which turns yellow when ripe. Moon and Stars is another heirloom with massive fruit.

CARE AND MAINTENANCE

Melons have shallow roots so keep them well mulched and never let the soil dry out. They

are hungry plants and should be given mulches of compost or manure or be fed regularly with an organic fertiliser, a liquid tea or pelletised chicken manure.

When the vines are about 2 m long, pinch out the growing tips to encourage branching. As the vine grows push it in the direction you want to grow it in.

Slide a flat piece of wood or a bundle of straw under the fruit as it ripens to avoid it rotting from contact with wet soil.

POLLINATION

Watermelon flowers are insect pollinated. See the section on Zucchini, Cucumber and Squash for pollination techniques.

HARVESTING

A week before melons are ripe for harvest, reduce watering to allow the sugars to concentrate in the fruit. Harvest watermelon when the undersides turn yellow and the fruit gives a dull hollow sound when tapped. Another indication of ripeness is when the tendril closest to the fruit has dried off. Each plant should produce three to six fruit.

Rockmelons are ready to harvest when the stem pulls easily from the fruit, which has turned a yellowish colour. They can then be ripened indoors for a day or two for full flavour.

Honeydews are ready to harvest when the skin has turned a whitish cream and the blossom end gives slightly when pressed. A slight twist should be enough for the fruit to slip from the stem.

All melons can be stored in the fridge for a week.

PESTS, DISEASES AND PROBLEMS

Caterpillars can be a nuisance. Use a homemade soap spray or derris dust to get rid of them.

Melons are prone to aphid attack. See Citrus on dealing with them. Encouraging wasps, hoverflies, lady beetles, lacewings and predatory midges, all natural predators of aphids, will soon get rid of them.

Avoiding overhead watering, especially in the late afternoon or evening, best prevents powdery mildew. Use a milk spray (recipe in Pests and Diseases section).

Leaf-eating beetles can be picked off if they are not too much of a problem.

PASSIONFRUIT

Of South American origin, passionfruit (*Passiflora edulis*) is a fast-growing vine with beautiful flowers. Indeed, parts of the star-shaped flower were thought by the Spanish conquistadors to resemble the symbol of crucifixion and therefore the passion of Christ on the cross—hence the name of the vine. Most originate from Brazil where the leaves and flowers are used for treating anxiety and insomnia.

WHERE TO GROW

Passionfruit grow on large self-clinging vines with tendrils that hold them to a climbing frame. They can grow from 2 to 10 metres tall and from 1 to 9 metres wide. Passionfruit likes full sun and, ideally, a warm north facing fence or climbing frame, sheltered away from strong winds. Soil needs to be well draining and rich and there should be no competition with other plants planted nearby.

VARIETIES

There are over 350 species of passionfruit, 50 of which produce fruit. Most popular is the black *Passiflora edulis*. Relatively hardy, it can be grown in most cool and temperate districts and will withstand light frost. In cooler climates buy a plant that has been grafted onto a hardy rootstock like Nellie Kelly.

Yellow and red passionfruit are more suited to the tropics and will crop more heavily if two vines are grown so they can cross-pollinate. In the tropics yellow-skinned Panama Gold and Panama Red with red skin do extremely well.

Banana passionfruit (*P. tripartita* var. *mollissima*) has been declared a weed in frost-free areas and should be avoided, as it is extremely vigorous.

WHEN TO PLANT

The best time to plant a passionfruit vine is during spring, after the last frost, or early summer. You should be able to pick fruit in about 18 months.

HOW TO PLANT

Passionfruit dislikes 'wet feet' (its roots being in soggy, wet soil), so if you have a clay or poorly draining soil you will need to prepare a raised bed or mound. Dig a hole three times the size of the pot and fill it with manure, compost and a couple of handfuls of slow release fertiliser or pelletised chicken manure. Water in well and leave it to settle. In the old days, passionfruit was always planted with an ox heart, sheep or lamb liver in the planting hole to provide the heavily feeding plant with iron. This is a good idea. If you cannot get offal, use pelletised chicken manure instead.

Soak the potted plant in its pot for half an hour in a bucket of water or weak seaweed solution. Tease out any spiralling roots and plant so that the soil level in the pot is at the same level as the ground and that the graft on the stem is not buried. Water in and sprinkle blood and bone liberally around the area. Mulch but ensure to keep it well clear of the stem.

Passionfruit is a vine, which needs the support of a trellis, a fence, a frame or an old tree. To train the vine, tie the new plant loosely to the support and pinch out the leading shoot to stimulate side shoots. As they grow tie them to the frame. When the plant has grown to the top of the support pinch out the tips of the shoots.

CARE AND MAINTENANCE

Passionfruit needs regular watering, particularly in hot weather when it should be watered twice a week, otherwise it will not fruit well. Every three weeks during its growing period feed it with weak fish emulsion. In spring and summer fertilise with manure, blood and bone or a high nitrogen fertiliser like citrus food. Keep the plant well mulched.

Never dig within 3 m of a passionfruit vine. If its roots are damaged or exposed it will send up very aggressive suckers, which are almost impossible to control.

Give your passionfruit a trim to keep it under control. If it becomes overgrown or the fruit fails to ripen, prune out some of the branches and dead shoots in late spring. Cut off any branches within 60 cm of the ground and any that have grown above the support. The fruit is produced on the new growth. Water well after pruning. Every couple of years give the vine a big prune in late spring, cutting the loose foliage and weaker branches back by two-thirds.

No matter how well you look after passionfruit its life span is usually only five or six years. When the vine becomes too old and diseased, dig it out. You must ensure to dig out all of the roots, as any left in the ground will sucker. Replant a new vine in a new place.

HARVESTING

Fully ripened fruit drops off the vine. If the fruit starts to wrinkle it is ready for harvesting. Passionfruit freezes well in ice cube trays.

PESTS, DISEASES AND PROBLEMS

Possums and cockatoos may try to raid your crops.

The passion vine hopper whose honeydew produces sooty mould may cause stunting and wilting. Hose off the hoppers and the sooty mould or apply horticultural oil spray.

If the plant is water-logged it may suffer from soil-borne diseases like fusarium wilt (see Pests and Diseases). They will not produce any fruit.

If leaves of a different shape appear below the graft or spring up around the plant cut them off, these are suckers from the grafted rootstock and will take over.

If the plant drops its leaves it may be suffering from collar rot or root rot. These are incurable fungal diseases. Dig up the plant and remove all of the roots. Do not compost them as they may still spread the infection. Don't plant another vine in the spot for three years. To avoid, keep mulch away from the base of the plant and try not to overwater.

A failure to bear fruit is often due to insufficient sunlight.

Fruit fly can be a problem. In some regions it is a legal requirement to cover spray for fruit fly. If you have an infestation make sure to collect all fruit as soon as it falls, net the vines and set up fruit fly baits.

Applying a horticultural oil in spring and summer when they breed can control scale and mealy bugs.

Aphids and vine-hoppers occasionally affect passionfruit. The leaves become mottled and distorted. See Pests and Diseases for controlling aphids.

If fruit lacks pulp it may be due to suckling bugs like mealy bug and scale or insufficient water, poor pollination or boron deficiency.

RHUBARB

Given that it is the stalks of rhubarb (*Rheum rhabarbarum*) that are harvested, it is botanically a vegetable. Wild or true rhubarb is thought to date back to 2700 BC China, where it was used as a purgative. Marco Polo mentions it in his travels and by the 1500s it was used medicinally in Europe. In the 18th century, Europe rediscovered rhubarb and it became known as the pie plant as it was primarily used in pies and tarts.

WHERE TO GROW

Rhubarb is a herbaceous perennial (that is, it grows actively during the spring, summer and autumn months then dies back to a dormant, below ground structure called a crown during winter). During its growing period it is a big plant (about 1 metre by 1 metre), so some care needs to be taken in choosing the site. Furthermore, it stays in the bed for several years. Rhubarb can be happily slotted in between other fruits or in an ornamental garden, or in a separate bed where it can be left undisturbed.

Best grown where there is a chilly winter, rhubarb will grow in the subtropics though it may not colour as deeply. It likes full sun, particularly in cool climates, but will tolerate semi-shade. It will not, however, tolerate poor drainage. In temperate climates some protection from hot afternoon sun is beneficial. Rhubarb is not recommended for the tropics.

WHEN TO PLANT

Winter. Rhubarb is best grown from crowns, available from winter to early spring from nurseries or online. Potted plants are available during spring and early summer but these are very slow growing as the crowns are yet to develop.

SOIL PREPARATION

Rhubarb will grow in any soil provided that plenty of compost, manure or blood and bone is added before planting. If your soil is acidic add some lime. If drainage is poor plant rhubarb in a raised bed.

HOW TO PLANT

Plant crowns 75 cm to 1 m apart with a similar distance between rows. Crowns should sit on the surface of the soil with the eyes or buds facing upwards and peeping just above the soil level. If they are planted too deeply the crown will rot. Water in with liquid seaweed or compost tea.

You can sow seed in spring in a seedbed or in pots and plant into its permanent position the following spring. Seeds will take three years until the plant will be ready for its first harvest.

VARIETIES

Rhubarb has red or green stalks. Sydney Crimson is the most readily available, Wandin Red, Glaskins, Perpetual Cherry Red are other varieties; Ever Red is suitable for pots. The colour of stems is largely determined by the variety but also by where they are grown. Generally, the colder the climate the more deeply red the stems. As it is inadvisable to pick all of the stalks of one plant at any one time, to get enough stalks for a meal you will need at least one plant for each member of the household.

CARE AND MAINTENANCE

Once the crown begins to shoot, rhubarb must have regular watering. Take care to never let rhubarb dry out, which may mean soaking it two or three times a week during summer. Its other crucial requirement is plenty of nutrition, so a couple of handfuls of compost and/or animal manure, pelletised chicken manure, a complete fertiliser, or blood and bone once a month during its growing season is necessary for healthy growth. It is a good idea every time you harvest any stalks to give the plant a liquid feed of fish or seaweed emulsion or compost tea. Mulch around the plant to help keep the soil moist, but take care not to cover the crown as it may rot.

After midsummer stop harvesting and leave the youngest stems in the centre of the plant. This directs energy into building up the roots for the following harvest. In autumn, the leaves will die back, remove spent stems and cover the crowns with a thick layer of straw or leaf mould to give some protection over winter. In spring after the last frost remove the mulch, loosen the soil around the crowns by gently pushing a garden fork into the soil around the perimeter of the plant and add in compost, manure or a handful of fruit and flower fertiliser. Pull out any weeds that try to grow in the crown.

Forcing pots are a traditional method used to bring on quick growth. By starving the plant of light they force it into production. Simply cover crowns with a bucket with the bottom cut out, a barrel, or a traditional terracotta forcing pot from late winter to early spring. A harvest will be ready in about four weeks. It is inadvisable to use forcing pots year in, year out as the crown will become exhausted and die.

Occasionally rhubarb will flower. This may be due to age, lack of water or infertile soil. Cut out the flowering stalk at the base (it is still edible). Give the plant some fertiliser, compost or manure or a liquid feed. To inhibit flowering make sure to divide the crown every four to five years.

Dividing rhubarb crowns

Every four to five years in late winter to early spring, when the plant is dormant, crowns need to be divided to reinvigorate the plants. When the crown is crowded stalks start to get small and spindly. Use a garden fork and lift the crown from the ground. Shake or hose off the soil and, with a sharp knife or pruning saw, cut the crown up into large pieces. Those with two or three well-developed shoots or eyes and no sign of rotting should be replanted. Replant immediately into enriched soil preferably in a new part of the garden.

HARVESTING AND STORAGE

The leaves of rhubarb contain oxalic acid and are poisonous to eat, though they are fine to compost. Rhubarb is harvested in summer. In its first year it is best not to harvest any of the stems, leaving them to nourish the crown. In the second year harvest a few stems only. In following years each plant should give you eight to 10 stems throughout the growing season. Never cut the stems, instead, when they are about 30 cm long gently pull them from the base of the plant, outside stalks first. You may need to give a twist. Never harvest all of the stalks from a plant, as some stems are required for photosynthesis to aid the next season's growth.

As soon as you have harvested the stalks cut off the leaves and compost them. Leaving foliage attached to the stem draws water from it, causing it to wilt. Store rhubarb by wrapping the stems in a damp tea towel or paper towel and keep them in the crisper for up to a week. Rhubarb can be frozen.

PESTS, DISEASES AND PROBLEMS

Rhubarb rarely suffers pests and diseases. Overhead watering may cause rust and rot. Crowns may rot due to fungus. If so, dig up the affected plant and throw it away. Replace with new stock in another place.

Thin stems indicate poor nutrition, lack of water or overly warm growing conditions.

STRAWBERRIES

Strawberries are, botanically, neither a fruit nor a berry, but the enlarged ends of the stamen. They are a member of the rose, or Rosaceae, family. The name strawberry (*Fragaria x ananassa*) is probably derived from the way the plant grows with the 'berries' strewn about the bush, or could be attributed to the common practice of resting the plants on a mulch of straw to protect them. Conventionally grown strawberries are among the most chemically contaminated crops and are a tasteless shadow of their luscious, home-grown cousin.

WHERE TO GROW

Strawberries must have an open position in full sun with good air circulation around them. Good drainage is also essential. Strawberries can make an excellent ground cover, or can be planted around the edge of the vegetable patch.

Strawberries do very well in pots and hanging baskets. In pots, use a good-quality potting mix enriched with compost and a handful of blood and bone. They must be watered regularly so

they do not dry out and fertilised more regularly than strawberries in the garden. Give them a weekly dose of liquid nutrients or seaweed solution during spring and summer. A large strawberry pot can contain up to six plants and can be planted at any time of the year.

WHEN TO PLANT

In the tropics and subtropics plant strawberries from March to May. Elsewhere, the best time to plant strawberries is from winter to early spring. Some cultivars are 'cool stored' and can be bought in pots at anytime and planted out.

SOIL PREPARATION

Good soil preparation is crucial for strawberries to help reduce the risk of pests and of soil-borne diseases. It also enhances flavour and yield. First dig over the soil and mix through copious amounts of compost and manure. Add one handful of blood and bone every square metre. Rake over the bed until you have a fine crumbly soil. If drainage is poor where you want to grow strawberries, make mounds of the soil about 15–20 cm high and plant on these or plant them in a raised garden bed. Strawberries like a slightly acid soil with a pH of between 5 and 6.5. Pine needles and peat both have an acidifying effect on soil. If your soil is alkaline consider growing strawberries in pots or add powdered sulphur before planting.

HOW TO PLANT

Strawberries can be bought in pots or as bare-rooted runners from nurseries or online. Ensure that the plants are virus free from registered growers. Strawberries can also be grown from 'runners' produced each year by the parent plants.

Plant individual runners or strawberry plants at least 40 cm apart, with a similar distance between the rows. The space between them is important to ensure adequate air circulation around the plants and to give them room to grow. When planting be careful not to bury the crown (the rosette at the base of the plant where the leaf stems emerge), sit it at ground level and push the soil up around the roots, otherwise the plant may rot. Water well after planting.

Many gardeners grow strawberries in black

plastic. It acts as a mulch, suppressing weeds, retaining moisture and protecting the fruit. Build the soil into ridges, water well, and then cover them with the plastic. Cut crosses in the plastic and push the strawberries through these into the soil.

VARIETIES

Cultivars perform differently in different climates, so it may be a case of experimenting with varieties until you find which one suits your climate. Cultivars also have different fruiting times so it is possible to prolong your harvest by planting different varieties. Some popular cultivars include Cambridge Rival, a small fruiting English heirloom, good for southern regions, Kunowase, a Japanese cultivar good for cooler regions and Lowanna, which grows in all regions and bears large fruit, as does Tioga, a Californian heirloom. In hotter regions try Earlisweet and Red Gauntlet.

CARE AND MAINTENANCE

Strawberries need to be kept well watered. The best practice is to water them from beneath as overhead watering encourages disease and pests. Fertilise strawberry plants every six weeks during spring while they are flowering. The best fertilisers for strawberries include potash, high potassium fertilisers for fruit and flowers, manure or liquid plant food, including compost tea. Finally, make sure to mulch around them when the berries start to form to keep the fruit clean and prevent rot, but make sure not to mulch over the crowns. Mulch can be straw, black plastic sheets, sugarcane, hay, pine needles or shop-bought mulching mats.

If there are more than four crowns on a plant pinch the excess out. With too many crowns the plant will concentrate more of its energy on leaf growth and less on producing fruit.

In early winter, tidy up the plants by removing diseased and damaged leaves, any old fruit and any runners. Apply compost and an organic fertiliser and re-mulch the crop in preparation for the new growing season.

Strawberries are easy to propagate. They send out runners, which take root wherever they touch the soil. Clip the stem between the runners and carefully lift the new plant from the soil. Choose the healthiest runners, which have formed a number of roots and replant. Strawberry plants should last for about three years.

Strawberries are pollinated by bees and other insects so encourage them into the garden by planting some flowers that will attract them, including daisies, basil and borage around the strawberries.

HARVESTING AND STORAGE

Strawberries are harvested from spring into autumn. They do not sweeten after harvesting so when the fruit has turned red, pinch and twist the stem or use scissors to cut it from the plant. Eat immediately or freeze as a puree.

PESTS, DISEASES AND PROBLEMS

Birds and possums love strawberries so it is a good idea to set up some sort of protection over the patch, by draping a net over stakes or fencing it with some wire mesh.

Strawberries are prone to powdery mildew and black spot. If they do get attacked, feed the plant with a liquid seaweed or compost tea and use it as a foliar spray as well, or use a registered fungicide. See the section on Pests and Diseases for other ways to deal with them.

Strawberries can suffer from mites. Use an organic dusting sulphur, white oil or paraffin oil. Clean up any leaf litter where mites may hide.

If aphids attack strawberries, use a soap spray or remove by hand.

Slugs and snails around strawberries can be dealt with by beer traps or slug and snail pellets.

Pale-coloured or distorted fruit may indicate excessive nitrogen, or calcium and boron deficiencies. Water in potash at the recommended rate as the plants begin to flower to help encourage fruit development.

Left: Strawberries behind wire mesh to keep out birds and possums.

PESTS AND DISEASES

At some time or another all gardeners are going to be confronted with various garden pests and diseased plants. Some, like slugs and snails, will affect all vegetables; others are peculiar to a particular type of fruit or vegetable and are dealt with in the section on that fruit or vegetable. It is important to be aware of what can strike your vegetables and when and how to take measures to avoid it.

Crop rotation is critical to avoiding a build-up of disease. Cleaning up diseased plants and composting them if you are hot composting or throwing them out is another. A wide number of agricultural sprays and chemicals are available to deal with diseases and viruses but, as the residues of these often remain in the soil or wash into waterways and they frequently kill off beneficial insects as well, it is a better practice to use natural homemade remedies where you can.

If you are unable to determine what the particular problem is you can always take a cutting to your local nursery for some advice. As a rule of thumb, the healthier the plant and the soil it is grown in the more resistant it is to pests and diseases.

If your fruit or vegetables are not looking well the first thing to determine is if they are getting sufficient light. You may need to thin out

some of the plants around them. This is often a cause of the fungal disease powdery mildew. Otherwise, the vegetable may not be getting enough water, or conversely, too much. It may need to be mulched or fertilised.

Some seasons will see conditions that are particularly bad for pests. This is one of the vagaries of gardening and of nature but does

not mean that the next season will be the same. There will always be good and bad seasons in the garden. Planting a big enough and diverse enough crop can help see you through.

As prevention is always better than cure, follow some organic gardening principles. Plant trap plants where you can. These plants attract pests away from the crops or confuse them. So include nasturtiums to attract aphids, zinnia to trap Japanese beetle, dill to lure away caterpillars, sage to confuse white cabbage butterfly and tansy to ward off aphids and fruit fly. Barriers and traps can be made around plants. Barriers of used coffee grounds, coarse river sand, saw dust or crushed eggshells around plants make it impossible for snails and slugs to crawl across. Other material and sticky glue barriers can be bought. Weeds often harbour pests so ensure the garden is cleared of them.

Not all bought sprays and insecticides are organically unacceptable. Pyrethrum, derived from the African daisy, can be used against aphids and caterpillars. Bordeaux, a fungicide made with hydrated lime and copper sulfate, can be used on fungal problems including potato and tomato blight and black spot. Insecticidal soap is acceptable to fight red spider mite, blackfly, green fly, whitefly and scale. Dipel (*Bacillus thuringiensis*) can generally be used on leaf eating caterpillars in organic gardens.

MINERAL DEFICIENCIES

Plants can suffer if there are mineral deficiencies in the soil. These become apparent by changes to the colour of the leaves. Container-grown vegetables are particularly at risk as the minerals are depleted over time from the potting mix.

Iron deficiencies, particularly in citrus, cause the new leaves to turn yellow with dark green veins. This is a problem in many alkaline soils, or where too much mushroom compost has been used. Water on iron chelates or spray them onto the plant, once a month, until the leaves turn green.

Nitrogen deficiency can affect all vegetables, except peas and beans. The leaves remain small and grow an unusually pale green. On brassicas, purplish tints may appear on the leaves. The vegetable will generally have poor growth and small fruit. To add nitrogen to the soil, fold in chicken manure, compost and/or blood and bone and nitrogen-rich fertilisers or grow a nitrogen-fixing green manure in the plot.

Potassium deficiency is likely in sandy soil when there has been a lot of rain. Potatoes, tomatoes and fruit are the most prone and will suffer from abnormally shaped, smallish leaves, often with brown scorch marks around the edges. Add potash. Blood and bone, seaweed meal, comfrey and wood ash will also boost potassium.

Phosphorous deficiency is manifested in poor growth and dull purplish leaves. Fruit will be small and bitter. Add rock phosphate, blood and bone or bonemeal.

Calcium deficiency is common in acidic soils. It is caused by erratic watering. Curling of shoots and young leaves is a symptom. In apples the fruit becomes pit marked, in carrots oval spots occur and the vegetable cracks, while in brassicas the insides can rot and go brown. Add lime.

Magnesium deficiency can strike potatoes, tomatoes, apples and berries, especially after heavy periods of rain. The older leaves change colour and then drop. Add dolomite and Epsom salts watered into the soil or sprayed on at a rate of 200 g per 10 litres.

COMMON PESTS AND BUGS

Some of the more common pests include aphids, scale, caterpillars, cabbage white butterfly and cut worms or curl grubs. While dealing with these, care needs to be taken not to harm beneficial insects, many of whom are the predatory insects natural enemy. Birds are a great consumer of pests and so should be encouraged. Gardeners will need to experiment with ways to get rid of the pests and see what works best.

Some of the more tried and true methods for dealing with various bugs are listed below.

CUTWORMS

Moth caterpillars lay their eggs in the soil and a fat C-shaped larvae develops. They feed at night on young seedlings, often cutting them off at ground level, or leaving them to wilt and die. They are difficult to get rid of, short of turning the patch over to chickens to forage for them. Turn

over the soil and expose them, then leave the plot fallow for a month. Keeping the area weed free and dusting the soil surface with derris dust may help. Cardboard coffee cups with the bottom cut out, old cans or bits of cardboard pressed into the soil can be used as collars to protect seedlings from cutworms, as do old vases or plastic drink bottles used as cloches.

APHIDS

Aphids are minute sap-sucking insects who produce a sticky, sooty mould. Where you have aphids you will have ants running up and down the plant trying to harvest the honeydew produced by the sooty mould. Citrus, fig and apples can be attacked. Rub off the aphids with your hands or give them a sharp spray with the hose. Try either the garlic spray or the vegetable oil spray listed below, or use a white oil or pyrethrum.

CATERPILLARS

Leaves that have been chewed off are evidence of caterpillars, which can be prodigious eaters. Use Dipel.

SLUGS AND SNAILS

Beer traps for snails and slugs

Dig old jars or cups into the ground at an angle with the lip level with the soil. Fill the jar with beer. A number of traps will need to be placed around the more vulnerable vegetables. The beer will need constant replacing.

CABBAGE WHITE BUTTERFLY

Cabbage white butterfly is the small, grayish-white moth with black-tipped forewings you see in droves in the warmer months circling your brassicas. They lay pale yellow eggs on the vegetable's outer leaves. When the caterpillars hatch they feed on the undersides of leaves gradually working their way to the centre. The caterpillars are a vivid green and can grow to a couple of centimetres long. The caterpillars can be handpicked off, but to thwart the butterfly you may need to spray with Dipel (*Bacillus thuringiensis* (Bt)). It is an organically approved spray, which takes three to four days to be effective. Dipel must be stored at below 21°C to remain viable.

Alternatively, make your own remedy for cabbage white butterfly with one tablespoon of

molasses and a few drops of liquid soap to 1 L of water and use it as a spray on both sides of the foliage.

Placing white eggshells or golfballs around the plants can outsmart the cabbage white butterfly, which can be tricked into thinking other moths are already at work on the plant and will go elsewhere.

CODLING MOTH

Codling moths are small grey-brown moths whose caterpillars burrow into fruit. Spray the affected areas with white oil, pyrethrum or derris dust and try hanging sticky traps.

DISEASES

While most pests and fungal diseases can be dealt with, plants that have been infected by a virus need to be dug up and destroyed. Most diseases are spread by insects. Make sure to always pull up plants you suspect of disease before it can be spread and pick up any fallen and rotting fruits.

FUNGAL DISEASES

The most common fungal diseases and ways to deal with them are as follows:

Powdery mildew looks like a whitish-grey coating over the leaves and stems of the plant. Cucurbits are particularly at risk, although it may also cover raspberries, fruit trees, brassicas and strawberries. Pick off the infected shoots and use a milk spray or bicarbonate of soda spray, or purchase a sulphur spray.

Rust affects silverbeet, spinach, beetroot and beans. Sulphur sprays can be used to control rust, or make a bicarb spray.

Clubroot is a fungal disease found in acidic soils. Brassicas are susceptible. The plants will droop and leaves and stems blacken. Pull up infected plants immediately. The roots will appear gnarled and stunted. Clubroot can stay in the soil for up to 20 years. Don't replant brassicas in the patch.

VIRUSES

Verticillium, fusarium and spotted wilt—particularly at risk are peas and beans, tomatoes, capsicum and cucurbits. The plant wilts and doesn't recover with watering. Remove all infected plants and destroy. Make sure to rotate crops and don't plant that crop again in that area for the next five or so years.

Blossom end rot is the blackspot that develops at the end of the vegetable, particularly tomatoes and capsicum. It is caused by irregular watering, allowing the soil to dry out and then watering heavily. Avoid this by heavy mulching and regular watering.

NATURAL REMEDIES

Natural remedies probably work better than bought insecticides and pesticides. They are non-poisonous and seem to be every bit as effective. They are safe around children and pets and do not harm beneficial insects or organisms. They do, however, need to be kept up as they biodegrade rapidly and are washed away with watering and rain. They all need to be applied until they are literally dripping off the plant.

Garlic spray

For aphids, caterpillars, scale, carrot root fly, onion fly, codling moths and snails. Put one bulb of garlic, three chillies and two tablespoons of water in a blender and blend until smooth. Add 1 L of water and one tablespoon of liquid soap. Add five feverfew leaves, if you have any. Strain and apply to affected plants with a spray gun. Another method for dealing with aphids is a light dusting of wood ash or lime on infected new shoots.

Soapy water spray

A soapy water spray made with soft soap or soap flakes and water is also a good spray to kill aphids. Remember that beneficial insects like lady beetles love aphids and some even feed on mites, while the larvae of the common lacewing eat caterpillars, aphids and other insects. These may well be enough to control any infestations in the garden.

Vegetable oil soap spray

For mites, scale and citrus leaf miner. Mix one cup of vegetable oil with a quarter of a cup of pure liquid soap. Dilute one tablespoon of the mix with 1 L of water and spray.

Espresso coffee snail killer

Dilute one part espresso with 10 parts water and use as a spray on foliage.

Milk spray

Milk spray for fungal diseases like powdery mildew on the cucumber family and tomatoes. Fungal diseases can be controlled by spraying with a mixture of two parts full-cream milk and eight parts water. Avoiding overhead watering is an important practice to prevent powdery mildew.

Bicarbonate of soda fungicide

For powdery mildew, black spot, tomato blight, leaf blight and rust. Mix 1 L water, two teaspoons bicarbonate of soda, one drop vegetable oil and one drop liquid or castile soap. Shake well. Spray.

Fruit fly baits

Maggots in fruit indicate fruit fly. The flies lay their eggs within the developing fruit, which then drops to the ground where the larvae pupates in the soil. Sticky pheromone traps, spinosad-based sprays or splash baiting systems are all methods of control.

Cover fruit with paper bags, cotton cloth or exclusion fabric and collect and dispose of all fallen fruit. Mulch trees and let chickens and ducks roam beneath the trees to eat the larvae.

To trap the female fruit fly, you can try making a homemade trap. Make a hole in a plastic drink bottle, insert a small funnel, which could be made by cutting the neck off another bottle, and pour in a mixture of one cup water, one teaspoon vanilla and one tablespoon of vinegar, bleach or ammonia. Diluted vegemite or molasses can work as well. Hang a number of the traps around the tree.

WHAT TO SOW WHEN GARDENING CALENDAR

A lot of seeds are best sown straight into the garden, carrots and radish for example. Others can be started off undercover in seed trays or pots 4 to 6 weeks before being planted out as seedlings into the garden. Sowing undercover will help ensure a continuous harvest and free up space in the garden. It is also a way to get a headstart on the growing season. The calendar below is a rough guide of when to sow or plant, as the weather differs from year to year it should be treated flexibly.

'Sow' indicates it is time to sow seeds directly into the garden,

'(U/C)' indicates seeds can be sown undercover into seed trays,

'plant' indicates time to plant the vegetable as a seedling, either bought from a nursery or from your own seed trays, sown in the previous month.

JANUARY	SOW	PLANT
Cool	Asian cabbage, beetroot, cauliflower, cress, Florence fennel, kale, kohlrabi, lettuce, mizuna, mustard, parsnip, radish, rocket, silverbeet, spring onions, swedes, tatsoi, turnip, winter carrots. **U/C:** Broccoli, Brussels sprouts, cauliflower, collards, kale, winter cabbage.	Asian cabbage, basil, broccoli, Brussels sprouts, cabbage, cauliflower, celery and celeriac, chives, cherry tomatoes, endive, kale, kohlrabi, leek, lettuce, marrow, melon, oregano, parsley, potato tubers, salsify, silverbeet, tarragon.
Temperate	Beans, beetroot, carrot, cauliflower, cress, cucumber, endive, Florence fennel, kohlrabi, lettuce, mustard, parsnip, radish, silverbeet, spring onion, squash, sweetcorn, turnip, zucchini. **U/C:** Broccoli, Brussels sprouts, cauliflower, collards, leek, onion, winter cabbage.	Broccoli, Brussels sprouts, cabbage, cauliflower, chives, cucumber, endive, herbs, kohlrabi, lettuce, marrows, mustard, salsify, shallots, silverbeet, spring onion, tomato, turnip, zucchini.
Subtropical	Asian cabbage, basil, beans, beetroot, capsicum, cress, eggplant, lettuce, marrow, melons, mustard, okra, radish, silverbeet, squash, swede, sweet corn, sweet potato, tomato, turnip, zucchini. **U/C:** Broccoli, cabbage, chilli, leek, onion.	Basil, capsicum, chilli, chives, cucumber, eggplant, herbs, loose-leaf lettuce, marrow, melons, mustard, okra, parsley, pumpkin, salsify, silverbeet, squash, tomato, zucchini.
Tropical During the wet season small seeds can be washed away with the rain so planting undercover is a good idea.	Snake beans and winged beans can be sown all year, cress, cucumber, eggplant, herbs, lettuce, mustard, okra, radish, squash, sweetcorn.	Basil, cress, cucumber, eggplant, lettuce, mustard, okra, squash, sweet potato, zucchini.

FEBRUARY

	SOW	PLANT
Cool	Asian greens, beetroot, carrot, cauliflower, cress, fennel, kohlrabi, parsnip, radish, rocket, shallots, silverbeet, tatsoi, turnip. **U/C:** Broccoli, cabbage cauliflower, collards, coriander, kale, leek, onion.	Broccoli, Brussels sprouts, cabbage, chives, cauliflower, celery and celeriac, kale, kohlrabi, lettuce, oregano, parsley, potato tubers, salsify, silverbeet, spring onion, strawberries.
Temperate	Beetroot, carrot, cauliflower, celery, cress, Florence fennel, kohlrabi, leek, lettuce, potato, radish, rocket, shallots, silverbeet, spinach, swede, turnip. **U/C:** Broccoli, cabbage, cauliflower, kale, leeks, onion.	Basil, beetroot, cauliflower, celery, coriander, cress, endive, Florence fennel, herbs, kohlrabi, lettuce, mizuna, mustards, pak choy, radish, rocket, salsify, shallots, silverbeet, spinach.
Subtropical	Beans, beetroot, capsicum, carrot, cress, cucumber, eggplant, kohlrabi, leek, lettuce, parsnip, radish, rocket, silverbeet, squash, swede, sweet corn, tomato, turnip, zucchini. **U/C:** Asian greens, broccoli, cabbage, celery and celeriac, collards, kale, kohlrabi, leeks, onion.	Capsicum, celery and celeriac, chilli, chives, cress, cucumber, eggplant, herbs, lettuce, melons, mustard, okra, pak choy, rocket, silverbeet, squash, sweet potato slips, tomato, zucchini.
Tropical	Beetroot, celery, chicory, chilli, chives, cress, cucumber, eggplant, herbs, open-hearted lettuce, radish, rocket, snake and winged beans, swede, sweet potato, turnip, zucchini.	Asparagus, basil, cabbage, capsicum, chicory, chilli, chives, cress, cucumber, eggplant, ginger, lettuce, potato tubers, swede, sweet potato.

237

MARCH

	SOW	PLANT
Cool	Asian greens, beetroot, cress, Florence fennel, garlic, kale, kohlrabi, leeks, mustard, radish, rocket, shallots, silverbeet, spinach, turnip. **U/C:** Brussels sprouts, cabbage, kale, leeks, onions.	Asian greens, broccoli, cabbage, cauliflower, celery, chives, collards, coriander, garlic, globe artichoke crowns, kale, leek, lettuce, mizuna, oregano, parsley, salsify, shallots, silverbeet, spring onion, strawberries.
Temperate	Asian greens, asparagus seed, beetroot, broccoli, cabbage, carrot, cauliflower, collards, cress, endive, kale, kohlrabi, lettuce, leeks, onions, parsnip, peas, radish, shallots, silverbeet, spinach, swede, turnip. **U/C:** Broccoli, cabbage, collards, kale, leeks.	Asian greens, beetroot, broccoli, Brussels sprouts, cabbage, cauliflower, celery, chives, coriander, cress, daikon, endive, fennel, globe artichoke, herbs, kale, kohlrabi, leek, lettuce, mizuna, mustard, onion, radish, salsify, shallots, silverbeet, spinach.
Subtropical	Asparagus seed, beans, beetroot, cabbage, capsicum, carrot, Asian greens, celery, cress, cucumber, eggplant, endive, fennel, kohlrabi, leek, lettuce, mustard, okra, onion, parsnip, peas, radish, rocket, shallots, silverbeet, spring onion, squash, sweet corn, turnip, tomato, zucchini. **U/C:** Asian greens, broccoli, cabbage, celery and celeriac, chicory, leeks, onion.	Cabbage, capsicum, celery, chilli, chives, celery and celeriac, chicory, cress, cucumber, eggplant, kohlrabi, lettuce, silverbeet, squash, sweet potato slips, tomato, zucchini.
Tropical	Asian cabbage, beans, beetroot, cress, cucumber, eggplant, endive, herbs, kohlrabi, lettuce, mustard, onion, parsnip, peas, radish, shallots, spring onion, sweet corn, turnip. **U/C:** Asian greens, capsicum, chilli, celery, collards, eggplant, kale, melons, spring onion, strawberries, tomato, zucchini.	Asian greens, basil, cabbage, capsicum, chicory, chilli, chives, choko, coriander, corn, cress, cucumber, daikon, eggplant, ginger, kohlrabi, lettuce, leeks, mizuna, okra, pak choy, parsley, radish, salsify, shallots, silverbeet, squash, strawberries, sweet potato, turnip, watermelon, zucchini.

239

APRIL	SOW	PLANT
Cool	Asian greens, broadbeans, Brussels sprouts, cress, daikon, fennel, garlic, lettuce, mustard, onions, radish, shallots, spinach, spring onion, turnip. **U/C:** Kale, kohlrabi, leeks, onions, silverbeet.	Asian greens, broccoli, cabbage, cauliflower, chives, collards, endive, fennel, garlic, globe artichoke, horseradish, kale, lettuce, leeks, mizuna, mustard, onion sets, rocket, salsify, shallots, silverbeet, spring onion, strawberries.
Temperate	Asian greens, asparagus seed, broad beans, broccoli, cabbage, cauliflower, celery, cress, fennel, kale, kohlrabi, leeks, lettuce, mustard, onion, peas, radish, shallots, spinach, spring onion, turnip. **U/C:** Kale, brassicas.	Asian greens, broccoli, Brussels sprouts, cabbage, cauliflower, celery, chives, collards, cress, endive, Florence fennel, garlic, globe artichoke, kale, kohlrabi, lettuce, leeks, mizuna, mustard, onion, pak choy, rocket, shallots, silverbeet, spinach, spring onion, strawberries.
Subtropical	Asian cabbage, beans, beetroot, broad beans, broccoli, cabbage, carrots, cauliflower, celery and celeriac, chicory, cress, kohlrabi, leek, lettuce, mustard, onion, parsnip, peas, potato, radish, salsify, shallots, silverbeet, spinach, turnip. **U/C:** Broccoli, Brussels sprouts, cabbage, cauliflower, celery and celeriac, chilli, collards, onion, strawberry seeds, tomato.	Asian cabbage, broccoli, cabbage, cauliflower, celery and celeriac, chicory, cress, kohlrabi, leek, lettuce, mustard, onion, salsify, shallots, silverbeet, spinach, spring onion, tomato.
Tropical	Asian cabbage, beans, beetroot, broccoli, cabbage, capsicum, celery, cress, herbs, kale, kohlrabi, leek, lettuce, melons, mustard, onion, parsnip, peas, potato, pumpkin, radish, rocket, salsify, shallots, silverbeet, spinach, sweet corn, winged beans, zucchini or luffa. **U/C:** Broccoli, Brussels sprouts, cabbage, celery, cauliflower, chilli, collards, spring onion, strawberry seeds, tomato.	Artichokes, asparagus, basil, berries, broccoli, cabbage, capsicum, chicory, chilli, chives, choko, coriander, cress, cucumber, daikon, eggplant, garlic, ginger, horseradish, kale, kohlrabi, leek, lettuce, okra, marrow, melons, mint, mizuna, mustard, silverbeet, spinach, zucchini.

MAY	SOW	PLANT
Cool	Asian greens, broad beans, chives, cress, garlic, leeks, lettuce, mustard, rocket, shallots, silverbeet, snow peas, spinach, turnip.	Asian greens, broccoli, Brussels sprouts, cabbage, cauliflower, chives, cress, garlic, globe artichoke crowns, Japanese turnip, Jerusalem artichoke, kale, leeks, lettuce, mizuna, mustard, onions, silverbeet, spring onion, strawberries, rocket.
Temperate	Asian greens, asparagus seed, broad beans, broccoli, cabbage, cauliflower, celery, cress, fennel, kale, leeks, lettuce, mustard, onion, peas, radish, rocket, shallots, silverbeet, spinach, spring onion, snow peas. **U/C:** Strawberry seeds.	Asian greens, broccoli, Brussels sprouts, cabbage, cauliflower, celery, chives, collards, cress, Florence fennel, garlic, globe artichoke crowns, kale, kohlrabi, leeks, lettuce, mizuna, mustard, onion, oregano, pak choy, parsley, rocket, shallots, spinach, spring onion, strawberries.
Subtropical	Asian cabbage, asparagus, beetroot, broad beans, broccoli, cabbage, carrot, cauliflower, celery, celeriac, chicory, cress, cucumber, daikon, endive, Florence fennel, garlic, ginger, herbs, horseradish, kale, kohlrabi, leek, lettuce, mustard, onion, parsnip, peas, radish, salsify, shallots, silverbeet, spinach, turnip. **U/C:** Onion, strawberry seed.	Asian cabbage, asparagus crowns, broccoli, cabbage, cauliflower, celery, celeriac, chicory, collards, coriander, cress, endive, Florence fennel, Jerusalem artichoke, kale, kohlrabi, leek, lettuce, mizuna, mustard, pak choy, parsley, silverbeet, snow peas, spinach, strawberries.
Tropical	Asian cabbage, asparagus seed, beans, beetroot, broccoli, cabbage, capsicum, carrot, celery, celeriac, chicory, chilli, cress, cucumber, eggplant, endive, Florence fennel, herbs, kale, kohlrabi, leek, lettuce, melons, mustard, parsnip, peas, potato, pumpkin, radish, rocket, shallots, silverbeet, spring onion, spinach, sweet corn, tomato, turnip, zucchini or luffa. **U/C:** Cabbage, collards, kale, tomato.	Asian greens, asparagus, basil, berries, broccoli, cabbage, capsicum, cauliflower, celery, chicory, chilli, chives, coriander, cress, cucumber, Florence fennel, garlic, kale, kohlrabi, leek, marrow, melons, mizuna, mustard, okra, salsify, silverbeet, spinach, strawberries, tomato.

JUNE	SOW	PLANT
Cool	Asian greens, broad beans, onions, peas, radish, shallots, snow peas, spinach, turnip. **U/C:** Brassicas (to plant out in August).	Asian greens, asparagus crowns, berries, chives, cress, globe artichoke crowns, Jerusalem artichoke, kale, mustard, onions, rhubarb crowns, strawberry crowns.
Temperate	Asian greens, asparagus seed, broad beans, cabbage, cress, lettuce, mustard, peas, rhubarb crowns, shallots, spinach, strawberry seed.	Asian greens, asparagus crowns, cabbage, cauliflower, cress, garlic, globe and Jerusalem artichoke, kale, lettuce, mustard, onion, shallots, spinach, spring onion, strawberries.
Subtropical	Asian greens, asparagus, beetroot, broad beans, broccoli, cabbage, carrot, cauliflower, celery and celeriac, cress, endive, garlic, herbs, kohlrabi, lettuce, mustard, onion, parsnip, peas, potato, radish, rhubarb crowns, rocket, salsify, shallots, silverbeet, snow peas, spinach, spring onion. **U/C:** Onion, tomato.	Asian greens, asparagus crowns, berries, broccoli, cabbage, cauliflower, celery, celeriac, chicory, cress, endive, English spinach, garlic, Jerusalem artichoke tubers, kale, kohlrabi, leek, lettuce, mustard, onion, rocket, silverbeet.
Tropical	Asian greens, asparagus, beans, beetroot, broccoli, cabbage, carrot, capsicum, celery, cress, endive, Florence fennel, herbs, kohlrabi, kale, leek, lettuce, melons, parsnip, peas, pumpkin, radish, shallots, silverbeet, snake and winged beans, spinach, spring onion, sweet corn, tomato, zucchini or luffa.	Asian greens, basil, borage, broccoli, cabbage, capsicum, celery, chives, choko, collards, cress, cucumber, daikon, dill, eggplant, endive, fennel, garlic, ginger, herbs, horseradish, kale, kohlrabi, leek, lettuce, marrow, melons, mizuna, mustard, okra, onion, pak choy, salsify, shallots, silverbeet, spinach, spring onions, squash, tomato.

245

JULY	SOW	PLANT
Cool	Broad beans, cress, mustard, peas, spinach. **U/C:** Brassicas (to plant out in August), onion.	Asparagus crowns, berries, chives, Jerusalem and globe artichoke, onions, rhubarb crowns, shallots, spinach, strawberries.
Temperate	Asian greens, asparagus seed, beetroot, broad beans, carrot, cauliflower, cress, endive, mustard, onion, parsnip, peas, rhubarb crowns, salsify, shallots, spinach. **U/C:** Cabbage, chilli, eggplant, leeks, lettuce.	Asparagus crowns, berries, globe and Jerusalem artichokes, cauliflower, cress, lettuce, mustard, onion, rhubarb, rocket, shallots, spinach, spring onion, strawberries.
Subtropical	Asian greens, asparagus, beetroot, broad beans, broccoli, cabbage, carrot, cauliflower, celery, cress, endive, herbs, kale, kohlrabi, leek, lettuce, mustard, parsnip, peas, radish, rhubarb, salsify, shallots, silverbeet, spinach, spring onion, zucchini. **U/C:** Basil, cabbage, capsicum, celery and celeriac, chilli, collards, eggplant, leeks, marrow, melons, okra, squash, tomato, zucchini.	Artichokes, Asian greens, beans, broccoli, cabbage, cauliflower, celery, chives, cress, cucumber, daikon, dill, endive, fennel, garlic, Jerusalem artichoke, kohlrabi, leek, lettuce, mustard, onion, rocket, shallots, silverbeet, spinach, tomato.
Tropical	Asian greens, asparagus seeds, beetroot, broccoli, cabbage, capsicum, carrot, cauliflower, celery, cress, endive, fennel, herbs, kale, leek, lettuce, melons, mustard,parsnip, peas, pumpkin, radish, rhubarb, shallots, silverbeet, snake and winged beans, spinach, spring onion, sweet corn, tomato, zucchini or luffa.	Asian cabbage, basil, broccoli, cabbage, capsicum, cauliflower, celery, chilli, chives, choko, collards, cress, daikon, eggplant, endive, fennel, garlic, ginger, herbs, kohlrabi, leek, lettuce, melons, mustard,pak choy, pumpkin, shallots, silverbeet, spinach, spring onion, squash, tomato,

AUGUST	SOW	PLANT
Cool	Asian brassicas, asparagus, broad beans, carrot, onion, parsnip, peas, potatoes, rhubarb, silverbeet, spinach, spring onion, swede, turnips, radish, rocket. **U/C (in pot):** Basil, broccoli, cabbage, eggplant, kale, leeks, lettuce, pumpkin, silverbeet, strawberry seeds, tomatoes, watermelon.	Asian greens, berries, cabbage, cauliflower, chives, globe and Jerusalem artichokes, kale, kohlrabi, onion, rhubarb, rocket, shallots, spinach, spring onion, strawberry crowns, swede.
Temperate	Artichoke, Asian greens, asparagus seed, beetroot, cabbage, carrot, celery, cress, endive, fennel, kohlrabi, lettuce, mustard, parsnip, peas, potato, radish, rhubarb, silverbeet, spring onion, sweet corn. **U/C (in seed tray):** Basil, broccoli, cabbage, capsicum, celery and celeriac, chilli, cucumber, eggplant, leeks, lettuce, tomato.	Asian greens, asparagus crowns, berries, celery, chicory, coriander, daikon, endive, globe and Jerusalem artichokes, horseradish, kohlrabi, lettuce, mustard, onion, oregano, parsley, rhubarb, rocket, sage, shallots, spring onions.
Subtropical	Asian greens, asparagus seed, bean, beetroot, broccoli, cabbage, capsicum, carrot, celery, cress, cucumber, endive, kohlrabi, lettuce, melons, mustard, parsnip, potato, pumpkin, radish, rhubarb, rocket, shallots, silverbeet, spring onion, sweet corn, swede, tomato, turnip, zucchini. **U/C:** Basil, cabbage, capsicum, celery and celeriac, chilli, collards, cucumber eggplant, leeks, marrow, melons, okra, squash, strawberries, tomatoes, zucchini.	Artichokes, Asian greens, asparagus, cabbage, celery, coriander, daikon, eggplant, endive, fennel, horseradish, kohlrabi, lettuce, melons, mustards, onion, parsley, pumpkin, rocket, shallots, silverbeet, snow peas, spring onion, squash, tomato, zucchini.
Tropical	Asian greens, cabbage, carrot, celery, cress, cucumber, endive, fennel, herbs, kohlrabi, lettuce, mustard, parsnip, pumpkin, radish, rhubarb, rocket, snake and winged beans, sweet corn.	Asian greens, asparagus, basil, cabbage, capsicum, celery, collards, cucumber, fennel, ginger, herbs, kohlrabi, leeks, marrows, mustards, okra, squash, taro, tomato, yam.

SEPTEMBER

	SOW	PLANT
Cool	Asian greens, asparagus seed, beetroot, cabbage, capsicum, carrots, cress, cucumber, endive, fennel, kale, kohlrabi, leek, mustard, onion, parsnip, peas, potatoes, radish, rhubarb, rocket, silverbeet, spring onion, summer spinach, swede, turnip. **U/C:** Basil, brassicas, broccoli, chilli, eggplants, leeks, lettuce, melons, onions, pumpkin, silverbeet, squash, strawberries, sweetcorn, tomatoes, zucchini.	Artichokes, Asian greens, asparagus, broccoli, cabbage, cauliflower, celery, chicory, chives, coriander, daikon, fennel, horseradish, kale, leeks, lettuce, onion, parsley, pumpkin, sage, shallots, silverbeet, spinach, spring onion, strawberries.
Temperate	Asian greens, asparagus, beans, beetroot, cabbage, capsicum, carrot, cauliflower, celery, cress, cucumber, eggplant, endive, fennel, kale, kohlrabi, leeks, lettuce, mustard, onions, parsnip, peas, potato, pumpkin, radish, rhubarb, rocket, silverbeet, spring onion, sweet corn, sweet potato, tomato. **U/C:** Basil, broccoli, Brussels sprouts, cabbage, capsicum, celery and celeriac, chilli, cucumber, eggplant, leeks.	Artichokes, Asian greens, asparagus, basil, berries, capsicum, cauliflower, celery, chicory, chilli, chives, coriander, cucumber, daikon, eggplant, endive, fennel, herbs, horseradish, Jerusalem artichoke crowns, kale, kohlrabi, leeks, mint, mustard, onions, pumpkin, rhubarb, salsify, silverbeet, snow pea, summer squash, sweet potato, tomato.
Subtropical	Asian greens, asparagus seed, beans, beetroot, broccoli, cabbage, capsicum, carrot, celeriac, celery, cucumber, lettuce, melons, mustard, potato, pumpkin, radish, rocket. **U/C:** Basil, cabbage, capsicum, celery and celeriac, chilli, collards, cucumber, eggplant, leeks, marrow, melons, shallots, silverbeet, spring onions, squash, strawberry seeds, sweet corn, tomato, zucchini.	Artichokes, basil, broccoli, cabbage, capsicum, chilli, coriander, cucumber, daikon, eggplant, endive, fennel, herbs, horseradish, Jerusalem artichoke, kohlrabi, leeks, lettuce, melons, mustard, okra, onion, parsley, pumpkin, rocket, salsify, shallots, silverbeet, snow peas, spring onion, squash, sweet potato, tomato, zucchini.
Tropical	Asian greens, asparagus, beans, capsicum, carrot, cucumber, eggplant, herbs, lettuce, mustard, radish, rhubarb seed, squash, sweet corn.	Basil, collards, ginger, okra, sweet potato, taro.

251

WHAT TO SOW WHEN

	SOW	PLANT
Cool	Asparagus seed, beans, beetroot, broccoli, cabbage, capsicum, carrot, cauliflower, Chinese cabbage, cucumber, endive, herbs, kale, kohlrabi, leeks, lettuce, mustard, okra, onions, parsnip, peas, potatoes, pumpkin, radish, rhubarb seeds, rocket, silverbeet, spring onion, squash, summer spinach, sweet corn, tomatoes. **U/C:** Celery and celeriac, chilli, eggplant, leeks, melons, pumpkin, sweet corn, tomatoes, zucchini.	Artichoke suckers, Asian greens, asparagus crowns, basil, broccoli, cabbage, cauliflower, celery, chicory, chilli, coriander, daikon, dill, endive, fennel, herbs, horseradish, kale, leek, lettuce, mint, pumpkin, shallots, silverbeet, spring onions, squash, strawberries, sweet corn, tarragon, tomatoes, zucchini, (for eggplant, capsicum, tomato use cloches).
Temperate	Beans, beetroot, cabbage, capsicum, carrots, cauliflower, celery, cucumber, eggplant, endive, kale, kohlrabi, leeks, lettuce, mustard, okra, parsnip, pumpkin, radish, rhubarb seeds, rocket, silverbeet, spring onion, sweet corn, sweet potato, tomato, zucchini. **U/C:** Brussels sprouts, celery and celeriac, melons, okra, tomato.	Artichoke suckers, Asian greens, asparagus, basil, berries, broccoli, cabbage, capsicum, cauliflower, celery, chicory, chilli, chives, cucumber, daikon, dill, eggplant, fennel, herbs, horseradish, kale, kohlrabi, leeks, lettuce, mustard, onions, pumpkin, radish, rocket, salsify, silverbeet, squash, sweet potato, tarragon, watermelon, zucchini.
Subtropical	Beans, beetroot, broccoli, cabbage, capsicum, carrots, cucumber, eggplant, lettuce, mustard, okra, pumpkin, radish, rhubarb seed, silverbeet, spring onions, squash, swede, sweet corn, tomato, turnip, zucchini. **U/C:** (For successional planting) Marrows, melons, okra, tomato, zucchini.	Basil, broccoli, cabbage, capsicum, celery, chilli, Chinese cabbage, chives, cucumber, eggplant, endive, fennel, herbs, leeks, melons, mint, pumpkin, rocket, silverbeet, squash, sweet potato, tomatoes, zucchini.
Tropical	Beetroot, carrots, capsicum, cucumber, eggplant, herbs, lettuce, mustard, okra, pumpkin, radish, rocket, snake beans, squash, sweetcorn.	Basil, capsicum, chives, cucumber, eggplant, ginger, herbs, lettuce, okra, pumpkin, squash, sweet potato.

NOVEMBER	SOW	PLANT
Cool	Asparagus seed, beans, beetroot, broccoli, Brussels sprouts, cabbage, capsicum, carrot, cauliflower, celery and celeriac, Chinese cabbage, cucumber, eggplant, endive, fennel, kale, kohlrabi, leek, lettuce, mustard, okra, parsnip, potatoes, pumpkin, radish, rhubarb seeds, rocket, silverbeet, spring onion, squash, summer spinach, swede, sweet corn, tomatoes, turnip, winter squash, zucchini. **U/C:** Broccoli, eggplant, sunflower, watermelon.	Asian greens, basil, broccoli, Brussels sprouts, cabbage, capsicum, cauliflower, celery, chicory, chilli, chives, coriander, cucumber, daikon, eggplant, fennel, globe artichokes suckers, herbs, horseradish, kale, kohlrabi, leek, lettuce, mint, potatoes, pumpkin, rosemary, sage, silverbeet, spring onions, squash, sweet corn, tomato, zucchini.
Temperate	Basil, beans, beetroot, broccoli, cabbage, capsicum, carrot, cauliflower, celery and celeriac, chicory, chilli, chives, cucumber, eggplant, endive, fennel, herbs, kohlrabi, leeks, lettuce, marrow, melons, mustard, okra, parsnip, potato, pumpkin, radish, rhubarb seeds, rocket, salsify, silverbeet, spring onion, squash, sweet corn, tomato, zucchini.	Basil, broccoli, cabbage, capsicum, cauliflower, celery and celeriac, chicory, chilli, chives, cucumber, eggplant, endive, Florence fennel, herbs, horseradish, kohlrabi, leeks, lettuce, marrow, melons, mustard, okra, parsnip, pumpkin, silverbeet, spring onion, squash, sweet potato, tomato, zucchini.
Subtropical	Asian greens, beans, beetroot, cabbage, capsicum, carrot, cress, cucumber, eggplant, lettuce, marrow, melons, mustard, potato, pumpkin, radish, rhubarb seed, rocket, silverbeet, spring onions, squash, swede, sweet corn, tomato, turnip, zucchini.	Basil, broccoli, cabbage, capsicum, chilli, chives, coriander and other herbs, cucumber, eggplant, horseradish, leeks, melons, pumpkin, salsify, silverbeet, squash, sweet potato, tomato, zucchini.
Tropical	Beetroot, capsicum, cress, cucumber, eggplant, herbs, lettuce, marrow, melons, mustard, okra, pumpkin, radish, rocket, snake and winged beans, squash, sweet corn, sweet potato.	Basil, eggplant, ginger, sweet potato.

DECEMBER	SOW	PLANT
Cool	Asparagus seed, beans, beetroot, broccoli, Brussels sprouts, cabbage, capsicum, carrot, cauliflower, celery, Chinese cabbage, cucumber, eggplant, endive, herbs, kale, kohlrabi, lettuce, melons, mustard, okra, onion, parsnip, potato, radish, rhubarb seeds, silverbeet, spring onion, squash, summer spinach, swede, sweet corn, turnip, zucchini. **U/C:** Kale and other brassicas.	Asian greens, basil, broccoli, Brussels sprouts, cabbage, capsicum, cauliflower, celery and celeriac, chilli, cucumber, eggplant, herbs, fennel, kale, leek, lettuce, marrow, melons, mint, onion, potatoes, salsify, silverbeet, spring onions, squash, sweet corn, tarragon, tomatoes, zucchini.
Temperate	Beans, beetroot, broccoli, Brussels sprouts, cabbage, capsicum, carrots, celery and celeriac, choko, cress, cucumber, eggplant, endive, herbs, kohlrabi, leeks, lettuce, marrow, melons, mustard, okra, parsnip, pumpkin, radish, rhubarb seeds, salsify, silverbeet, spring onion, squash, sweet corn, tomato.	Broccoli, cabbage, capsicum, cauliflower, celeriac, celery, cucumber, eggplant, endive, herbs, lettuce, marrow, melons, okra, pumpkin, silverbeet, spring onion, squash, tomato.
Subtropical	Beans, beetroot, cabbage, capsicum, carrots, cucumber, eggplant, herbs, lettuce, marrow, melons, okra, pumpkin, radish, rhubarb seed, silverbeet, spring onions, sweet corn, sweet potato, tomato, winter squash, zucchini.	Basil, capsicum, chilli, chives, choko, cucumber, eggplant, herbs, lettuce, marrow, melons, okra, pumpkin, silverbeet, squash, sweet potato, tomato, zucchini.
Tropical	Beetroot, capsicum, cucumber, eggplant, herbs, lettuce, melons, okra, pumpkin, radish, snake beans, sweet corn, winter squash.	Capsicum, cucumber, eggplant, herbs, melons, okra, open-hearted lettuce, pumpkin, sweet potato, winter squash.

COMMON GARDENING TERMS

Acid soil—soil on the pH scale between 0 and 7, 'sour' soil.

Alkaline soil—soil on the pH scale between 7 and 14, 'sweet' soil.

Allium—of the onion family includes chives, spring onions, garlic, leeks and shallots.

Annuals—plants whose life cycle lasts only one year or less.

Biennial—plants that need two years to complete their cycle of growth and setting seed. Continue throughout the year like perennials but don't have a second season of growth. In the second year they set seed.

Blanch (for storage)—plunge the chopped up vegetables into a pot of boiling water for 1–2 minutes, drain and rinse under cold water before freezing.

Blanching—covering the top of a plant to prevent sunlight turning stalks green and preventing bitterness.

Bolting—plants running into flower and then to seed prematurely.

Brassicas—from the cabbage family, includes broccoli, cauliflower, Brussels sprouts, Asian greens, turnips, mustards, kale and kohlrabi.

Broadcast sowing—throwing the seed around as you would if feeding birds.

Cloche – a cover or frame placed over plants to protect them or preserve warmth.

Comfrey and borage—are herbs that are excellent additions to the compost heap and make excellent mulches or teas.

Compost—decomposed organic material.

Compost tea—a handful of compost thrown into a bucket of water to make a tonic for plants.

Cross-pollinated—some plants need to have their flowers pollinated from flowers of other plants of the same species, the process of the transfer of the pollen.

Crown or rhizome—the underground stem of the plant that sends up the shoot growth.

Cucurbit—cucumber family. Includes cucumbers, pumpkins, melons, zucchini, luffa and squash.

Cultivar—a cultivated variety.

Dibbler—a garden tool, not unlike a stick, to push small holes in the ground for planting seeds in.

Drill—shallow grooves made in the soil for sowing seed. Press a rake handle into the surface of the soil to mark out the straight lines.

Dolomite—a mixture of limestone and dolomite (a carbonate salt of magnesium and calcium).

Drip line—the edge of foliage of a tree, that is, the area under the plant or tree where the foliage ends. Fertiliser is applied to the soil directly on the dripline around the tree.

Friable soil—is soil that is readily crumbled and easily broken up when handled.

Fruiting spurs—growths on laterals of fruit trees that develop into the fruit.

Germination—the process by which the seed starts to grow into the seedling.

Hardening off—tender plants raised in pots are moved outdoors during warm days and back at night to accustom them to higher temperatures.

Humus—organic matter that is fully broken down.

Hybrid—a plant developed by crossing parent plants or cultivars to create a plant with particular characteristics.

Lateral—branch that develops fruit spurs.

Lateral bud—buds growing from the leaf axils on the side of the stem.

Leader—the central leader is the upright main branch of a tree.

Legumes—peas and beans (and wattles), they fix nitrogen in the soil though the action of bacteria in their root nodes.

Lime—a form of calcium. It is used to alter acidity in acid soils, to make them more alkaline.

Loam—is rich friable soil with the right mix of clay, sand and humus.

Mulch—materials like compost, straw, pea straw and hay, decomposed leaf mould and stones or black plastic placed on the soil surface around plants to retain moisture, deter weeds and moderate the soil temperature.

Organic matter—material that is either from a plant or animal.

Perennials—plants that live for 3 years or more.

Pollination—the pollen from the male flower or male part of the flower is placed on the female flower part, or stigma.

Root crops—carrots, beetroot, parsnips, for example, grown in the ground.

Pricking out seedlings—when young seedlings grown in trays have developed a couple of leaves, transplant into small individual pots. Use a dibbler or pencil to lever the seedling gently from the tray. Handle seedlings by leaves not stem.

Seed leaves—the first set of leaves on a seedling, will differ from the true leaves, which develop later.

Sub-soil—the layer of soil under the topsoil.

Spent straw—straw that has been used in the chicken coop and is enriched with chicken manure. It is an excellent addition to the compost heap or for mulching around plants.

Terminal bud—a bud at the tip of a stem. In many plants the terminal bud releases a hormone (auxin), which suppresses the development of lateral buds. If removed, the lateral buds will develop.

Thinning—cutting or pulling out seedlings after germination to allow more space for the healthiest seedlings to grow on.

Tuber—the storage organ of the plant, formed at the end of the roots or stolons.

Variety—the term used for a sub-division of a species (known as a cultivar if it is a cultivated species).

Viability—the ability of seed to germinate.

INDEX

BIBLIOGRAPHY

Colin Campbell, *Garden Talk*, Hyland House Publishing, 2009.

The Complete Book of Herbs, Reader's Digest (Australia), 2008.

Peter Cundall, *The Practical Australian Gardener*, Penguin Books, 2007.

Michel & Jude Fanton, *The Seed Savers' Handbook*, The Seed Savers' Network, 2010.

Organic Gardening in Australia, ed. Pauline Pears, DK 2006.

Bob Flowerdew's Organic Bible, Kyle Cathie Limited, 2003.

Jacqueline French, *Organic Gardening in Australia*, Reed Books Pty Ltd, 1986

Larry Zuckerman, *The Potato: How the humble spud rescued the Western World*, Faber & Faber 1998.

Josh Byrne, *The Green Gardener, Sustainable gardening in your own backyard*, Viking 2006

Luis Glowinski, *The Complete Book of Fruit Growing in Australia*, Hachette Australia, 1991

Judy McMaugh, *What Garden, Pest or Disease is That?* New Holland Publishers (Australia) Pty Ltd, 2000.

Jekka McVicar, *Jekka's Complete Herb Book*, Simon and Schuster. 2007

David R. Murray, *Successful Organic Gardening*, 2nd ed, Kangaroo Press, 2006.

Sue Strickland, *The Organic Garden*, Hamlyn Publishing Group Limited, 1990.

Garlic: Effects on Cardiovascular Risks and Disease, Protective Effects Against Cancer, and Clinical Adverse Effects, AHRQ, Evidence Reports, Agency for Healthcare Research and Quality (US) Oct 2000.

Richard Stirzaker, Out of the Scientist's Garden, A Story of Water and Food, CSIRO Publishing, 2010.

WA Department of Agriculture and Food, Garden note series

CSIRO fact sheet, Greening of potatoes, www.csiro.au/resources/green-potatoes.html

Gardening Australia Magazine, ABC

Organic Gardening Magazine, ABC

J. Conacher, *Pests, Predators and Pesticides*, Organic Growers Assoc. WA 1979.

Resources
www.diggers.com.au
www.greenharvest.com.au
www.ecogarden.com.au
www. seedsavers.net
www.theitaliangardener.com.au
www.edenseeds.com.au
www.greenpatchseeds.com.au

Other
www.bugsforbugs.com.au
www.biologicalservices.com.au
www.organicgrowers.org.au

ACKNOWLEDGEMENTS

We are particularly grateful to Arthur and Rosemary Lathouris, whose amazing garden is extensively featured in this book. We are also grateful for the generosity of the following gardeners:

Ian and Viv Mackenzie
Murray and Chris Wilcox
Will Smith, Norman Lindsay Gallery
M & R Vella Fresh Vegies
The Hawkesbury Vegetable Farm
Pine Crest Orchard
Pine End Organic Farm
Watkins Orchard
Urban Graze Millthorpe
Blue Mountains Community Garden
Myoori Place
Doug Pritchard and Lois Carson
Alethea Mathouris
Janelle Matouk

Special thanks to Alan Eagle of Hawkesbury Harvest.

Nor would this book have been written without the years of accumulated knowledge, thoughtful advice and practical know-how from my forever-gardening father Les Chivers and his brother Gordon. It is, in the end, a documentation of their grandfathers, their fathers and their own gardening tips and advice.

ABOUT THE AUTHORS

Former criminal lawyer, Alison Chivers moved to the Blue Mountains of New South Wales in a treechange, to provide her family with an upbringing more like her own. Alison and her family now produce their own food and tries to live sustainably in the bush.

Mary Canning is a former lawyer and recruitment consultant who, on moving to the Blue Mountains with her family, was able to nurture her deep love for photography. She has documented private gardens, a vineyard, a Botanic Garden and producers on the Hawkesbury Harvest Farm Gate Trail, together with work for a national gardening magazine.

First published in Australia in 2012 by
Reed New Holland, an imprint of New Holland Publishers Pty Ltd
Sydney • London • Auckland

www.newhollandpublishers.com

1/66 Gibbes Street Chatswood NSW 2067 Australia
131-151 Great Titchfield Street London WIW 5BB United Kingdom
5/39 Woodside Ave Northcote Auckland 0627 New Zealand

National Library of Australia Cataloguing-in-Publication entry:
        ISBN: 9781877069918 (pbk.)

Publisher: Fiona Schultz
Publishing director: Lliane Clarke
Project editor: Jodi De Vantier
Designer: Kimberley Pearce
Production director: Olga Dementiev
Printer: Toppan Leefung Printing Ltd (China)

10 9 8 7 6 5 4 3 2

Follow New Holland Publishers on Facebook:
www.facebook.com/NewHollandPublishers
and Twitter: @NewHollandAU